The Race of Sound

Refiguring American Music
A series edited by RONALD RADANO, JOSH KUN, AND NINA SUN EIDSHEIM
CHARLES MCGOVERN, CONTRIBUTING EDITOR

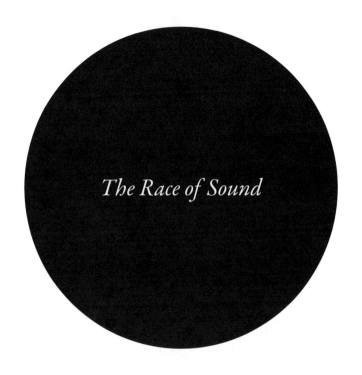

The Race of Sound

LISTENING, TIMBRE, AND VOCALITY

IN AFRICAN AMERICAN MUSIC NINA SUN EIDSHEIM

Duke University Press   Durham and London   2019

© 2019 Nina Sun Eidsheim
All rights reserved
Printed in the United States of America on acid-free paper ∞
Designed by Courtney Leigh Baker and
typeset in Garamond Premier Pro by Copperline Book Services

Library of Congress Cataloging-in-Publication Data
Title: The race of sound : listening, timbre, and vocality
in African American music / Nina Sun Eidsheim.
Description: Durham : Duke University Press, 2018. | Series: Refiguring
American music | Includes bibliographical references and index.
Identifiers: LCCN 2018022952 (print) | LCCN 2018035119 (ebook) |
ISBN 9780822372646 (ebook) | ISBN 9780822368564
(hardcover : alk. paper) | ISBN 9780822368687 (pbk. : alk. paper)
Subjects: LCSH: African Americans—Music—Social aspects.
| Music and race—United States. | Voice culture—Social aspects—
United States. | Tone color (Music)—Social aspects—United States.
| Music—Social aspects—United States. | Singing—Social aspects—
United States. | Anderson, Marian, 1897–1993. | Holiday, Billie,
1915–1959. | Scott, Jimmy, 1925–2014. | Vocaloid (Computer file)
Classification: LCC ML3917.U6 (ebook) | LCC ML3917.U6 E35 2018
(print) | DDC 781.2/308996073—dc23
LC record available at https://lccn.loc.gov/2018022952

Cover art: Nick Cave, *Soundsuit*, 2017. © Nick Cave.
Photo by James Prinz Photography. Courtesy of the artist
and Jack Shainman Gallery, New York.

This title is freely available in an open access edition thanks
to generous support from the UCLA Library.

To Julie

This is a call to enhance love, but not just private love. This is a call to enhance public love—justice. This is a call to intentionally support the creation of structures informed by and informing our sense of social justice and spirituality. This is a call to become responsible for the institutional structures we inhabit and that inhabit us. This is a call for self- and world-making and for the bridge between them, as well as recognition that the world is deeply spiritual even at its most secular. It is a call to create and live the predicate for a beloved community.

—JOHN A. POWELL, *Racing to Justice*

Widening Circles

I live my life in widening circles
that reach out across the world.
I may not complete this last one
but I give myself to it.
I circle around God, around the primordial tower.
I've been circling for thousands of years
and I still don't know: am I a falcon,
a storm, or a great song?

—RAINER MARIA RILKE, *Book of Hours*

Contents

Acknowledgments

The idea at the core of the themes and topics with which I have wrestled in this book has been my companion since I was a teenager—but these themes came into sharper relief after I moved from Norway to the United States, where I experienced race as an insider to some communities and as an outsider to others. This change of location and culture also afforded me a clearer view of the listening practices of the culture in which I was brought up. A term coined by Mendi Obadike, "acousmatic blackness," crystallized the many questions that arose from these observations regarding vocal and listening practice. Since I first encountered it in 2005, I've continuously meditated on and worked with acousmatic blackness as a concept and as an analytical framework. In addition to Obadike's teachings, many interlocutors along the way have helped me work through them at whichever stage I found myself in our respective encounters. Even with the fear of omitting some, I still wish to name them.

First, many thanks to my editor, Ken Wissoker, for his editorial vision and for truly understanding and trusting in my work. To Jade Brooks, Judith Hoover, Olivia Polk, Christopher Robinson, Liz Smith, and the entire Duke University Press production team, for steering this manuscript through the production process. And to the three anonymous readers for their tremendous efforts in reviewing the manuscript. I cannot thank you enough for your generosity and for the depth of your intellectual exchanges with this work.

Thank you to my UCLA colleague Jody Kreiman, professor of head and neck surgery and linguistics, for countless conversations over the past five years, for coteaching with me two graduate seminars related to voice, and for collaborating on some of the research for chapter 3.

I was fortunate to have a very special research assistant for all things Vocaloid. Katie Forgy was an expert guide, bringing me up to speed in a world with which I was unfamiliar; she also provided technical expertise. Her interest in the topic reignited mine! Gabriel Lee and David Utzinger worked with me on designing figures and music examples, respectively, and they executed all things technical in that area. Alexandra Apolloni and Schuyler Whelden offered detailed suggestions on the entire manuscript.

Special thanks to past and present colleagues in the Department of Musicology at the University of California, Los Angeles: Olivia Bloechl, Robert Fink, Mark Kligman, Raymond Knapp, Elisabeth Le Guin, David MacFayden, Mitchell Morris, Tamara Levitz, Jessica Schwartz, Shana Redmond, and Elizabeth Upton; and to graduate students at UCLA and beyond (especially Robbie Beahrs, Jacob Johnson, Ryan Koons, Joanna Love, Tiffany Naiman, Caitlin Marshall, Helen Rowen, David Utzinger, Schuyler Whelden, Helga Zambrano; and to Alexandra Apolloni, Monica Chieffo, Mike D'Errico, Breena Loraine, and Jillian Rogers for working closely with me on multiple projects). Thanks are also due to the exceptional UCLA Council of Advisors, Joseph Bristow and Anastasia Loukaitous-Sideris; Deans David Schaberg and Judi Smith; Associate Dean for Diversity and Inclusion Maite Zubiaurre; and Lauren Na, Reem Hanna-Harwell, and Barbara van Nostrand and the rest of the humanities administrative group and the Herb Alpert School of Music staff, who together make everything possible.

For generously engaging me in conversation and sharing resources at critical junctures, I thank Shane Butler, Faedra Carpenter, Hyun Hannah Kyong Chang, Suzanne Cusick, J. Martin Daughtry, Joanna Demers, Emily Dolan, Ryan Dohoney, Tor Dyrbo, Veit Erlman, David Gutkin, Stan Hawkins, David Howes, Vijay Iyer, Brandon LaBelle, Douglas Kahn, Brian Kane, Jody Kreiman, Josh Kun, Alejandro Madrid, Susan McClary, Katherine Meizel, Mara Mills, Matthew Morrison, Jamie Niesbet, Marina Peterson, Benjamin Piekut, Matthew Rahaim, Alexander Rehding, Ronald Radano, Juliana Snapper, Jason Stanyek, Kira Thurman, Alexander Weheliye, Amanda Weidman, Zachary Wallmark, Rachel Beckles Willson, and Deborah Wong.

Special thanks to Jann Pasler, George Lewis, Wadada Leo Smith, John Shepherd, Miller Puckette, Adriene Jenik, George Lipsitz, Deborah Wong, Andy Fry, Steven Schick, and Eula Biss, who first helped me to critically articulate the kernels of the ideas with which I grapple herein.

To Daphne A. Brooks for inviting me to be part of the Black Sound and the Archive working group at Yale, and, earlier, the Black Feminist Sonic Studies Group at Princeton, and to its stellar lineup of Farah Jasmine Griffin, Emily Lordi, Mendi Obadike, Imani Perry, Salamishah Tillet, and Gayle Wald; to my co-convener, Annette Schlichter, and members of the University of California multicampus research group Keys to Voice Studies: Terminology, Methodology, and Questions across Disciplines (especially Theresa Allison, Christine

Bacareza Balance, Robbie Beahrs, Shane Butler, Julene Johnson, Patricia Keating, Sarah Kessler, Peter Krapp, Jody Kreiman, Caitlin Marshall, Miller Puckette, Annelie Rugg, Mary Ann Smart, James Steintrager, and Carole-Anne Tyler); to the UC Humanities Research Center residency research group Vocal Matters: Technologies of Self and the Materiality of Voice (my co-convener Annette Schlichter and participants Jonathan Alexander, David Kasunic, Katherine Kinney, Caitlin Marshall, and Carole-Anne Tyler); to the Cornell University Society for the Humanities (Brandon LaBelle, Norie Neumark, Emily Thompson, Marcus Boon, Jeannette S. Jouili, Damien Keane, Eric Lott, Jonathan Skinner, Jennifer Stoever-Ackerman, Duane Corpis, Ziad Fahmy, Roger Moseley, Trevor Pinch, Sarah Ensor, Nicholás Knouf, Miloje Despic, Michael Jonik, James Nisbet, Brian Hanrahan, Eliot Bates); and to participants invited to the symposium Vocal Matters: Embodied Subjectivities and the Materiality of Voice (Joseph Auner, Charles Hirschkind, Mara Mills, Jason Stanyek, Jonathan Sterne, and Alexander Weheliye)—thank you!

Many of the ideas herein were first presented in talks and roundtable discussions. I thank all of those who have engaged me in questions and conversation. For the invitation to speak about the ideas developed in this book, I thank Juliana Pistorius and Jason Stanyek at Oxford University; Ryan Doheney and Hans Thomalla at Northwestern University School of Music; Stan Hawkins and the University of Oslo and Tormod W. Anundsen at University of Agder, Kristiansand; graduate students at Indiana University; Zeynep Bulut and the ICI Berlin Institute for Critical Inquiry; Daphne Brooks and the Princeton Center for African American Studies; Dylan Robinson, Robbie Beahrs, and Benjamin Brinner at the UC Berkeley Department of Music; Martha Feldman and David Levin at the University of Chicago Neubauer Collegium for Culture and Society; Konstantinos Thomaidis and Ben Macpherson at the Centre for Interdisciplinary Voice Studies; the Society for Ethnomusicology; the American Musicological Society; and the International Conference Crossroads in Cultural Studies.

I extend a special category of gratefulness to the amazing writing communities of which I am part. For sustenance, sanguine advice, and good laughs my thanks goes to Sara, Muriel, Katherine, Leslie, Juliana, Lauri, Jessica, Julie, Ray, Sherie, David, Tracy, Kathy, Emily, Tavishi, and Jørgen.

Thanks to family and friends near and far for continued patience as I constantly seem to be in the process of finishing a book and don't take enough time to play.

I extend gratitude to Luisfer for patience beyond measure, for good laughs, and for always taking care of our family with a light touch. To Nicolás, the greatest teacher—who, at four years old, in response to my question about how he sings beautiful tones, pontificates, "I feel them with my heart, and my brain tells my voice how to make them."

I dedicate this book to my luminous friend Julie. Julie and I have spent countless hours writing in each other's company. With her, I have shared many intimate musings on work and life. I also dedicate this book to William and Tildy. William has talked through all of these ideas with me—I thank him for that. My beautiful friend Tildy has read and commented on practically every sentence I've ever published—her patience and friendship are legendary.

Much earlier forms of parts of this book have appeared elsewhere: "The Micropolitics of Listening to Vocal Timbre," *Postmodern Culture* 24, no. 3; "Voice as Action: Towards a Model for Analyzing the Dynamic Construction of Racialized Voice," *Current Musicology* 93, no. 1 (2012): 9–34; "Marian Anderson and 'Sonic Blackness' in American Opera," *American Quarterly* 63, no. 3 (2011): 641–71; "Synthesizing Race: Towards an Analysis of the Performativity of Vocal Timbre," *TRANS-Transcultural Music Review* 13, no. 7 (2009); "Race and the Aesthetics of Vocal Timbre," in *Rethinking Difference in Music Scholarship*, edited by Olivia Bloechl, Jeffrey Kallberg, and Melanie Lowe (New York: Cambridge University Press, 2015), 338–65.

For permission to reproduce images, I thank the Marian Anderson Collection, Rare Book and Manuscript Library, University of Pennsylvania, and CMG Worldwidc.com; the Library of Birmingham; Misha; Robert Gillam; Vanmark; Don Hunstein / Sony Music Entertainment; Sara Krulwich / The New York Times / Redux; the Lincoln Center.

Additional research support was awarded by the UCLA Council of Research Grant; UC Institute for Research in the Arts Performance Practice and Arts Grant; UCLA Research Enabling Grant; Miles Levin Essay award at the Mannes Institute on Musical Aesthetics; the UCLA Center for the Study of Women's Faculty Research Grant; the Woodrow Wilson–Mellon Foundation; the Department of Musicology and the Herb Alpert School of Music, UCLA; the Office of the Dean of Humanities, UCLA; the American Council of Learned Societies' Charles A. Ryskamp Research Fellowship; and the UC President's Faculty Research Fellowship in the Humanities.

THE ACOUSMATIC QUESTION

Who Is This?

JULIET: My ears have not yet drunk a hundred words
Of that tongue's uttering, yet I know the sound.
Art thou not Romeo, and a Montague?

—William Shakespeare, *Romeo and Juliet*, act 2, scene 2

UNWANTED VISITOR: I don't much like the tone of your voice.

—*Monty Python's Flying Circus*, season 1, episode 9

The second voice that you heard
sounded like the voice of a black man; is that correct?

—*California v. O.J. Simpson* (1995)

President Obama is "talk[ing] white."

—Ralph Nader to the *Rocky Mountain News*, 2008

Whether the vocalizer is heard over the radio or the phone, as part of a movie soundtrack or in person—positioned far away and therefore hard to see or speaking right in front of the listener—the foundational question asked in the act of listening to a human voice is *Who is this? Who is speaking?* Regardless of whether the vocalizer is visible or invisible to the listener, we are called into positing this most basic question—a question of an acousmatic nature.

The specific term, originally connected with the concept of *musique acousmatique*, originates with Pierre Schaeffer. Deriving the term's root from an ancient Greek legend that described Pythagoras's disciples listening to him through a curtain, Schaeffer defined it as "acousmatic, adjective: referring to a sound that one hears without seeing the causes behind it."[1] Originating with an electronic music composer, the term contains an assumption about the particular affordances of a particular historical-technical moment. That moment arrived with the introduction of recording technology, which made it possible to sever the link between a sound and its source. In playing back the recorded sound, the source did not need to be present or active. Famously, Victor Records' iconic logo showed a loyal dog desperately seeking the source of "his master's voice" (as the original painting was titled), even as the master lay dead in the casket upon which the dog sat.[2] While the acousmatic has been explicitly theorized in relation to the advent of recording and telephonic technology, scholars have even traced the phenomenon of the division between sound and source to ancient times, when tension was created by the unavailability of the source to the listener.[3]

While the circumstances of the severing of sound and source vary, the impetus behind asking the question is the same: the acousmatic question arises from the assumption that, in asking, it is possible to elicit an answer. It is assumed that if I listen carefully to a sound—in the absence of a visually presented or otherwise known source—I should be able to identify a source, and that any limitations are due to inexperience or ignorance. For instance, through attentive and informed listening, I should be able to know a lot about the vocalizer, and possibly about his or her identity. If I do not already know the person, I should still be able to glean general information about him or her—from broader identity markers to fine-grained assessments regarding health, mood, or emotional state—and discern the speaker's attempts to falsely communicate emotions or truth statements, or even to speak as another through imitation or impersonation.[4]

In the context of the human voice, this assumption about the possibility of knowing sound in the first place extends to a second assumption: that it is possible to know a person. The acousmatic situation arises from the assumption that voice and sound are of an a priori stable nature and that we can identify degrees of fidelity to and divergence from this state. This position is grounded in a belief—and truth claims—about the voice as a cue to interiority, essence, and unmediated identity.[5]

We assume that when we ask the acousmatic question we will learn something about an individual. We assume that when we ask the acousmatic question we inquire about the essential nature of a person. The premise of the acousmatic question is that voice is stable and knowable. As Joanna Demers describes the act of *reduced listening* within an electronic music context, where we aim to hear the sound of a creaking door without associating that sound with the actual door, "Schaeffer starts from the point that we *must* already know," and so the goal in reduced listening is to "ignore what we know."[6]

In contrast to Schaeffer's position, I posit that the reason we ask *Who is this?* when we listen to voices is precisely that we cannot know the answer to that question. In this book I will argue that we ask that very question not because a possible ontology of vocal uniqueness will deliver us to the doorstep of an answer but because of voice's inability to be unique and yield precise answers. In Adriana Cavarero's classic formulation, a human voice is "a unique voice that signifies nothing but itself."[7] For Cavarero, a humanist, the voice is "the vital and unrepeatable uniqueness of every human being."[8] Building on a story by Italo Calvino about an eavesdropping monarch, in which hearing a single and unrepeatable voice changes the king's relationship to the world, Cavarero poses a challenge for herself and her readers. "This challenge . . . consists in thinking of the relationship between voice and speech as one of uniqueness, that although it resounds first of all in the voice that is not speech, also continues to resound in the speech to which the human voice is constitutively destined."[9] While I am extremely sympathetic to the project of listening intently as a humanizing endeavor, in contrast to Cavarero and Calvino's king, what I identify as *listening through the acousmatic question* arises from the *impossibility that the question will yield a firm answer*. Therefore, despite common assumptions, we don't ask the acousmatic question—*Who is this?*—because voice can be known and we may unequivocally arrive at a correct answer. We think that we already know, but in fact we know very little. We ask the question because voice and vocal identity are *not* situated at a unified locus that can be unilaterally identified. We ask the acousmatic question because it is not possible to know voice, vocal identity, and meaning as such; we can know them only in their multidimensional, always unfolding processes and practices, indeed in their multiplicities. This fundamental instability is why we keep asking the acousmatic question.

Therefore the question's impetus is counterintuitive. In the face of common sense, the key to the question does not lie in its ability to produce a reliable answer when asked. Its import lies in the contradiction that it cannot fully be answered—and thus must be continuously pursued. In the totality of the chain of impossible-to-answer questions, we find our response.

Part of the reason many definitions of voice fail to capture its nuance is that the voice is a complex event that, in addition to its myriad acoustic signals, consists of action, material, and social dynamics.[10] Voice's complexity, and the social and cultural fabrics within which both voice and listening are formed, remain underexamined. Thus, while they do not provide access to a stable essence, voice-based assessments regarding race result in a number of discriminatory evaluations and acts. They are used in court cases, as the epigraph from the *California v. Simpson* case exemplifies. Potential renters who telephone regarding advertised rentals are at a disadvantage if they are perceived as nonwhite.[11] Similarly there is historical precedent for expectations regarding singers' ethnic or racial backgrounds in relation to musical genre, vocal ability, and vocal sound. With a growing group of scholars, I seek to create awareness of timbral discrimination in the same way that consciousness has been raised around, for instance, skin color and hair texture.

While I consider my scholarly coming of age to have begun with readings in American, African American, gender, popular culture, and postcolonial studies, my background and expertise lie in experimental music, music theory, vocal performance and pedagogy, and voice studies.[12] I have observed the ossification of terms and concepts in both areas, from ideas as seemingly straightforward as pitch to concepts that are acknowledged to be more complex, such as genre, musical interpretation, gender, and race. To me, the racialization of vocal timbre exemplifies both sides' processes of ossification—from vocal training and music theory to critical studies. Thus I cross disciplinary boundaries and build on work from music theory, the scientific and material aspects of timbre, and voice studies in order to debunk myths about race as an essential category. The analogy I have observed is this: In the same way that culturally derived systems of pitches organized into scales render a given vibrational field *in tune* or *out of tune*, a culturally derived system of race renders a given vibrational field attached to a person as a *white voice*, a *black voice*—that is, "in tune" with expected correlations between skin color and vocal timbre—or someone who *sounds white or black*, meaning that the vocalization did not correspond to (was "out of tune" with) the ways in which the person as a whole was taxonomized.

In my earlier book, *Sensing Sound: Singing and Listening as Vibrational Practice*, I focused on the materially contingent aspect of sound. I called for attention to unfolding material relationships, for example, noting that what we conventionally think of as "the same sound," say, the pitch A played in quarter notes at a pulse of 60 transmitted through air, would not be perceived as the same sound if transmitted underwater. Sound travels faster when transmitted through water, and the body's material composition also transmits sound differently—primarily directly to the inner ear via bone conduction, compared to via the ear drum when receiving the signal through air. The two books are companion volumes, two sides of the same coin. *Sensing Sound* shows what the naturalization of sonic parameters and ways of measuring sound does to the general experience of listening to voice, while this book seeks to show the political and ethical dimensions of such practices as they produce blackness through the acousmatic question.

Specifically, in *The Race of Sound: Listening, Timbre, and Vocality in African American Music*, I extend my previous argument by drawing out the parallel between the multiplicity of the thick event and the multiplicity of a person. Both sound and person are complex events reduced to a moniker, a placeholder that nonetheless is taken to stand in for the unnamable event. That is, in the same way that what I have described as the vocal moment is complex as a *thick event*, with the limited parameter of *sound* selected as the aspect that defines it, complex phenomena such as human voices are further defined by socially, culturally, and economically driven categories such as race, class, and gender. In the former situation, voice is often reduced to its textually driven or notatable meaning content (language, pitch, rhythm, etc.). In the latter situation, vocal timbre—an elusive and understudied phenomenon[13]—is often used to make truth claims about voice and the person emitting the vocal sound. While most racial essentialization of physical characteristics has been critically confronted (if far from eradicated), the West's long history of entwining voice and vocal timbre with subjectivity and interiority has contributed to such truth claims remaining stagnant. Having noted this lack of research around vocal timbre, then, what *can* we know about timbre, the vocal apparatuses, and so on? Not much.

Vocal timbre is also often referred to as vocal "quality": the color, vocal imprint, and sound of the voice.[14] Vocal timbre is often described by analogy to color and, as the case studies in this book discuss, many of these analogies closely resemble or imply racialized descriptions. The origin of the idea that colors may be connected with music is not racial; rather it is based on mathematical and synesthetic principles derived in antiquity from the relationships between music and form, light, intervals, and timbre. Today timbre is the parameter most closely associated with color, possibly due to the German word for timbre, *Klangfarbe*, or tone-color.[15] (The English *timbre* is derived from French.) Thus the terms "coloring" and "tone-coloring" can be used to signify timbral variation without necessarily implying any racial connotations. However, as I observe in chapters 1, 2, and 5, when colors are evoked in vocal descriptions, they are drawn upon specifically in order to create a sonic analogy with skin tone, and thus to racialize the sound.

The American National Standards Institute (ANSI), an organization that offers precise standards for everything from the size of nuts and bolts made in different factories to the permitted decibel level in residential neighborhoods, defines timbre in the negative: "that attribute of auditory sensation in terms of which a listener can judge that two sounds similarly presented and having the same loudness and pitch are dissimilar."[16] In other words, in this definition timbre is everything expect pitch and loudness.

What is "everything" except pitch and loudness when considering voice? If two voices sing the same pitch at the same dynamic and for the same duration, *timbre* is what allows us to distinguish between them. Timbre is also everything that allows listeners to distinguish between two different instruments that play the same pitch at the same dynamic, with the same duration. And it is important to point out that "everything else" is not an objective set of data. It is the *listener* who detects timbre and who names the "everything else."[17] Indeed "like pitch and loudness, quality results from an interaction between a listener and a signal," as Jody Kreiman succinctly puts it. Here she formulates the dilemma of the acousmatic question in speech science terms.[18] As there is no stable sound to be known, only that which comes into articulation because of a specific material relationality, there is no a priori voice to be known prior to the one formulated in response to the acousmatic question.

But if voice is a co-articulation, are its physical makeup and its sound unrelated? And what can we say about the physical makeup of the voice and the ways we can hear the overall physical structure of that materially specific organ and its vocal production? Generally speaking, the sound of the voice is determined by the diameter and length of the vocal tract and the size of the vocal folds. Neither of these components is fixed, and therefore they are adjustable and a number of modalities work together to create and refine vocal sounds. How does this translate to sound? Does it mean that those with statistically similar physical vocal apparatuses sound the same, or so similar that we group them together?

Comparing a large group that is distinguished into two groups—prepubescent boy and girl vocal apparatuses—there are no statistically significant physiological differences in terms of laryngeal size or overall vocal tract length.[19] Boy and girl voices are split into these two distinctions through enculturation. And gender differentiation takes place for both vocalizers and perceivers. Vocalizers signal gender through word choice, intonation, speed, rhythm, prosody, level of nuance, and so on. Perceivers bring gendered expectations to the vocal scene and are thus unable to hear a voice outside gendered terms. So, the girl/boy question exemplifies a case in which the physicality is the same, but the sound and the perception brought to the sound differ.

While we do have considerable knowledge about the general physical changes the vocal apparatus undergoes throughout a typical lifespan, it is important to acknowledge voices at the outer edges of these spectra as well as the considerable area of overlap between male and female voices. Moreover, while voices also undergo physical transformation with hormonal treatment, regardless of physical alteration, it is daily vocal practice that makes a given register feel comfortable.[20] In other words, we can begin with a set of statistics about the human body, but a number of forces combine to bring out one set of this body's potentialities while dampening others—and it is with this culture- and value-driven process that *The Race of Sound* is concerned. I aim to indirectly, but nonetheless intentionally, address the ways in which sociophysical conditioning (rather than skin color or some other measurement) structures the naming of race. I wish to enumerate some of the many ways in which the advantage of accumulated privilege is preserved, not only across historical time and geographic space but also in sounds, to create the recognition of nonwhite vocal timbre.[21] Thus I build on Obadike's keen observation that hip-hop music may summon the presence of blackness without an accompanying black body. Extending this concept to the case of African American singers, I suggest that her term and concept *acousmatic blackness* may also capture the perceived presence of the black body in a vocal timbre, whether or not that body is determined to be black by other metrics.[22] The acousmatic question is the audile technique, or the measuring tape, used to determine the degree to which blackness is present. And because of the acousmatic question's inability to yield a precise answer, any identification of black vocal timbre is, by definition, blackness formed in response to the acousmatic question.

If voices that are similarly constituted exhibit distinctly different vocal sonorous characters, are voices that have different physical makeups bound to physicalities? No. As we will see in chapter 5, a young girl can sound like a mature woman, and we know that impersonators cross not only race and class but also age and gender. Voices that are physically similar may sound completely different, and voices that are physically different may be mistaken for one another. In other words, the sound of a given voice transcends assumed physical characteristics and the ways in which we rely on such characteristics to make sense of one another. Thus while voice is materially specific, a specific voice's sonic potentiality—such as a girl's voice or a boy's voice—and, indeed, its execution can exceed imagination.

The image I have used to explain this idea is that of the falling tree, as in the classic question *If a tree falls in the forest and no one is there to hear it, does it make a sound?* Through this question our understanding of and relationship to a multifaceted event is reduced to what we perceive as sound. And, I posited, in the same way that we reduce the rich, multifaceted, heterogeneous, and undefinable composite event of a falling tree to mere sound, we reduce the *thick event* of vocality through another question: the silent acousmatic question *Who is this?* When we ask the acousmatic question, we reduce vocal events in a manner similar to the way we reduce the falling tree to sound, and in so doing we ignore multiplicity and infinity in order to fix what is unfixable under a single naturalized concept. In short, the question *What is the sound of the falling tree?* reduces the thick event to one aspect—say, sound—while the question *Who made that sound?* discounts enculturation, technique and style, and an infinity of unrealized manifestations in favor of preconceived essence and meaning.

The naming and critical analysis achieved with the aid of this question pair serve as "a portal, opening up a new and previously inaccessible way of thinking about something," as Jan Meyer and Ray Land put it. They explain that such a portal is often enabled through the articulation of a "threshold concept," a distillation that "represents how people 'think' in a particular discipline, or how they perceive, apprehend, or experience particular phenomena within that discipline (or more generally)."[23] Linda Adler-Kassner and Elizabeth Wardle describe threshold concepts as "naming what we know."[24] Thus "a consequence of comprehending a threshold concept . . . [may] be a transformed internal view of subject matter, subject landscape, or even world view."[25] For my particular work, crystalizing how most people think about sound—they reduce it through naming—has been transformative. This insight has given me the critical tools to understand the process through which vocal timbre is racialized.

Returning to the question about the falling tree, the first layer of this analogy is the reduction to sound of the physical and multisensory event of singing. The second layer is the reduction of the thick event to a *quantifiable* sound with inherent meaning and attendant value. As mentioned, from the perspective of singing and listening as vibrational practice, meanings and values are not inherent; instead they are derived from listening communities' values. One of the primary values that drives the society and culture that give rise to the music discussed in this book is difference. This difference is imagined as race, which is not unconnected to other imagined categories, but is articulated within a complex matrix of intersectionality. Hence the thick event—a continuous vibrational field with undulating energies (flesh, bones, ligaments, teeth, air, longitudinal pressure in a material medium, molecules, and much more)—is reduced to socially and culturally categorized and evaluated vocal sounds, such as pitch and voice, as essential markers.

An underlying assumption about vocal sounds' power to identify is present in a wide range of observations about voice. For example, as the epigraphs above illustrate, after minimal exposure to Romeo's voice, Juliet hears it as in tune with her recollection of his voice and his broader membership in the Montague clan. In the *Monty Python* comment the speaker considers his interlocutor to be attitudinally out of line, thus akin to a false note. His observation not only offers suggestions regarding the interlocutor's possible ranges of tones, but also carries information about the speaker himself: a person situated lower in a social hierarchy would not deliver such a judgment publicly. And the question in the 1995 court case *California v. O.J. Simpson*, "The second voice that you heard sounded like the voice of a black man . . . ?," is based on the assumption of a priori categories. Uncritically acting on the assessment that the voice "sounded like . . . a black man" assumes that voice points to the stable category of "black man who has emitted such a voice." And since the system sets up binaries of true or false and guilt or innocence, whether according to a pitch system or a racialized system, those who fail to fall within the "true" category are, by default, marked as false. President Barack Obama, for example, is called out for failing to align vocally with the timbres expected of the race the listeners have assigned to him.[26] While drawn from very different archives and ultimately with very different outcomes, assumptions about possible "misalignment" are fueled by listeners who use the voice as "truth statements," such as Juliet's perceived alignment of Romeo's true measure of love. In sum, an assumption about stable and knowable sound provides a conceptual framework that reduces the thick event to sound, to the question of being in tune, or to racial timbral categories.

What Does the Acousmatic Question Offer Insight Into?

Having established that there is no unified or stable voice, we may draw the following lessons from the in-depth readings of vocal cases treated in the chapters that follow. They can be summarized into three interrelated correctives that better capture what voice is and what we identify when we identify voice:

- Voice is not singular; it is collective.
- Voice is not innate; it is cultural.
- Voice's source is not the singer; it is the listener.

In extending my analytical toolkit in order to understand more about the thick vocal event, I am particularly concerned with vocal timbre—an elusive concept that, as mentioned earlier, may be defined broadly as everything about the sound of the voice except duration and pitch.[27] Timbre is used as a basis for considerations of identity and state, including age, mood, and musical genre.[28] It is used diagnostically in terms of health and is considered part of the acoustic signal and airflow.

While these definitions address timbre's richness and complexity, what unifies these vastly different analytics, methodologies, and scholarly discourses is the assumption that timbre is static and knowable. In other words, there is a perceived sense of inevitability in each of these approaches. Vocal timbre is assessed when it is understood as a knowable entity, or in the context of correcting or creating a particular type of timbre. My suggested correctives address these false assumptions and provide an alternative explanation for the formation of timbral meaning. Hence in the following redefinitions of voice, the broader phenomena of voice, vocal timbre, and timbre are not knowable entities but processes.[29] The perception of vocal timbre thus entails dealing with slices of a thick event—a multitude of intermingling phenomena set within a complex dynamic of power and deferral over who gets to assign the meaning that ultimately affects the very medium it seeks to define.

First, voice is not singular; it is collective.[30] The voice is not a distinct entity, but rather part of a continuous material field. The so-called physical individual voice, then, is part of a continuum, a concentration of energy that we interpret and define as a distinct voice. (As we will see in this book, imagining separate and distinct voices requires many acrobatic framings!) The voice is composed of a collection of bodily organs involved in the production of sound, the acoustical conditions in which it is emitted and sensed, and the style and technique involved in its lifetime of training, what Farah Jasmine Griffin calls "cultural style."[31] No one part of this collection of styles and techniques involves race essentially or entails the uniqueness of the speaker; it is instead a performance of cultural style. James Baldwin observes the collective performance of race thus: "I began to suspect that white people did not act as they did because they were white, but for some other reason."[32] That is, Baldwin's insight is that "whiteness" is a particular performance of culture. The performance of whiteness is followed by the assumption that any such traits are either expressions or false performances of essence. Recall, it is this deep-seated belief that is expressed in the observation that Obama "talks white." In the absence of underlying assumptions regarding the (performed) sound of whiteness and which bodies have the right to perform such sonorities, there would be no reason to make such a point. Because the voice is not distinct and separate, it possesses neither the capacity to signal innate and unmediated qualities nor a stable identity. This is the case in what I call the measurable and the symbolic realms.

Moreover the voice is not unique, in part because it is not a static organ. It is not an isolated and distinct entity; instead it is shaped by the overall physical environment of the body: the nutrition to which it has access (or of which it is deprived) and the fresh air it enjoys (or harmful particles it inhales). It is the physical body and vocal apparatus that are trained and entrained each time a voice voices, and that develop accordingly. Vocal tissue, mass, musculature, and ligaments renew and are entrained in the same way as the rest of our bodies. Research and knowledge that show how the body is a result of its overall environment also apply to the part of the body that is the voice. Because we often focus on the sound and assume that there is an unchanging relationship between the entity we believe to be a static, distinct human and the vocal sound we hear, we also assume that the voice is intrinsic and unchangeable. However, just as the body possesses different qualities, or is able to carry out different activities, depending on how it has been nurtured and conditioned, so too is the voice an overall continuation and expression of the environment in which it participates.

Second, in this way, voice is not innate; it is cultural. Vocal choices are based on the vocalizer's position within the collective rather than arising solely as individual expression. Vocal communities share an invisible and often unconscious and inexplicable synchronicity of vocal movements and vocal performance, gravitationally attracted by the dynamics of the culture in which the vocalizer participates. This takes place, for example, through the vocal body's movements, habituation of practice, proprioception (self-monitoring), listening, and the specific practices adapted to and expressing a given culture's ideal. Neither speakers nor singers use the entire range of their voices' infinite timbral potentialities.[33] In other words, the decisive factor in honing each voice's potentiality and developing expertise in a timbral area is not individual preference but collective pressure and encouragement.

With the multitude of timbral choices involved in learning how to use the voice, voices tend to be developed based on collective rather than singular preference. The process that determines which select areas of our vocal potential we attend to, and that therefore will be understood as innate, is a social one. What we conceive of as a single voice, then, is a manifestation of a given culture's understanding of the vocalizer and his or her role within that culture. That is, voice is a manifestation of a shared vocal practice.

Third, as we've already begun to see, the voice does not arise solely from the vocalizer; it is created just as much within the process of listening. This means

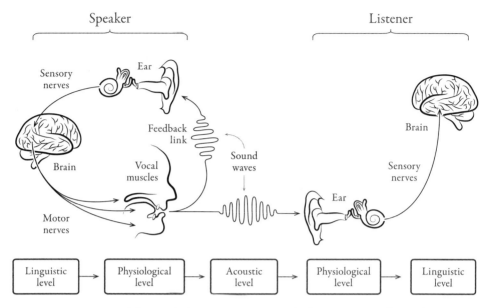

FIGURE INTRO.1 The speech chain. Peter B. Denes and Elliot N. Pinson, *The Speech Chain: The Physics and Biology of Spoken Language* (New York: W. H. Freeman, 1993), 5.

that the voices heard are ultimately identified, recognized, and named by listeners at large. In hearing a voice, one also brings forth a series of assumptions about the nature of voice. The speech chain—the now-ubiquitous model of the voice conceived by the linguists Peter Denes and Elliot Pinson—includes two general areas: the speaker and the listener (see figure Intro.1).[34] Information transmission from speaker to listener can be condensed into the following parts: the speaker's brain → motor neurons → sound generation → the listener's ear → the listener's brain.[35] This model usefully expanded the previous model of speech by considering speech in the context of communication (versus distinct and separate processes). As Denes and Pinson outline, the speech chain is incomplete without the listener.

I will go one step further in suggesting that the listener, including both other listeners and auto-listening, is so strong, and indeed so overriding, that in order to understand the process of evaluating and defining vocal timbre and voices, it is more useful to consider the process from the listener's point of view.[36] And I could flip the directionality of the speech chain, calling it the listener-voice chain, with the listener as the focal point (see figure Intro.2). This is because, on the one hand, actual vocal output is determined by the speaker's listening to his or her own voice and considering how the community hears it, and by the

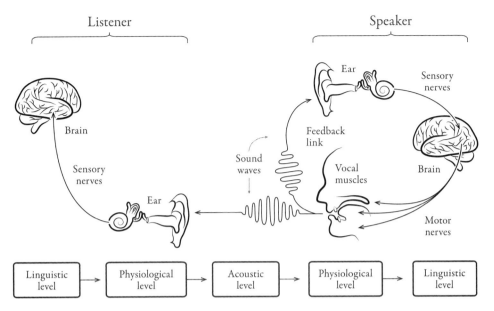

FIGURE INTRO.2 Listener-speaker model.

countless concrete instances in which he or she is vocally corrected, directly or indirectly, by other people. On the other hand, regardless of the actual vocal signal emitted, listeners will produce their own assessment of what they did hear. We actually *assign value* when we pose and respond to the acousmatic question.

Identifying the voice as located within the listener returns us to the first two correctives. Because a human vocalizer exists and vocalizes within a community, listeners' assessments directly affect and entrain the vocalizer materially and thus sonically, and direct the vocalizer's auto-listening. The assumptions, expectations, and conventions of a given culture, and that culture's impression of who the vocalizer is, are overlaid onto its acceptance or rejection of the vocalizer, akin to what Marcel Mauss describes as bodily technologies.[37] Furthermore, as Carter G. Woodson and Michel Foucault have both noted in reference to different cultural circumstances, adopting those listening practices and self-monitoring the voice is a condition of participation in a culture.[38] As Foucault indicates, monitoring is relocated within the individual and thus does not need to be reinforced on a level higher in the structures of power. In a nutshell, this tripartite cycle explains why, by asking the acousmatic question, the listener cycles between the vocal apparatus as part of a continuous material field and vocal acts that accord with the values and dynamics of the culture within which they are practiced and heard. Ultimately it is why we cannot expect to yield a singular and unambiguous answer to the question *Who are they?*

Roadblocks and Processes on the Way
toward Insights into Voice

In conversations and interactions with voice scholars working in a wide variety of fields, I have found that each study seems less interesting by itself than when considered together with seemingly related (and seemingly unrelated) voice research. However, while numerous fields and areas of research hold voice at the center of their work, their definitions of voice, methodologies, and epistemological and ontological assumptions vary widely. In some cases the object of study has no correlation, yet in other cases the same phenomenon (or aspects of it) is studied in multiple fields but vocabulary is not shared, or differences in epistemological horizons and methodology seem insurmountable.

Synthesizing across fields, I observe a split in ontology, epistemology, methods, and the very object "voice" into what appear to be two general camps: the position that assumes the voice is measurable and the position that assumes voice is an expression of the symbolic.[39] (Hereafter I will refer to them as *measurable* and *symbolic*.) The categories "measurable" and "symbolic" can broadly be thought of as "essential and strategic remappings of nature and culture."[40] As a result of the split between these two major positions, the same phenomenon is approached, scrutinized, and discussed using two sets of disparate vocabularies, resulting in a roadblock separating disciplines. The *measurable* position is concerned with organizing the material voice in ways that can be defined and replicated. Examples include movement of the air molecules and tissue, articulations of the mouth and tongue, timbral definition, the metrics of a vocal genre, and more. This position understands voice as a measurable, material entity that develops in a linear, causal relationship. It considers factors such as bodily health and socially and culturally formed habits and practices that are directly vocal or that somehow affect vocal or listening practice. The definition of voice is limited to aspects that can be measured and quantified, such as acoustic signal, air flow, and articulation. These are all interpretations that slice the thick material event into segments that allow for the articulation of testable questions and replicable experiments. The measurable voice is understood as largely straightforward in regard to its signaling. To slightly caricature this position, any emotional, cultural, or social investments in voice can be generalized as stemming from an evolutionary explanation. Those who take this position formulate and address questions with the assumption and intention that they can and will be answered in unambiguous terms. The answers to questions posed or the confirmed outcome of the thesis are aimed at broader application or transferability. *The measurable position aspires to show us something about the universality of vocal function.*

In contrast, the *symbolic* position is concerned with the ways in which vocal sound presentations are interpreted. Broadly described, this position considers how dynamics (of power, for example) are played out through the acceptance of meaning-making. Here, what I conceive as the thick material vocal event is also segmented, significant only in its symbolic capacity, and often conceptually detached from the material sound or phenomenon. Whether the voice is read and understood as sound, as text, or even as implicated with the body, this analysis assumes that the power and impact of voice take place only on the symbolic level. In other words, for voice to have a different meaning, it is the symbolism that must be changed. However, as with the measurable position, the voice comes to be so intimately associated with whichever symbolic position is taken that considering the connection between the thick event of the voice and the given symbolism as a true choice becomes challenging.

Scholars operating from this type of position investigate the historical and cultural reasons the voice is understood in such a manner rather than evolutionarily. They formulate and investigate questions in order to address a very particular situation and, indeed, to help formulate how this situation is distinct and how it contributes to an understanding of why an answer or position is not transferable to another situation. The value of such a research project's outcome lies precisely in its level of detail, in a fine-grained and finely textured engagement. *The symbolic position aspires to show us something about the voice's fine-grained specificity and overall complexity and the impossibility of any findings being directly ported to another situation.*

We may now turn to the roadblocks. Considering voice from only one of these perspectives fails to take into account both the ways in which the symbolic is derived from material positions and how the symbolic informs everything from the units of measurement used to the types of questions formulated in material positions. As mentioned, part of the reason for the divide between the two positions is that, due to its richness, voice is studied in multiple disciplines, which are often so different that they are not considered by one another.[41] Voice is at the center of research in vastly different areas of inquiry, such as (to mention a few) musicology, ethnomusicology, anthropology, film, gender, and sound studies on the one hand; linguistics, biology and evolutionary studies, acoustics, mechanical engineering, and head and neck surgery on the other. As a result of their assumed ontologies, epistemologies, and research

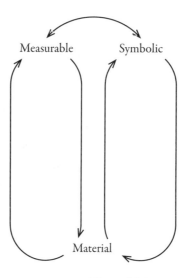

FIGURE INTRO.3 The model shows
the interplay among the symbolic, the
measurable, and the material.

methodologies, each of these positions yields distinct, often non-overlapping, voice objects, for example voice as subjectivity, voice as evidence of reproductive fitness, and voice as libretto.

In summary, voice scholarship in general, and the potential field of voice studies (which I see as explicitly transdisciplinary) in particular, possess built-in problems in regard to cross-fertilization. Within these two camps—the measurable and the symbolic—the voice has been formulated as two entirely different objects, and because of this there have been no grounds, reason, or purpose for their scholars to interact. The interactions have mainly consisted in pointing out the errors in the other camp's assumptions about and definitions of voice. However, the past five years have seen a shift toward interest in transdisciplinary conversation.[42] The third position I wish to advocate in this book is that the symbolic and measurable dimensions are never detached; they always already work in tandem with the *material* dimension. The symbolic and the measurable are both re-created in the material, and the material gives rise to that which we understand as the symbolic or the measurable (see figure Intro.3).[43]

What is the tactic or perspective that shows us how to connect the symbolic and the measurable? How may we dissolve the roadblocks? For me, the answer is a practice-based methodological approach to vocalization, explained in more detail below, that allows us to simultaneously address the naturalized aspects of both the measurable and the symbolic. This approach is grounded in the material and considers the flow among the three areas: symbolic, measurable, and material. In making these connections, I look to the pioneering work of Robbie Beahrs, Shane Butler, J. Martin Daughtry, Cornelia Fales, Sarah Kessler, Katherine Kinney, Jody Kreiman and Diana Sidtis, Theodore Levin, Caitlin Marshall, Kay Norton, Ana María Ochoa Gautier, Kasia Pisanski, Matthew Rahaim, Annette Schlichter, and Amanda Weidman, to name a few, all of whom work from a rigorous sensibility regarding voice's material- and meaning-making powers.[44]

While most of these scholars would probably not describe their work in this way, I find that an interesting common thread among them is their sensitivity to the practical application or use of voice in their approaches. Here I want to gesture toward an area of inquiry into voice, involving vocal practices such as singing, acting, vocal therapy, and more, that is often not considered scholarship but that has allowed me and many of the above-mentioned scholars to consider the dynamic between the measurable and the symbolic. Specifically, in addition to these positions, I am interested in an aspect of the performative perspective that I call *critical performance practice* and discuss in more depth below. Such a methodology allows me to map the relations and track the consequences between the material and the semiotic.

Voice's Manifestations of the Measured and the Symbolic

It is a truism that the body has been objectified and used as a measure of race and as evidence of innate racial difference. This book shows that voice is equally objectified, entrained, and used as a "measure" of race (i.e., a feature that is believed to represent something specific but has the power to do so only through social consensus). Created internally and crossing from the internal to the external, the voice holds a special position in the sonorous landscape, herein addressed as experienced through Western thought. The voice is thought to reveal the true nature of the body. As I have discussed elsewhere, measurements of skull shape and size and taxonomies of the relative development of different races and ethnicities were graphically charted in *The Family Group of the Katarrhinen* and *Inventing the Family of Man* and *Types of Mankind*.[45] These figures sought to convey at a glance the idea that different human and animal groups that represented a wide spectrum of beings on a single evolutionary timeline—from the primitive (apes, Africans) to the highly evolved (Aryans)—lived side by side at the same time. Because of the medicalization of vocal pedagogy that also took place at this time, the relative developments were believed to be audible or, in today's big data language, "sonified" through vocal timbre.[46] The term "measuring," then, refers to the ways in which the body's physical dimensions (crania and height) were, to some extent, measured. These dimensions, taken with those not measured (e.g., internal tissue and organs), were thought to be made audible to a given community of listeners through the voice, much like masses of data are sonified to make them easier to process.

These perceived quantitative findings on the measures of the subhuman not only arose from but also reinforced a belief in difference in the metaphysical sphere: the difference between fully human and not fully human, and the existence or nonexistence of the soul. The impact of such a perverse attitude is not limited to those claiming superiority, but, as W. E. B. Du Bois has shown, through enculturation "a peculiar sensation" develops. It is "this double-consciousness, this sense of always looking at one's self through the eyes of others." One begins "measuring one's soul by the tape of a world."[47] The metaphysical isolation of "black folk[s]" is totalizing.[48] And, when thinking back to Aristotle— "Voice (phōnē) is a kind of sound characteristic of what has soul in it"—we are reminded of the long-standing connection between soul and voice.[49]

What the seemingly objective measuring and naming of the symbolic really allows is manifestation of the power dynamic at play—and that manifestation then takes on a life of its own. In the antebellum era, slave owners and non-slaves began to hear the sounds of slaves' voices as a distinct vocal timbre, first in what was understood as self-exclusion and evidence of subhumanness (in their "noisy" voices), then in the reification of blackness.[50] Ronald Radano has described the process in this way: "The tendency to devalue Negro music, to reify blackness and to turn it into a natural resource, also sustained the perception of its difference, its status as an objectionable, illicit form of black cultural property, which, in turn, established its negative value." The "inalienable, unexchangeable qualities of black musical animation" are traded in the exchange of blackness through the form of black vocality.[51] Understood as a natural resource, vocal timbre is also measured in its value.

Echoing the language of Radano and Arjun Appadurai, through "exchange and re-imagined uses"—evaluated, quantified, given a sticker prize, and thus appraised, assessed, calculated, weighed and measured—body, soul, and voice take on the social life of things.[52] This book tells stories about the ways such values are traded on the back of the voice but also instilled in the voice through formal and informal pedagogies. Throughout I do argue that listening *is* akin to measuring. The two techniques are similar in that they are both socially and culturally constructed: neither will work unless a community buys into them.

Assessments such as "a white voice" and "an overly loud voice" mean nothing unless the listening community that assesses the voice knows the designation to which these concepts refer—akin to the agreed-upon definition of "one meter" or "in tune"/"out of tune."

The effectiveness of any measuring tool is reliant on a community's agreement about and adherence to the measuring convention; thus the articulation of the two positions discussed earlier—the measurable and the symbolic—does not take place in a vacuum. It affects the definition, perceptions, and indeed the material makeup and expression of the voice. In any investigation that has articulated a measurable entity (decibel, pitch, enharmonic sound) or symbolic position (imitation, gendered performance, coy expression), a formulation of the vocal object has already taken place. Rather than dealing with the messy variables that accompany it, the thick vocal event has already been pruned into the select aspect of voice that was already assumed at the outset. I think of this as akin to working with rigged evidence.

Expressed as a formula, this process unfolds as follows: the symbolic (as manifested by concepts ranging from gender to decibel) is used to shape the material; the material is shaped accordingly and emits precisely the signal that the symbolic purports to describe or capture; this signal is then *measured*; and a (false and rigged) correlation is logged and used as confirmation of the existence of the phenomenon and/or meaning envisioned by the symbolic. Thus, considering the triangulation of the measurable-symbolic-material aspect of the voice shows us the dynamic and codependent processes played out in the perception of every utterance and evaluation (see figure Intro. 3). With attention to that process, preconceived aspects of the symbolic and the material are denaturalized.[53]

The process of projecting, arranging, and manifesting the vocal object results in a self-fulfilling prophecy. Below I offer a list of some ways in which this takes form. In each case, a pivot is created around listener-determined timbral meaning or measurement. The listener then adjusts various aspects of his or her perception of the thick vocal event to offer coherence around the assumed or projected meaning. The specific areas I address include the sense of coherence (according to a given society's measuring tools) between singer's timbre and visual appearance, ethnic or racial identity, genre assignment, and affiliations with vocal communities. This process is born from the assumption that voice is unique and innate.

Scholarship seems to be continually refining the processes of raising awareness and critiquing such labeling. Thus when I assert that it's not racism itself but what underlies racism (assumptions about essence and the need to define) that is the root of racist thought and action, I point to the assumption that *there is something there* to recognize and define. Child, middle-aged woman, African American, or white—all of these definitions depend on the assumption that there is something there to name correctly. Work that makes these definitions salient is important, as it underpins untold nightmares that are played out daily. Where my own work differs, however, is that I am not primarily concerned with offering up more fine-grained discernment.

For example, Angela Davis reframed female vocalists within African American culture and African American artists within American popular music in her massively influential 1999 *Blues Legacies and Black Feminism: Gertrude "Ma" Rainey, Bessie Smith, and Billie Holiday.* While Davis and other scholars seek to address artists who have been marginalized in some way—including household names who have not received social or monetary recognition congruent with their artistic offering and cultural impact—to me, at the end of the day, these scholars are mounting arguments that deal in issues of fidelity. While I admire the overall thrusts of scholars like Davis, I cannot but note that the main ways in which such arguments and theses are forwarded relate to the types of contextual information that are considered or not considered when interpreting and judging an artist's level of excellence, impact, beauty, relevance, and so on.

In her close readings of Gertrude "Ma" Rainey, Bessie Smith, and Billie Holiday, Davis makes a case for recalibrating the lens through which African American blueswomen are considered, thus recognizing an agency and artistry that were not originally attributed to them. Indeed, Davis corrects the idea that Holiday was someone who passively "worked primarily with the idiom of white popular song" to someone who "illuminated the ideological constructions of gender and . . . insinuated [herself] into women's emotional lives." Through her vocal work, Davis asserts, Holiday "transform[ed] already existing material into her own form of modern jazz" and "relocated [that material] in a specifically African-American cultural tradition and simultaneously challenged the boundaries of that tradition." Bringing in comparisons to "African Americans' historical appropriation of the English language," Davis compares Holiday's contributions to the "literary feat of Harriet Jacobs," who, in the narrative *Incidents in the Life of Slave Girl,* "appropriated and transformed the nineteenth-century sentimental novel and, in the process, revealed new ways of thinking about black female sexuality." By bringing in additional context, such as Herbert Marcuse's notion of the "aesthetic dimension," Davis hears Holiday as "transform[ing] social relations aesthetically beyond the shallow notions of love contained in the songs."[54]

The assumption underlying these interpretations of Holiday's work is that the goal is to sharpen our interpretive lens, and that, by doing so, the reading will more closely capture the truth. One of its major premises is that the way we have heard Holiday before is not quite correct; that is, we have heard her correctly only after Davis's analysis heard her with proper fidelity. While I am in favor of expanding the ways we might listen to Holiday, and of Davis's endeavor to remove the myths and inaccuracies surrounding Holiday, my approach and contribution differ from those that seek to claim the most accurate interpretation. Ultimately I seek to disassemble any promise of "accuracy." I will go as far as to argue that its pursuit is a dead-end street.

In this area I align with Jacques Derrida's belief that the search for meaning consists of a series of deferrals. (But I do not align with his prioritization of written language.) By insisting on returning to the category of the listener, which embodies the category of the originator of meaning, I am not insisting on a more perfect understanding of the voice. Instead I aim to confront the continually developing understanding of meaning, the choices and power structures at its base, and the selective choices even the most conscientious listeners must carry out in order to make sense of a voice.

In this way scholars from different disciplines are committed to dismantling "transcendental racial categories."[55] However, as a scholar, what work is left for me once I have demonstrated that the categories are not transcendental? I am skeptical that it's possible to reinvigorate agency by offering up (another) fidelity, however nuanced. Measuring and invoking meaning (the symbolic), even if in a more refined way, will produce the same result in the long run—that is, will legitimize what I think of as the cult of fidelity. We may move further into style and technique, understanding what makes up the performance and focusing on the details, and ultimately coming out on the side of a vibrational field engaged through vibrational practice—and we may stop there without renaming. Thus I have used anomalous examples in order to move away from categories and names and toward intermaterial vibrational practice, and I analyze that practice from the perspective of style and technique.

So is there a way we might name or notate something without also ossifying it in the process? Looking to film studies, I find much resonance with the work of Michael Boyce Gillespie, whose work is "founded on the belief that the idea of black film is always a question, never an answer," and with his notion of "the enactment of film blackness," which relates to my notion of voice as the "performance/construction of the event." Gillespie contributes a refinement of the definition of blackness by examining twentieth- and twenty-first-century American cinema, showing that "film blackness" is a performance taking place within a production and that it is much more nuanced than any idea of blackness can capture. Gillespie also articulates options for black film as starting points for interpretation. For example, in a reading of *Medicine for Melancholy*, Gillespie writes that the film offers "film blackness as a meditation on romance, place, and ruin." In the end, because Gillespie resists the temptation to replace existing categories with another renamed, more finely grained category, he opens up spaces for additional ways to perform, inhabit, and imagine blackness.[56]

While insistent that his work is not concerned with race specifically, the composer, improviser, and trumpeter Wadada Leo Smith offers an example in his notational system of opening space while avoiding the reassignment of meaning. Called Ankhrasmation, the notation system "is a compositional language he developed using multidimensional visual symbols as stimuli for improvisation."[57] The notation system stresses that meaning is both personal and contextual. For example, if all members of an ensemble are assigned to play a red half-triangle, each will need to research the meaning of "triangle" and "red." The half-triangle is a velocity unit. Smith explains, "Each person will take that velocity unit and determine how fast or slow that velocity unit develops, depending on which symbol it is—but even if they all have the same symbol, it would by nature never come out to be the same velocity." For red, Smith uses the symbolic references of blood and cherry to illustrate the process the musician might engage. On the one hand, "if it's referenced as blood, then they have to go and do the research and find out about all the properties of blood and come up with some reference of how blood is used in humans or other creatures. Then they start to transform that data about blood into musical property." On the other hand, "if you take the cherry, the cherry's got an outer skin that's red, and it also has a pit inside of it. It has a stem that comes out of the center of it. And you would take all of those elements and break them down into different parts and research them."[58] The Ankhrasmation system is realized through each participant's individual associative chain, which, of course, has also been developed within a lifetime of enculturation. These individual reference points are emphasized and indeed make up the music. Smith's system offers a radical departure from the traditional Western staff system and from interpretations of singers' legacy and impact, as exemplified in the ubiquitous perceptions of and work on Holiday, whereby pitches and people are processed through a series of (Derridean) deferrals and an ongoing dispute about which interpretation is most accurate.

My listening-to-listening framework, addressed in detail below, attempts to consider all symbols and meanings from an Ankhrasmation point of view, asserting that there is no *in tune* or *out of tune*, no "voice of a black man"; there is no single *most accurate* red triangle sound, but rather each designation is already the result of chains of associations made by an individual under the pressures of the social and cultural contexts in which that individual participates. Thus thinking about Davis and other scholars through Ankhrasmation makes explicit a focus on both the context and the meaning based on it rather than on an improvement in meaning. There is no attempt at calibrating the lens for a more accurate assessment; there is instead an aim to be more explicit about the dynamism and instability of meaning-making, resisting the gravitational pull toward reassignment of meaning.

I am following Farah Jasmine Griffin, Emily Lordi, and Robert O'Meally, who represent "models of scholarly works designated to dismantle the myth that black women singers naturally express their hard lives through their songs."[59] I want to stress that I deeply respect these scholars and that my work would not have been possible without theirs. While we have similar aims—to shed myths and inaccuracies—they tend to emphasize more detailed and complex contextualization that facilitates deeper reading. They also emphasize a more accurate analysis with the goal of higher fidelity (e.g., reading Holiday's rhythmic sophistication as a Jazz Genius with an untimely death and as an *auteur* through her lyric interpretations). Taking Smith's lead through Ankhrasmation rather than aiming for higher fidelity, I use the data to point to what I conceive as the fiction of fidelity.

While my assumption is that all measurements and constructions merely label and manifest dynamics of power as they are played out, measurement and construction also constitute a game that works only when everyone participates and continuously re-creates and reifies. The measured and the symbolic paradigms take place within the body through explicit and implicit pedagogy. Vocal culture is performed and formed in the flesh. I examine this phenomenon by observing a very particular kind of vocal training. When listeners connect a singer with a particular community, their listening is filtered through assumptions about that community and the music and vocal genres with which its people are most commonly associated. For example, when an African American singer, such as Marian Anderson, is connected more with a community of minstrelsy and spirituals than with opera, she is heard, and expectations about her are formed, through that filter. When a timbre is understood as gendered in a particular way, and a singer's voice precludes association with that gendered meaning, listeners create alternative identities for the singer. In the example of the jazz and ballad singer Jimmy Scott, the categories of female, sex, and death are inserted in place of Scott himself. Because the myth of vocal essentialism and innateness runs so deep, we create complex, schizophrenic, layered listening situations in order to compensate for confrontations with the nonessential nature of voice—confrontations caused, for instance, by vocal like-ness, imitation, or ventriloquism. And finally, the sound of a particular racial-ized genre—soul—is reproduced through vocal synthesis and dresses in the imagery of blackface. In other words, through listening, the symbolic mani-fested by way of the material is used to confirm itself. Consequentially voice as evidence becomes an unexamined truism: the evidence is rigged.

Let's return to the issue regarding the possible function, if any, of the acous-matic question. What I have realized, by attuning to sixty years' worth of in-stances of listening to race in the United States,[60] is that posing the acousmatic question—*Who is this?*—will never tell you who the singer is. Attending to the acousmatic question tells you only who is listening: who you are. Indeed, who *we are*.

The Micropolitics of Listening

Because listening is never neutral, but rather always actively produces mean-ing, it is a political act. Through listening, we name and define. We get to say, "This is the voice of a black man." We get to say, "That singer doesn't sound sincere." And we get to say, "This singer doesn't sound like herself." As I hope I have made clear by now, not only do we, as listeners, get to label the vocalizer; we also manifest the symbolic in the material. Because voices are communal technologies attuned to cultural values, what the community hears, and the meanings it assigns, are accordingly aligned. In other words, through listening we enact and activate.

This book advocates the return of the acousmatic question to the listener, and ultimately to ourselves: *Who am I, who hears this?* On which assumptions and values are my observations based (or, to put it more strongly, to which are they tethered), and from which position(s) within a given society do I observe? This book seeks to provide tools that can help denaturalize both the listening process and the voices it names.

Through such listening we enact the micropolitics of timbre: the process of discernment involved in listening to and naming voices. "Micro" refers to the smaller unit or entity of vocal expression, in comparison with "macro" units such as notes, durations, phonemes, words, phrases, sentences, and so on. "Mi-cro" also refers to the way these sentiments are activated by a listener. While there is a relationship between hegemonic definitions and naming, the activa-tion and realization of these definitions' potential take place one by one, ear by ear. The rubber hits the road where and when the neighbor, friend, family, stranger, and, most crucially, the vocalizer himself or herself hears and names the voice based on these factors. It is both the curse and the beauty of the collective process that, through listening, we can either reinforce or refuse to engage naturalized notions and values. Listening is not a neutral assessment of degrees of fidelity but instead is always already a critical performance—that is, a political act.[61]

Because, within the figure of sound framework, vocal timbre and the so-called measurable object or given meaning (or symbol) seem to conform to one another so closely, there is no analytical space within which to assert a third point: the role of the interpretant. Therefore, again, rather than examining what is purportedly heard, I suggest we step back in order to examine listening practice and the frames around it that yield given outcomes. In other words, we can apply Peirce-like operations in order to acknowledge the third party.[62] I propose that we examine racialized vocal timbre (and any other qualities that are understood as essential) in order to move from an analysis of sound to an analysis of *how that sound is listened to.*

With *The Race of Sound*, then, I wish to hurl against the wall the long-overdue and much-underexamined connection between the perceived meaning of vocal timbre and vocalization. By offering new methodologies with which to examine vocal timbre, sound, and listening, I wish primarily to offer an intervention in American studies, race and ethnicity studies, and cultural studies, and secondarily in sound and voice studies, musicology, and ethnomusicology. Specifically I wish to address the problematics of voice as they are played out through the dynamics of race in late twentieth-century American popular music. I do so by taking seriously the important and penetrating critiques offered by these areas of scholarship regarding race, gender, ethnicity, and identity, and by detailing how they take form in the broad and elusive arena of vocal timbre. Drawing on my knowledge in music, sound studies, and voice studies, I wish to offer an additional perspective on how social divisions and power relationships are carried out through the space of vocal timbre, which seems to be one of the last areas still viewed as an essential trait.

Because of general assumptions regarding music and voice—that their major currency is sound and that vocal sounds are essential and unmediated expressions—readings of vocal timbre have remained impenetrable to critical investigation. In the same way that hair, body movement, dialect, accent, and style have been critically examined and thus are no longer available as ammunition for arguments about race as essence, *The Race of Sound* shows how timbre is institutionalized and internalized as a meaningful measurement of traits believed by a given society to be essential to people, and demonstrates the falsity of such correlative argument. The internalization of the disciplining of ears—or, in Jonathan Sterne's evocative term, "audile techniques"—is described by Du Bois, as noted earlier, as "souls being measured by the tape of a world."[63]

As a musicologist, scholar of voice and sound studies, singer, and voice teacher, I consider vocal timbre here within a contemporary music context while keeping a keen ear tuned to historically situated racial dynamics surrounding physiology, how these dynamics are connected to notions of voice, and the ways in which racialized listening is formed. In carrying out this work, I build on critical-analytical traditions that detail the construction of identity and essential categories, including race and gender. I examine how structures of power burrow down into flesh and are realized through it; how the articulation of power structures is self-regulated by those who live within them; how the technology of narrative comes into play; how knowledge is situated; and how everyday life is performed.[64] I also dig into and listen deeply to the sonic archive in a detailed examination of vocal timbre.

Engaging perspectives from performance studies, I address concerns in critical race studies and sound studies and extend them to the site of vocal timbre. Thus my questions find a parallel in theater scholarship's inquiry into the performed spoken voice. Faedra Chatard Carpenter is also "struck" by the phenomenon that, "despite the widely accepted recognition that race is a social construct, Americans still talk about what *sounds black* or *sounds white* in simplified racial terms."[65] I share goals with scholars of avant-garde music, jazz, and literature, such as Fred Moten, who is concerned with the rematerialization of the visual through sound and with the objectification of persons based on the ways in which their visual presentation is understood.[66] I also share objectives with Daphne Brooks, Emily Lordi, Jennifer Lynn Stoever, and Gayle Wald, all of whom critically engage the catalogue of the African American experience. Their activist approach to scholarship includes listening to that experience as it is archived in the form of vocal micro-sonorities and inflections within the context of popular music production, representation, and reception.[67]

Moreover I build on Josh Kun's work on the "American audio-racial imagination," which posits that considering music's potential function as a form of survival—considering "audiotopia"—offers key insights into racial relations and dynamics.[68] Developing an awareness of and a vocabulary to describe the American audio-racial imagination is to better articulate and thus develop critical analysis with which to address the "peculiar sensation, this double-consciousness, this sense of always looking at one's self through the eyes of others"[69]—or, to paraphrase Baldwin, this sense of always hearing one's voice through the ears of others. In developing our awareness, we take on the collective response to the acousmatic question. Since all predicates heard in the voice are judgments made by acculturated listeners, heard voices reflect the norms and values of those listeners. Parsing encultured responses to the acousmatic question builds a critical apparatus that aids in denaturalizing, in the context of the belief that it is possible to know sound (e.g., F-sharp, quarter note, in 60 metronome tempo), or disidentifying, in the context of the belief that it is possible to know people and to know them through their voices (e.g., the belief that President Obama is "tal[king] white"), through critical interventions such as the micropolitics of listening. In building on these strategies and perspectives, I wish to understand and detail the material-symbolic projection, manifestation, performance, and perception of vocal timbre in general, and racialized vocal timbre in particular.[70]

Listening to Listening

While working through specific issues related to voice, *The Race of Sound* is a book about how ideas and ways of listening manifest. Attuning to how we observe voices offers one poignant way of witnessing concepts and active processes of thought in manifestation and in practice. Thus by listening to listening we can trace voice back to ideas.[71] And by doing so, we can consider the sound and the meaning attached to it as several of many interesting data points that can help us understand the voice as a collective expression of a cultural fabric, and as arising through listening.

In *The Race of Sound* I propose that we can better understand voice by examining *listening* to voice, because (1) attitudes around the voice as essential, innate, and unmediated are deeply engrained; (2) voice is always already produced through social relationships, within which it is heard and reproduced; (3) critique on the symbolic level remains a critique of systems of thought, seemingly separate from the material and sonorous voice and the sensorium involved in experiencing that voice; (4) research on the quantifiable material level is seldom connected to the symbolic power dynamic, a dynamic acted out through listening (whether with human ears or machines); and finally (5) the limit to knowing voice lies in what we understand about listening to it; hence to know voice we must examine the listening practices that structure voice.

That which is manifested through listening is consequently measured and used to confirm ideas and ways of thinking and the ways in which they manifest. That is, voice has long been believed to be essential, innate, and unmediated, and consequently any meaning derived from it is unavailable for critical examination. Listening to listening, I propose, enables analysis of the voice—even as it is an essentialized object—and offers a space within which we may do more than automatically re-essentialize it. In order to listen to listening, though, we must first observe listeners' naturalized behaviors and assumptions.

Methodology

Because my basic definition of voice is that it does not exist a priori, I developed a methodology that responds to this perspective. By listening to listening in order to become clearer about the auditory practices that structure voice, analyses that are intended to identify the most accurate figure of sound are no longer relevant. Listening to listening urgently calls for new analytical tools so as not to replicate essentialisms. Fundamentally, listening to listening also calls previous data into question and expands our notion of what can count as data. In short, it reorients the researcher. To that new landscape, critical performance practice applies an analysis that resists renaming, resists replacing one existing category with another. In laying bare the ways voices are produced and listened to, and in building the ability to note where naming takes place, critical performance practice can also resist another renaming. When we consider voice through critical performance practice, a measurement of the naturalization of voice is introduced, and this analytical framework allows us to step outside of and question the endless loop of essentializations and of increasingly nuanced categorizations. Thus we can see that both naming and resistance to naming vocal timbre are political. It is this process that I call the micropolitics of voice.

As mentioned, considerations of the thick vocal event have tended to fall into two camps, involving attention to either the measurable or the symbolic. I often compare the rich vocal event to the falling of a tree. In this scenario, material considerations encompass considerations of the atoms; the shift in the tree's position from vertical to horizontal; the actualization of some of the shifting air molecules into sounds; and how the ecosystem shifts from living to dead, with the tree becoming nutrition for insects, fungi, moss, and more. Symbolic considerations can include concern with the pitch of the falling tree's sound and the range of possible meanings and interpretations of that sound. In a vocal event such as vocal fry, a material position would concern itself with the function of the vocal folds in sonic production; a reading of a spectrogram that could, for example, consider the pattern regularity or irregularity; the impact on the vocal cords; and more.[72] From the symbolic position, vocal fry would be considered in terms of its meaning and signaling, including its gendered and generational dimensions.[73]

Aiding me in coming to *The Race of Sound*'s conclusions was an experiential and experimental approach based on embodied knowledge of singing and listening. I developed multiple experiments into the more streamlined *critical performance practice methodology* expounded earlier. The methodological tool of critical performance practice synthesizes and combines the book's correctives (voice is a collective, encultured performance, unfolding over time, and situated within a culture) with my performance-based tenets concerning voice.[74] Carrying out critical performance practice means testing and examining materially and performatively symbolic positions on the voice and tracking any insights, findings, and conclusions to the symbolic realm—even if a symbolic interpretation seems beyond evolutionary logic. Critical performance practice methodology offers a tool that allows tracking between, among, and within the measurable, symbolic, and articulated (or performative) modes.

How is the methodology of critical performance practice implemented, in practical terms? Critical performance practice applies narrative analysis to objects, timbres, and discourse based on listeners' observations. It aims to tell the story not of whether a voice is authentic or maintains fidelity to a given idea, but of how a given vocalizer is associated with a particular category, culturally created group, or genre. In this way critical performance practice methodology can address performances carried out through listening. Responding to the myth of voice as essence, critical performance practice re-creates the isolated and bifurcated listening that takes place in upholding such a myth. For example, by working through the triangulated and mutually influential areas of the material, the measurable, and the symbolic; by testing through vocal teaching and practice; and by assuming that vocal events are collective, encultured, and manifested through listening, we can test and debunk hypotheses (e.g., that there is an innate black vocal timbre). And by tracking how vibrating air molecules are eventually performed, experienced, and interpreted by a human being who is situated within a particular cultural context, we can learn more about the ways the symbolic is embedded within the material and the material is not disconnected from the symbolic.

Built on the assumption that voice is neither innate nor unmediated, critical performance practice methodology is able to test any meaning that arises through listening, as well as track measurable categories back to the concept(s) and relational dynamics that gave rise to them in the first place. Moreover this work does not stop with a critical diagnostic. By engaging critical performance practice we are able not only to identify, analyze, and offer critical positions but also to propose critical performative strategies that can contribute to untangling notions of voice as innate, essential, singular, defined statically, and a priori.

To summarize, racialized timbre exists as a species under the figure of sound and is used as proof of race because the figure of sound assumes that it indeed identifies an example of a phenomenon that exists in nature—an essence. However, there are two incompatible phenomena. The first paradigm, the figure of sound, is a particular way of listening to things. When you listen to it in this way, it produces a restrictive outcome: it allows only certain namings and situations wherein multiple naming possibilities nonetheless exist and within which reaching a certain threshold moves us into a situation of contested namings. Race exists vocally for most people because they approach voice through the paradigm of the figure of sound, wherein voice can be named and the naming ritual is limited to the names into which a given responder to the acousmatic question is enculturated.

The route to a better name is to step away from the paradigm of the figure of sound altogether—and here we use the acousmatic question to propel this lateral movement. Applying the acousmatic question to listening to listening allows a more precise question to come into relief: Why do *I* hear this person in this way? In our focal shift from the singer to the listener, we not only move to a second paradigm, from essence to performance, but we can also hear the performance as the product of combined processes of entrainment, style, and technique.

At first the answers to the questions—the singers' very singing is in itself an answer to the question "Who is singing?" and to "Why do I hear this person in this way?"—look exactly the same. However, what establishes the difference between entrainment as understood through the figure of sound and entrainment as understood through style is *agency*. Through agency, a space for discernment is cleared and the trick of race is subverted. If, as Ta-Nehisi Coates notes, "race is the child of racism, not the father," *style* is singers' and listeners' selective use of a lifetime of formal and informal pedagogy, even if this education took place within a racist society. Specifically, as a community member and a scholar, in order to discern style and technique I "listen in detail" to how we listen to timbre.[75] The acousmatic question introduces a technique that can lead us to the revelation that not only is timbre not essential, but when the figure of sound paradigm collapses, something is there. What is revealed is entrainment and style and technique. We move from immersion within the figure of sound paradigm to what is exposed when peeling off its veil.

Style and technique, then, constitute an approach, an analytical mode, and a description of a condition. They constitute an *approach* when a given vocalizer plays with the material condition and feels compelled to name the practice and its product. Here technique refers to an inner vocal choreography, the actual movements the singer executes, and, more specifically, singers' employment of vocal technique to create the types of sounds they want to make. Style refers to the overall stylization of the vocalization and to the elusive differentiation that, for example, causes two equal, perfectly presented renditions to be identified as a romantic versus a baroque rendition of a piece. Style and technique constitute an *analytical mode* when, on being confronted with the acousmatic condition, listeners listen within an inquisitive frame. They may ask themselves: What is the material play? What are the ranges of ways I could name these performative choices? Doing so, listeners recognize the material-symbolic play on the part of both vocalizer and listener. Style and technique constitute a *description of a condition* when we understand that voice is not identified a priori.

If the meaning of vocal timbre is explained entirely through the singer's execution of technique and communication of style, and listeners' interpretations of these aspects, a certain type of imbalance may be felt. Analysis of technique and style does not seem to have the capacity to account for the racism played out through the voice as a tool of systematic oppression. For example, racial mimicry from antebellum to present-day minstrelsy cannot be excused as merely trading in stylized vocal techniques. As Eric Lott has noted, an imbalance of power and the related inability of one side to negotiate create a situation of cultural theft and imperialism.[76] To me, the very structure of power within which entrainment and subsequent vocalization take place is the issue, not which exact timbres were unconsciously entrained and which were deliberately performed. The issue is the fact that a timbre performed by one person is understood as essence (e.g., a so-called white timbre performed by a person understood as white), while the same timbre performed by another person is understood as an imitation (e.g., a so-called white timbre performed by a person understood as African American). In other words, the same timbral performance is assigned a different meaning depending on the power structure within which the vocalizer and listener are situated. And entrainment as essence, versus as style and technique, is not defined by any external, measurable parameters.

However, I would argue that, by carefully attending to style and technique, as listeners (both as vocalizers and as listeners of other vocalizers) we can develop tools that will help us to distinguish between, for example, "racial mimicry" and "mimicry of racial mimicry," to draw on Daphne Brooks's and Anne Anlin Cheng's vocabulary.[77] Within the context of the United States, the former trades in what Radano has described as "animation" of blackness.[78] The latter, however, engages vocal technique and style in a recognition of complex cultural origins—where any recognized sonic markers have developed through a fraught power dynamic in an explicit process of creating difference. Indeed, to invoke Radano again, "thinking about black music this way, finally, helps us recognize how it emerged and evolved according to identifiable social processes

TABLE INTRO.1. Beliefs about the Material and Beliefs about What Is Named

	Belief about the material	Belief about what is named
Essence	Material is essential	Names essence
Entrained	Material is given/formed	Names the condition
Style/technique	Material is chosen/selected	Names the choice

along the symbolic boundaries that structured a profoundly racialized world."[79] The actualization of any given phase within the politics of listening, as shown in table Intro.1, depends entirely on how listeners heed the acousmatic question.

By questioning erroneous ideas about sound as essence—fixed entities that are possible to know—we may turn our attention to what I call sound as a vibrational practice, a practice that is materially dependent and contingent. When we bring discussion regarding the metaphysics of sound into the realm of people's voices and identity politics, the parallel is this: I have identified that a given sound does not exist as such a priori, and hence cannot be identified as correct or incorrect. Thus sounds cannot be considered in terms of their relative fidelity or falseness (*falsk*, as "out of tune" is phrased in Norwegian). I complicate this basic observation about sound and extend the problematics to voice. By doing so, I dispel the notion that timbre is unique, is singular, and arises from the singer. Hence the notion of voice as essence is also dispelled. In that way, I can show what the naturalization of parameters and ways of measuring sound do to the more general experience of voice and listening. I can also foreground the explicit political and ethical dimension of such practices.

While much of my previous work on voice and race has carefully traced the entrainment of timbre, here I attempt to account for overlapping possibilities of entrainment used in the service of the figure of sound and as a resource in the expression of agency. Entrainment may take place within a constrained existence, such as the conditions of slavery or gender inequality, where the entrainment of the body is total. Entrainment can also take place within the choice to undertake a particular vocal practice, within a vocal practice's resistance against hegemony, and in a play whose vocal roles may be forced upon a person, within which the vocalizer may potentially redefine the very definition of that vocal practice. That is, what we have referred to as vocal "mimicry of racial mimicry" may be connected to familiar positions, what Gayatri Spivak describes as "strategic essentialism" and Jose Muñoz considers "disidentifications."[80] By closely examining entrainment's complex condition, we may conceive of certain uses of entrained vocal features as *technique and style*.

By extracting the thread of *technique and style* from the totality of entrainment, I can turn the acousmatic question into a productive one, a method of critical practice.[81] This practice does more than name the choice the singer makes. In listening, we can be more precise, zooming in to aspects of "strategic essentialism" or performative "misrepresentations." Listening in to how we listen and how we respond to the acousmatic question *Who is this?* opens us to a type of micropolitics of listening, where the determination of race, essentialism, and naturalized concepts can be analyzed and contested by the listener as well as the vocalizer.

Thus, by practicing listening to listening, applying the critical performance practice analytical framework, and either flagging or performing the micropolitics of listening—that is, by hearing that there is nothing unique or natural about voice while taking steps to decipher its encultured process—*The Race of Sound* offers a significant challenge. I challenge both everyday listening to and indexing African American voices, and Cavarero's theory of the "vocal ontology of uniqueness."[82] While Cavarero ties the sound of the voice to the uniqueness of the vocalizer's body in order to offer a relational ontology and politics, I advance the micropolitics of listening, a process that does not assume any indexical connection between voices and bodies. In fact I began by noting that racialized listening does not necessarily stem from racism, and I can now show that, (most likely) inadvertently, Cavarero's "vocal ontology of uniqueness" assumes the very same logic that supports racialized perception of vocal timbre.

Chapter Overview

In each of the chapters I deconstruct how a given voice is created through (1) projection by the listener rather than by the vocalizer alone. I show how and where that process actively and concretely affects the singer's body or vocal presentation and detail how these concepts are (2) manifested in the singer, explaining (3) which symbolic position is projected over them. The breakdown of this process offers details of the politics that are carried out through vocal timbre. Additionally, within the chapters I discuss and offer examples of the different phases of the micropolitics of listening. The micropolitics of listening includes both reinscribing essence through entrainment and moving away from essence by harnessing entrainment toward self-determined style and technique.

I can also offer another way to think about this book: it argues that when listeners identify vocal performances as black, they are really offering a naturalized shorthand for deeply informed and considered cultural expressions that are always, in the here and now, actualized through vocal style and technique.

Each chapter discusses different aspects of these naturalization processes and the performances of their conflations. In other words, singing is always made up of entrainment, style, and technique but is generally mistaken for essence. And when voice is mistaken for essence, other aspects of the vocalizer that are believed to be essential are conflated with voice and are forced into a causal relationship, performing the erroneous logic that an essential black body gives rise to an essential black voice.

In chapter 1, "Formal and Informal Pedagogies," I set out a case against vocal timbre's ability to sound the essence of a person. The chapter presents as an alternative explanation that vocal timbre is a result of the material condition of the voice as formed through continuous entrainment. Specifically I offer a consideration of voice as always already a continuous formal and informal pedagogical enterprise. Voice teachers' projection of race and/or ethnicity as unmediated essence, which would be expressed in an authentic voice and would result from the training, is used as evidence of the singer belonging to a given ethnic community. This chapter's analyses and concerns join the tradition of critical pedagogy. By considering the deep impact that voice teachers have on the formation of vocal timbre, I investigate the ways in which overall perceptions of race and ethnicity, paired with convictions about voice as an essential and unmediated expression of interiority, play decisive roles in vocal training. I argue that what takes place during formal voice lessons, where teachers' sentiments about their students' identities (including race and ethnicity) are present in vocal evaluations and pedagogical prescriptions, is similar to informal voice lessons. That is, by investigating a very controlled situation of entrainment within formal voice lessons, I make a broader argument about the ways everyday vocal training is manifest corporeally and vocally. As such, we understand that voices are equally entrained through repetitions called forth at teachers' urgings or in seeking recognition within a classroom or broader social setting. That is, the material voice manifests cultural and societal values and dynamics of power in its habituation of ligaments, muscles, and tendons, and sounds timbral identity categories accordingly.

In chapter 2, "Phantom Genealogy," I show how the values of a historical-political moment set the agenda for entrainment. I not only show that the voice is entrained but also discuss how stories about essence are constructed. Thus I argue that perception of timbre is shaped through narratives about the singer and the voice—specifically by which artistic, genre, repertoire, ethnic, or racial genealogies are drawn around the singer. By arranging the narrative arc within which a voice is heard, perceptions can be radically directed, opportunities presented for the singers can open and close, and the artist's voice and career can be shaped. For example, applying such a reading, we see that Marian Anderson was placed within the narrative genealogy constituted by the historical perception of slaves' voices, burlesque opera, and minstrel shows. Her career, her voice, and its perception were thus shaped by such complex filters and identity markers, including the notions of black voice and the suffering voice of the spiritual, that became so strongly associated with her that she was not allowed to move beyond their projection onto her voice. As such, this chapter traces the fraught history of African American singers in integrated U.S. opera to the mid-nineteenth and early twentieth centuries. While a singer can certainly relate a narrative through timbre alone, individual singers are heard in particular ways depending on the context within which they are placed. In these cases the racial imagination may not manifest by directly shaping flesh and its consequent vocal production. Rather it manifests through timbre that is experienced as racialized simply through the musical, genre, or repertoire genealogies connected to the voice. The ways in which we hear a particular voice are drawn as networks among people, genres, repertoires, and racialized conceptions of music, and a singer's vocal timbre is directed through that filter.

In chapter 3, "Familiarity as Strangeness," I show that, although we are all subject to vocal entrainment, it is possible to use it as the basis of what I call "style and technique." Style and technique means that the singer is making choices in regard to his or her vocal sound and expression and has honed his or her vocal technique to reflect these choices. I also show that, ultimately, the listener is integral to recognition of the singer's voice as essence. Specifically this chapter examines timbre in regard to particular vocal pitch ranges and their relationship to gender. Gender is not primarily cued through pitch, as is commonly assumed; timbre is a stronger cue to gender. Jimmy Scott, who was born with Kallmann syndrome, which affects male hormonal levels and prevents the onset of puberty, is commonly believed to signal gender ambiguity through vocal tessitura. By considering Scott in relation to comparable black male singers, I show that his vocal range was also occupied by many of his peers whose voices were not read in the same gender-ambiguous ways. I posit that the gender ambiguity through which Scott is perceived is due to timbre, particularly through his failure to exhibit falsetto in the higher register. In other words, a singer can sing in a higher vocal register and signal (black) masculinity by exhibiting the otherness of that vocal register through falsetto.[83] In contrast, Scott sang with great timbral integration, sounding no timbral break into falsetto. Thus while Scott himself insisted on his heterosexual male identity, his producers and audiences manifested ambiguity toward his gender and state of being through imagery, descriptions, and castings. My discussion shows that listeners undertake extreme measures when a voice does not fit within preconceived, culturally dependent notions—such as Scott's voice, which challenged the popular image of masculine blackness.

The stages of the politics of listening are also reflected in the digital realm. In chapter 4, "Race as Zeros and Ones," I focus on the ways audiences are integral to the process of creating the singer through digital entrainment—the fashioning of sound and image using digital tools—which is produced on the basis of assumed essence. Here I revisit the vocal synthesis software Vocaloid, which I first critiqued in 2008 for producing and reinforcing racial musical and vocal stereotypes. Surprisingly, over the past few years music producers and online user communities (with significant overlap with the anime community) have refused the racialized presentation of the vocal synthesis software, imposing their own characters over the voices. The Vocaloid vocal synthesis system and the artistic activities around it provide a striking example of how voices are manifested through a combination of sound, music, genre, and visual and textual (re-)presentation. Zero-G and other companies that work with the Vocaloid system eventually listened to their users' application of the software and their full artistic creation of characters that subverted the companies' original bid. Zero-G et al. have responded in kind, working with users in creative competitions and crowdsourcing the imagery, names, and textual descriptions of newly issued synthetic voices.

Chapter 5, "Bifurcated Listening," showcases audiences' oscillation between aligning the performer with style and technique and aligning him or her with essence. It is in this unsettled space that we can understand the singer as having agency. In examining the concrete tools of singing, this chapter reveals a new avenue in the reading and analysis of voices. I tackle how the reception of vocal icons such as Billie Holiday complicates and contradicts the simultaneously applied practices. On the one hand, Holiday's voice is deemed unequaled in its power due to the authenticity it communicates, which is believed to be beyond the performer's control. On the other hand, Holiday's distinctive voice is a prized sound for imitation. And when that imitation is successful, the fact that Holiday's life experience overlays that of the artist who erases herself while channeling the grain of her voice poses multiple intriguing questions, making the vocal moment even more poignant. Observing how the position that voice is essential, unmediated expression is upheld while recognizing *vocal imitation*, we can see that such attention requires a rearrangement of listening into a bifurcated perception that can simultaneously hold the "essential" voice of one singer and the recognizable voice of another in a contradictory grasp. In other words, the recognition of ventriloquism counters the premise that an inimitable voice has been imitated.

The sixth and final chapter, "Widening Rings of Being," calls for the study of voice as style and technique. By developing detailed knowledge about the arbitrary and adoptable patterning of voices, we can grasp the institutionalization and internalization of race that takes place through daily vocal and listening practices. I posit that race and ethnicity are merely aspects of a continuous field of style and technique that are distinguished from its limitless potentiality only through naming. In other words, *The Race of Sound* suggests that in order to more fully understand the operationalization of race through vocal timbre, we must turn our inquiry to the listener who materializes his or her own values when naming voice. The chapter and book close by posing an open-ended question: What protective mechanism does the naming of voice serve for the listener? What would listeners have to confront within themselves if they were not able to rely on the mechanism of measuring voice?

FORMAL AND INFORMAL PEDAGOGIES

Believing in Race, Teaching Race, Hearing Race

The cultural belief that voices are the unmediated expression and evidence of transpersonal categories, such as gender and race, is strong. When discussing this reality, I often invoke the example of Charles Clifford, an African American man who, in 1999, was convicted for selling drugs on the basis that the perceived sound of his voice made him culpable for the crime.[1] Yet Clifford's imprisonment—a result of what his lawyers called "linguistic profiling"—runs against the grain of influential humanities scholarship that has carefully demonstrated that audiovisual markers of race are highly subjective. Moreover linguists have convincingly shown that word choices and pronunciation are tied to speech communities rather than to innate qualities. In my own field of musicology, critics have noted that influences of vocal styles originating in a given community are complex and often extend beyond social circles and across time, as well as musicians' strategic essentialist positioning. Then again, none of these inquiries has systematically mapped the way vocal timbre is entrained and perceived through racialized listening practices, thereby debunking the assumption that voice is an unmediated essence. This is particularly the case in relation to the large body of scholarship that has explored the rich cultural and performance history of diverse forms of African American music.

Although it may sound at first like a complete exaggeration, it is nonetheless true to say that the extensive scholarship on North American and African American musical traditions has never methodically demystified racial suppositions about vocal timbre. This striking problem is deeply embedded in a long history of practices that involve measuring race. Audile techniques that render African American vocal timbre largely unquestioned today can be traced back to aspects of nineteenth-century scientific racism. The belief that the perceived racial component of vocal timbre could be scientifically measured originates in debates about craniometry, the pseudo-science that calibrated humans by race. My research shows that formal and informal vocal pedagogy and listening practices, which were built upon these very assumptions, understood that, like a resonating chamber, voice "sounded" the cranial dimensions—measurements that were already racialized. Although I am specifically concerned with the cultural-historical formation of one category of vocal timbre, I address the broader concern that researchers in the humanities have no method with which to account adequately for the micropolitics of timbral difference to which voice is still subjected.

Racialized conceptions of vocal timbre persist. But why has vocal timbre resisted analysis when most aspects of the racialized body have been critically treated? I contend that fundamental misconceptions about voice and vocal timbre have prevented careful and critical analysis. Therefore, if we think about this problem simply through questions around race, and avoid examining basic understandings of voice, we will fail to get to the root of how categories, including race, are constructed through vocal timbre. In other words, we will easily note the attitudes about people that are overlaid on top of voice, but we will not be able to identify the distinct building blocks with which racialized timbre is projected, perceived, manifested, and sustained.

However, if we do change underlying conceptions that sound and voice are expressions of essence, we may be able to analyze, and create adequate responses to, the racialization of vocal timbre. Thus, by critically examining a given group's listening responses and judgments regarding connections between vocal timbre and a given social category, race, or ethnicity, we may begin to deconstruct the deeply held conceptions about sound, voice, and vocal timbre that give rise to racialized judgments. I'm quite aware of the work this entails and of the minute details that need attention, but I am also confident that once we identify our basic misconceptions about sound, voice, and vocal timbre, the process of listening to voices and the critical-analytical tools we use to discourse about voice will be healthier and transferable across fields.

Recall, then, in the introductory chapter, I identified three correctives to broad misconceptions about voice:

- Voice is not innate; it is cultural.
- Voice is not unique; is it collective.
- Voice's source is not the singer; it's the listener.

In this chapter I will further investigate these correctives and misconceptions by examining the vocal-pedagogical process as it unfolds during formal and informal lessons (i.e., everyday socialization). By doing so, we can better track the phase in the micropolitics of listening that I term entrainment. Specifically it is the figure of sound, as it pertains to racialized vocal timbral categories, that is entrained. In other words, the figure of sound is entrained into voices and is subsequently used to authenticate the very value system from which it was born. Voices that are heard and even those voices that sound according to racial timbral categories are akin to planted evidence in a criminal investigation: objects or biological traces intended to serve as proof of a fabricated story of difference. While the actual vocal apparatus or vocal sound has not been replaced by another person's vocal apparatus or sound, daily formal and informal voice lessons plant an investment in race into both vocalizers' bodies and listeners' assessments. In short, this chapter outlines the cultural-pedagogical work carried out to maintain the figure of sound.

By identifying the processes involved in decisions around the broad areas of enunciation, articulation, and intonation, we can begin to grasp—and deconstruct—the constructed aspect of timbre. Together these broad vocal processes contribute to oral and vocal tract shape, which in large part indirectly determines timbral characteristics. Vocalizers can also directly influence timbre by, for example, making a concerted effort to sound happy, disinterested, or stern. As choices around enunciation, articulation, and intonation are repeatedly made, they begin to form a pattern of vocalization that feels natural or second-nature to the vocalizer and is recognized as his or her default and consistent vocalization pattern by the people around him or her. Taking this process as a starting point, we may begin to deconstruct any notion that voice is innate and unique. By denaturalizing timbre and placing it on par with word, enunciation, and intonation choices, we see that voice is not innate and that timbre is also formed as a result of vocalization patterns that are repeated hourly and daily and are favored (or not) depending on their result. In other words, vocalizers adopt, keep, switch between, or discontinue timbral patterns.

Voice is not unique. Vocalization and the resulting timbre are as encultured as is self-expression through fashion. Akin to the ways we are habituated to dress, walk, or throw a ball "like a girl," each vocal engagement is connected to a collective practice that depends on habituated micro-vocal maneuvers. This daily vocalization practice habituates flesh, muscles, and ligaments, leading to an altered vocal apparatus that, in turn, leads to altered sounds. Finally, the source of the voice is not only the vocalizer, because any statement about a voice arises from a listener's assessment. Thus, relevant to our inquiry into race and vocal timbre, a given listener's attitudes about race will influence which aspects of a voice he or she will notice and how he or she will make meaning from them. It is when such basic assumptions about voice go unquestioned that we also fail to examine our responses to the acousmatic question: *Who is it who is speaking*?

I seek to explain responses to the acousmatic question through the three correctives about voice: voice is not innate, not unique, nor the singer. In identifying these correctives, I am indebted to Foucault, who famously discussed "the body as an object and target of power." The distinguishing aspect of the modern body, he claimed, is that it "is manipulated, shaped, trained," and "obeys, responds, becomes skillful and increases its forces." Not unlike a machine, it is "built, rebuilt, operationalized and modified."[2] We may productively consider the formation of this modern body through the concept of *body technologies*. Coined by Mauss, this term describes "one of the fundamental moments in history itself: education of the vision, education in walking—ascending, descending, running."[3] Jonathan Sterne has added "the education and shaping of audition" to this list, and here I add the phenomenon of vocal timbre.[4] While we all move, hear, and sing in idiosyncratic ways, body technologies intone these actions so they both project and affirm social structures of recognition—for example, "masculine" strides, "girl-like" throwing, or "upper-class" enunciation—or, in Michael and Linda Hutcheon's formulation, "To train the voice is to train the body."[5] As Mauss points out, phenomenology assumes culture. I come to my consideration of voice with the assumption that vocal-timbral recognition is a type of encultured behavioral knowledge that manifests dynamics of difference and normativity. Specifically, sonic timbral markers that suggest a person's race or gender hold little meaning or power outside the cultural context within which they are defined.

Thus, naming vocal timbre is a kind of knowledge. That is, within the range of responses to the acousmatic question—the seemingly innocent *Who is this?*—the dynamic of power relations is played out. In response to the question, a statement is offered; therefore, it is in our trust in the question's validity, and in the assumption that it can be answered, that the micropolitics of timbre is carried out. The power dynamic is enacted through the incessant validation of culturally and socially tinged assessments of vocal timbre as knowledge.

Encultured actions create a certain set of behaviors, and these behaviors are set within the play of power. Vocal timbre is an area of body politics that has not yet been thoroughly examined as encultured performance. I wish to look more deeply at this area of human activity in order to denaturalize timbre and to illuminate some of the ways in which timbre, and listening to timbre, are encultured. I also want to examine vocal timbre as a means of considering how we may intervene in the continuous cycle of vocal-timbral naturalization. Thus this chapter considers formal and informal vocal training in order to understand how racialized vocal timbre is taught and how the physical vocal apparatus is molded and habituated as a result of encultured listening practices.

One way to break away from this cycle, I posit, is to consider a given response to the acousmatic question from the perspective of critical performance practice—that is, to critically examine and experiment by reproducing the vocal practices that created particular timbres, and to test assumptions about essentialized timbre by experimenting with the range of timbres a given voice has the capacity to produce. Such a performative approach can allow us to deconstruct and denaturalize our responses to the acousmatic question. It can also help us identify and name the building blocks from which such naturalized notions are constructed. And by deconstructing notions of voice as innate, singular, and arising solely from within the vocalizer, we can begin to recognize the micropolitics that are carried out through listening. Finally, this allows us to begin to detail the incestuous process of assessing, manifesting, and validating, and thus to denaturalize vocal timbres. In this first chapter of *The Race of Sound*, then, I aim to establish in greater detail how misconceptions about voice affect not only its experience and perception but also the materiality of a voice and its vocalizer. This process, I assert, takes place through both formal and informal vocal instruction.

Sounding Race

As ocean depth is measured by taking soundings (historically using rope; now using sonar), race is sounded, or assessed, through the process of listening. Classical vocal artists undergo intense training, much of which is dedicated to learning to hear their own voices as the experts hear them. A decade of daily practice, weekly (or more) private lessons, monthly or quarterly master classes, sustained participation within the milieu of classical singers and musicians in the form of summer workshops or university or conservatory training, and opera apprenticeship programs constitute the pedagogical structure and business model for this world. The path toward a professional vocal career is an immersive experience and lifestyle. The following discussion draws on specific examples from the world of classical vocal training. It offers a foundation from which to discuss how any feedback given to a vocalizer about vocal usage contributes to his or her subsequent vocal choices and habituation. I seek to examine how general attitudes around sound play out when voices are listened to within the context of deeply held assumptions regarding difference.

The observations are drawn from my sixteen years of intense and direct participant observation of selected classical vocal music communities and training.[6] While I am still in touch with the classical vocal world, my immersion in the community, including what I refer to as my period of participant observation, took place in Norway and Denmark (1991–99), New York City (1995–99), and southern California (1999–2007). In addition, over a period of a year I conducted thirteen interviews with voice teachers.[7] In these conversations I asked general questions regarding what constitutes vocal timbre, how vocal timbre is developed, and what kinds of information vocal timbre is able to convey about the singer. When correct singing—in terms of vocal weight and color, both crucial issues in vocal pedagogy—was discussed, issues of race, ethnicity, and vocal timbre arose. In the thirteen interviews I carried out, all but two teachers told me that they can always tell the ethnicity of the singer by his or her vocal timbre. In the following discussion, I will draw on the sentiments expressed in all the interviews. However, two interviewees stood out as crystallizing these sentiments in their statements, and therefore the specific quotes are pulled from those conversations.[8]

Besides my in-depth knowledge of this performance and its associated pedagogical tradition, another reason to consider the relatively exclusive vocal practice of the classical music world is that, in general, teachers and practitioners of this vocal art are some of the most sensitive to—and systematic adopters of—timbral enculturation. Moreover I chose to concentrate on teachers and practitioners of classical music because of the genre's strict adherence to the written score, and of its uniformity in both pronunciation and overall performance practice. That is, for this study, the practice's institutionalization offered a type of baseline. However, I do not take classical vocal practitioners as exceptional or as different from other vocalizers. To the contrary, I take them to be "first adopters," and indeed, broadly speaking, the practice is only a subset of formal and informal vocal pedagogy. Like a kind of subspecies that shows certain characteristics more strongly than the general population, classical vocal pedagogical practices can be read as an advance warning system of danger. According to my analysis, despite classical voice professionals' extensive vocal education, this subset of experts does not succeed in breaking the cycle of racialized timbre or in laying bare the process of enculturation. To the contrary, many continue to amplify and re-present these beliefs on respected and prestigious stages.

Vocal timbre is both elusive and poorly understood in the performing arts, humanities, medicine, and sciences alike, yet entrenched positions are held tightly in each area of specialization. Vocal timbre, and what a given timbre signals, is one of those things most people assume they know. For example, most people trust timbre over words if, say, the words "I'm okay" seem to be contradicted timbrally, or if a voice on the radio sounds like it is an older black man or a young white woman. Classical voice teachers hold clearly articulated positions regarding timbre and its meaning. Rather than the unarticulated taxonomy most listen from, voice teachers' work is to align vocal training with the vocal characters arising from particular cultural moments. Thus classical voice teachers train and pair timbre profiles with conceptual areas such as identity and authenticity. For both the layperson and the voice teacher, timbre is a barometer of one's inner state and health and is broadly held, continuously assessed, and reliably acted upon. In fact vocal timbre is used as a diagnostic for gendered mental health issues ("She's hysterical") and as a diagnostic for truth statements ("She's lying"). Major plots in both Western literature generally and the Bible specifically hinge on the characters' ability to judge authenticity vocally.

Voice teachers tend to crystallize these general sentiments into two prevalent concerns around guiding the aesthetic development of vocal timbre: first, the question of what constitutes healthy and natural singing for the student; second, the need to avoid homogenizing students' voices in favor of allowing each singer's "true timbre" to emerge. When we discussed the "correctness" of vocal weight and tone color, which are crucial topics in vocal pedagogy, issues of what kinds of information these aspects convey about a singer also arose. Specifically, when fleshed out, conversations that began on topics of "healthy" vocal use and the "authentic" timbre of a given singer's voice ended by discussing race and ethnicity.

The notion of "correctness" in vocal weight and tone color returns to issues of maintaining healthy, authentic, and beautiful voices. Interestingly, practices that the teachers I interviewed considered "healthy" and "honest" were ultimately correlated with each student's race and ethnicity.[9] One way to describe this situation is that, even when it was not referred to explicitly, race was discussed under the cloak of singing "healthily" or "authentically." Because race has been thoroughly naturalized, what I describe as racialized vocal timbre is conceived by voice teachers as simply a healthy way of singing that promotes a nonhomogenized sound and that allows students to be "themselves."[10] Voice teachers and students commonly conceive of voices as unrealized or repressed due to any number of causes, from bad vocal habits—often conceptualized as "tensions"—to evidence of underlying physiological or mental issues. In short, a "healthy"-sounding voice is assumed to be a voice freed from blockages, and thus is assumed to be an unmediated sonorous conduit for the subject. It follows that whatever voice teachers understand as the singer's "inner essence" will be equated with a sound voice and will be listened for during vocal "diagnosis."[11]

For example, Dorothy, a soprano and professor of voice for seventeen years, told me that she can invariably identify whether a student is, for example, Armenian, Russian, or Korean from the student's vocal timbre, but she frames her classification of students as a concern about *vocal health*: "There are principles of what is healthy, a balanced sound and all of that, and if [voice teachers] observe that rule, then how can they not hear an Armenian sound or Korean sound and cultivate it?"[12] In this statement Dorothy reasons that if the voice is trained along principles designed to promote a vital, balanced sound, it will "naturally" display its inherent ethnicity, thereby conflating race, national identity, and vocal health.[13]

Rather than considering this strategy as a race- or ethnicity-based categorization of voices, Allison, another longtime teacher, views what she calls "ethnic timbre" as the "unique color" and vocal "fingerprint" of the student, yet associated with a racially categorized group. Pedagogy, then, becomes a matter of bringing out the "true sound" of the student's voice—and that true sound happens to be connected to his or her perceived race or ethnicity. Allison regards this pedagogical philosophy as a means of allowing each student to maintain an element of individuality within the highly cultivated and stylized world of classical singing. During the interview process, I frequently heard such statements regarding the *individuality* of a voice, by which my interviewees meant, I believe, the opposite: "an ethnic vocal timbre," determined by *socially* constructed notions of ethnicity. Indeed, an ethic of multiculturalism has permeated vocal pedagogy; Allison goes so far as to criticize ignorant teachers, who have not been exposed to a variety of "ethnic timbres," for "homogenizing" their students' sounds. And most teachers with whom I spoke stressed the importance of being literate readers of "ethnic" vocal timbres.

When we began to discuss what might cause the varied timbres of different ethnicities, Allison explained that the Central and South American timbre is influenced by Latin people's connection to their bodies. In her view, inhabitants of Latin cultures are motivated by bodily drives, while North American inhabitants are moved by cerebral concerns. She explained that singers' connections to their bodies affect their sounds: "The Mexican culture, for example, is, to me, a very visceral culture. It's not a super heady culture. I think we in the United States of America tend to be more cognitive. You know, the whole Puritan ethics where sex is bad and you just disallow that you have anything below your waist. You know, that is a primary drive in people." To clarify her sense of the connection between body and timbre, I asked Allison whether she believed that some cultures come by that body-voice connection more naturally, so that even if a singer from one of those cultures studied with an American teacher, or a teacher who is not particularly focused on the development of the body-voice connection, his or her voice would still sound the connection that was "in" him or her from the beginning, and thus would differ from the voice of an Anglo-American growing up in the United States. Allison responded:

> Yes. I think [Latin Americans] naturally have that connection.... They're ... connected to their bodies ... and their guts [said with throaty, "gut sound"], and they make music from their hearts. In European repertoire they talk about that "she broke my heart, I will just lay down and die now" [said with a very "proper" voice], and in Hispanic music, the Latino music: "She broke my heart, she ripped it out of my chest and stomped it on the floor!" [nearly screaming]. And that's how their music sounds. It's very gut. Americans—we don't operate on that level, we tend to be a visual or cognitive society.

Allison expressed her claims in compassionate language and avowed a commitment to allowing the "natural" and "individual" voice to remain untouched through intense classical vocal training. Yet several interviewees used these notions of "naturalness" and "individuality" synonymously (if unconsciously) with ethnic, national, or racial difference.

While Allison and Dorothy articulated strong ideas regarding authenticity, the singer's "real" voice, and ethnicity, all but two of the interviewees touched on these ideas in some way. And, as we will see below, their sentiments are shared by musicologists. While these appraisals are offered as personal assessments, evaluations cannot be assigned as their personal beliefs, but must be seen as examples of broad and pervasive cultural beliefs. Who cannot recall having made such judgments? These teachers carrying out one-on-one sessions with their voice students are doing what the broader sociocultural milieu sanctions by consuming such trained voices. This reinforcement parallels racialization in other corporeal realms, such as skin hue and hair texture. What is today cloaked in concepts of health, authenticity, and self-expression was, only half a century ago, unhesitatingly described as race and racial qualities.

In a 1957 encyclopedia entry titled "Primitive Music," for example, the musicologist Marius Schneider posits, "Every being has its own sound or its own song, the timbre and rhythm of which embody the mystic substance of the owner."[14] Alan P. Merriam and Valerie Merriam observe, "Races are held to have special and mystic abilities, and what the anthropologist attributes to learning and to culture, Schneider attributes to race."[15] In Schneider's own words, some musical characteristics are "bound up with certain racial factors.... In fact, the innermost essence of the more intensely specialized types of song cannot be transmitted at all . . . since the dynamic and vocal timbre which is inseparably bound up with it cannot be acquired by learning."[16] According to Schneider, whichever vocal qualities are heard as expressing "certain racial factors" are understood within this listening framework as nonnegotiable expressions. The consequence of such a listening position is that meaning is formed within a rigid and closed cycle.

Historically speaking, my informants' investment in race, as classical vocal pedagogues, is far from anomalous, although their frankness on this question is worth noting.[17] As mentioned earlier, all but two teachers claimed to hear singers' ethnicities in their vocal timbres. That is, teachers' perceptions of students' ethnicities shape their understanding of how the students might develop as singers, and further direct teachers' ears.[18] These beliefs lead mentors to encourage certain timbral features over others, which causes the re-enculturation of racialized vocal timbre. Not only do these specific teachers teach in this way, but vocal pedagogical ideologies as a whole are built on specific ideas of timbre.

In fact the classical vocal pedagogy practiced today in southern California (and elsewhere in the United States) can be traced back to the formation, during the mid-nineteenth century, of what John Potter has called the modern classical voice. For Potter, the formalization of vocal pedagogy grounded in scientific principles marks the transition from the premodern to the modern classical voice.[19] Modern classical vocal pedagogy's advances and its questionable notion of "the natural" were aided in part by findings encouraged and enabled by colonial racial dynamics and research resting on colonial power structures. As Potter observed, the ideologies powering the formation of the modern classical voice are still present in current vocal practices.[20] Despite having substantial specific knowledge about voice, voice teachers—like most people—hear race (or health or authenticity) as communicated through essential timbral qualities that are presumed to tell us something unmediated about a person's internal state.[21]

As noted in the introduction, I suggest that these racialized assessments do not flow directly from, nor are they solely enabled by, racial sentiment in a given culture and society. It is not, contrary to the expression, turtles all the way down. Instead, I would argue, this type of listening is propped up by general assumptions about the nature of sound and its ontology (i.e., assumptions regarding what we can know about sound and its meaning). It is these underlying misconceptions about sound that lead, on the one hand, to misconstrued notions of voice and to unfounded trust in a given response to the acousmatic question, on the other. That is, the type of listening reported above is supported by unexamined assumptions regarding what kinds of meaning sound is capable of communicating.

Thus, while not comparable in effect or ramification, listening assessments ranging from mood, gender, age, health, authenticity, class, ethnicity, and racial tone arise from a general framework that involves the possibility of quantifying and knowing sound. All of these assessments are enabled by the naturalization of sound as a specific knowable entity (e.g., A-sharp) and as a more ambiguous knowable entity (e.g., as authentic or truthful). While, of course, many racialized assessments do arise from an investment in difference, some arise from a less informed place, a place of wanting to "be right"—to "name the right sound," to adhere to fidelity—an impulse that is nonetheless equally impactful.

In the same way that I argue within this book that a particular voice is not unique, but rather is created and understood within a specific milieu, I suggest that the vocal teachers' way of listening is not necessarily directly tied to personal racism, sexism, or any other prejudice. What underpins their assessments are the general beliefs that we can identify and know sound and that essential traits are audible in vocal timbre. Once the assumption that sound is knowable is in place, values and beliefs within a given society—around, say, race, ethnicity, gender, age, or class—then also become "knowable" through sound. Concepts such as "correctness," "health," and "authenticity" are vacated prior to their use within a cultural and social situation. Hence, because sound in general, and vocal timbre in particular, have no a priori meaning, whichever sentiments, positions, and values a given society deems important fill this vacuum. In other words, the assumption that we can know sound, and that the meaning we infer from it is stable (and indeed essential), allows for the *projection of beliefs about people onto the sound*. Thus denaturalization of concepts about race and timbre depend on a more general denaturalization of basic assumptions and attitudes about sound. In a nutshell, the naturalization of voice leads us to believe that what we decipher through voice exists in that voice, and the naturalization of race leads us to listen for race everywhere. But this destructive cycle cannot be broken on the level of judgments about race and voice, because it does not rest there. Instead we must look to the more general level of the epistemology of sound and the process of listening to voice.

Recall that the acousmatic question's assumption that the voice is essential and innate, and that asking and responding to the question can lead to an objective assessment of the vocalizer, is rooted in broader assumptions about sound. That is, a constellation of beliefs in a stable, knowable sound—what I call the figure of sound (FoS).[22] Observations about voice, such as "healthy," "authentic," "Asian," and "speaks white," are really statements built upon the idea of an existing, knowable, sound with a given meaning. We are conditioned to *hear what we listen for* and to assume that what we hear is indisputable, and this conditioning acts much like planted evidence. As I see it, the dominant Western notions of music making and listening are founded on this paradigm of the figure of sound. Listening that is formed and that takes place within this paradigm is listening that knows *only* how to listen for and through difference from a fixed referent. Because the FoS paradigm assumes a fixed referent, it fosters a specific kind of listening wherein the primary goal is to identify difference from that referent. In other words, within this paradigm, making sound and listening are about degrees of fidelity to an imagined a priori sound and our ability to identify that fidelity. For example, we note observations such as the following response to the acousmatic question:

- This is "ma" (as opposed to "pa," and "ma" is different from "pa").
- This is B-flat (different from other pitches).
- This is a too-high or "out of tune" G-sharp (it is not faithful to the a priori G-sharp).

Yet the paradigm of the figure of sound does not end with the drive to know and identify a sound such as, say, G-sharp as the second scale degree of the key of F-sharp major. Nor does it end the drive to know and identify sounds on a unit level, such as syllables, words, or pitches. The paradigm of the figure of sound extends into timbre, and such timbral assessments are used to establish basic information around a sound source in response to the acousmatic question:

- This is a flute (different from other instruments, say, a clarinet).

Nonetheless, beyond basic distinctions such as flute versus clarinet, timbre is often bound up with the assessment of value and identity. For example, in the FoS paradigm, listening to human voices can lead to appraisals such as "This is the sound of a woman's voice," based on perceived similarities between a given sound and other, specifically female, human voices and their dissimilarities to male and children's voices.[23] Likewise the observation that someone is "talking white" has at least two layers: the assumption that the speaker is not white and the assumption that the unexpected racialized vocal style is out of place, necessitating attention to the perceived clash of identity and timbre.[24] The statement comes out of a comparison with what the listener believes should have been the case. Because Obama is understood to be a black man, his voice is compared to the FoS of "black man." When his voice is not understood as consonant with that FoS, its infidelity to the FoS is called out. In other words, this observation exemplifies assumptions that race is quantifiable and knowable and that race is timbrally conveyed. This is but one example of how the figure of sound is also bound up with the assumed meaning of an identity, which is often derived from values and assumptions related to visual cues.

Listening within the FoS framework effectuates a circular logic. This logic is akin to a self-fulfilling prophecy that sets up a prediction that it directly or indirectly causes to be true. Per Robert Merton's description, the self-fulfilling prophecy is "in the beginning, a *false* definition of the situation evoking a new behavior which makes the original false conception come *true*." He continues, "This specious validity of the self-fulfilling prophecy perpetuates a reign of error. For the prophet will cite the actual course of events as proof that he was right from the very beginning."[25] In the case of racialized vocal timbre, the "false definition" is the belief in race as an essential trait, which causes us to fail to attend to the many ways in which timbre is learned and performed, including those we associate with race, ethnicity, or authenticity. We then listen for those phenomena that we believe to exist; we subsequently hear them, and because we hear them, we believe the perceived meaning to be verified.

For example, "black voice" is an observation born from an encultured notion of sound that expects fidelity to a referent and listens for difference. When voices are reduced to fixed sounds and undergo assessment, they cannot help but be heard within binaries or scale degrees of fidelity and difference. Moreover, due to the ways vocal timbre has historically been aligned with and metaphorized as interiority and truth, the stakes and ramifications of such assessment involve more than just sounds. What is measured is a person's degree of fidelity to and difference from a dominant category. I bring two observations to this reading of a timbral micropolitics.[26] First, the persistence of the metaphor of vocal timbre as the unmediated sound of selfhood and subjectivity means that a given society's beliefs lie at the core of its citizens' personhood. Second, culturally trained ears assume, and thus perceive, only formalized vocal practices as encultured. Moreover they tend to perceive enculturation only in certain components of the trained voice, while believing others to be "natural." The naturalization of the untrained voice as an expression of "essential identity" and the naturalization of aspects of the trained voice according to racial categories are both functions of the micropolitics of timbre.

Independent of the "actual" or intended sound, what a listener ultimately hears depends to a large extent on his or her assumptions regarding the ontology of sound. For example, the belief that it is possible to know something firm about a sound and its source deeply affects the meaning the listener will form around that sound. Such belief arises from assumptions that sound can be known, is stable, and can be unequivocally recognized and unambiguously named. Furthermore such belief assumes a deep connection between sound and its apparent signification, an assumption regarding significance that is taken on through enculturation. Considering the statements made by the voice teachers in light of the broader listening framework helps us to see how, when listening through the FoS, we will listen for and, indeed, hear according to categories aligned with values within a given society (e.g., race). However, we do not need direct feedback (in the form of overt praise, recognition, misrecognition, or punishment) from a teacher or other authority figure in order to fall in line.

The FoS is based on the general practice of listening for similarity to and difference from it, and on the perceived implication of the listener in this process. Such listening springs from the assumed connection between a given sound's source and its apparent meaning. Therefore, while some of the statements from my interviews may be taken as extremely provocative, I chose these because they are helpful in identifying the FoS's framing of timbral phenomena as personal, innate, and essential rather than as stylistic performance choices. On the level of the FoS, while observations such as "This is a soprano," "This is a woman's voice," "This person is happy," or "This person is sad" are not driven by the same urgency, they're based on the same type of listening. There are no technical differences between these seemingly innocuous observations and the types of observations made by the voice teachers.

Believing Race, Practicing Race, Creating Race

One of the many paradoxes related to timbre is that while vocal timbre is understood as essential, classical vocal pedagogy is built upon the very notion that it is possible to construct timbre. For the initiated ear, the classical vocal soundscape can be heard through such blocks of timbral construction. While for most people, classically trained voices might simply sound "classical" or "operatic," tone quality is further and more specifically refined within subgroups, directed by aesthetic and pedagogical concerns. A national school of singing implies both a preferred tone quality and the technique that produces that quality. Tone quality and technique function symbiotically on a national and regional scale and result in differing pedagogical schemes and a corresponding shaping of the voice according to a national tone ideal. (Perhaps the most commonly known national schools of singing are the English, French, German, and Italian, but there are also the Nordic and Slavic.)[27] We know that the sounds of these various schools are the result of aesthetic preference and of vocal technique designed to accommodate this preference.[28] We also know that they are *not* recognized as the unmediated expression of a people, contra nineteenth-century romantic nationalism.[29] A national school of singing simply refers to a region's preferred tonal quality (and the vocal technique that engenders it) and does not, of course, necessarily indicate the nationality of the singer. A Norwegian singer may be educated in a conservatory in Germany and thus develop a German tone. A teacher schooled in Italy might teach in Paris, passing on his or her Italian technique and tone ideal.

The phenomenon of national schools of singing is understood as contextually contingent and acquired. The processes involved in forming vocal timbre are formalized and recognized in extreme detail, even if the resulting timbres are understood within the signifying process only by those with knowledge of the cues. While most people have the ability to recognize operatic timbral characteristics in general, not everyone can distinguish between the various national schools of singing. However, for those initiated into operatic timbre, the national schools are quite distinct from one another.

While national schools of singing seem to most people to be only an esoteric detail, for those invested in these distinctions, the preferred national tone that one must perform in order to remain within the group is a serious matter. This is where we can sense the resonance between judgments about what somebody should sound like ("Obama should sound black") and what they might sound like ("Obama talks white"). The French Ministry of Culture, for example, has employed official inspectors to observe regional conservatories of music in order to evaluate their vocal pedagogy. Richard Miller reports that in the decades after World War II, some inspectors were especially adamant that their concept of proper onset be taught in French conservatories.[30] The preferred onset among these inspectors was an "attack," a very strong beginning that is created by a powerful inward thrust of the abdomen. This forces the vocal folds to deal with a high level of airflow, and in response the larynx resists the excess airflow by fixing the vocal folds in a single position. The result is a "held" sound that is slightly above pitch, with a pushed and sharp-sounding phonation. This sound is now characteristic of the French onset and, because the attack sets up a tense position of the vocal folds, of the French line.[31]

It is also important to note that within the geographical area of a single national school there are many different spoken dialects. In some areas these dialects are so different that they are nearly separate languages. In countries such as Switzerland, students at a single conservatory might have four different mother tongues. However, phonation and, as a result, pronunciation differ in song and speech, and singers learn very carefully how to pronounce words when singing, even in their first language. Even singers with different mother tongues or dialects are unified under a single national school or a single teacher's tonal ideal. In summary, the presence of national schools of singing not only exemplifies the malleability of the human voice and the enormous impact that teachers' and institutions' tonal ideals and pedagogical practices have on the ultimate sound of a classical singer's voice, but also shows that we are fully aware of, and aesthetically depend on, the constructedness of vocal timbre in formally trained voices.

Translated to my tripartite diagnostics, this shows that we know voices are not innate, but cultural, and that voices are not intrinsic, but are shaped by a pedagogical collective. However, feeling this intuitively and knowing it intellectually can be challenging. While we know that voice is malleable and construct pedagogies based on this premise, and while timbre is simultaneously naturalized, essentialized, and used to evidence uniqueness, legible FoSs are embedded in flesh through the process of formal and informal pedagogy. Many of these vocal legibility projects are self-directed and so fluidly part of everyday life that their timbral formation processes are not accessible to us. Vocal timbral constraints are not straightforward; they are categories into which we ourselves shape our voices as well as categories that are pushed upon us, both of which are part of a broader sociocultural landscape. Therefore, while we have acquired knowledge in vocal pedagogy and vocal anatomy and could put that knowledge together with how social categories, including vocal timbral categories, are performed and thus embedded into flesh, it has nevertheless been challenging to decipher the constructedness of timbre and to debunk the myth of its authenticity.

Vocal work is about legibility to the listener.[32] The listener should here be understood both as an external listener who comes from the same group as the vocalizer and listens for sameness and belonging to that group, and as a listener outside the vocalizer's group who can identify the vocalizer as different from himself or herself and as part of a given group. The listener is also the vocalizer, who goes through the same listening exercise of identifying with and against others. By bringing meaning to the voice, we not only affect it discursively but also, because of voice's physical formation according to its practice, *form* the voice's material existence according to that meaning. Participation in a collective requires vocal legibility. Conforming to notions of legibility shapes the voice. That legibility is not a single monolithic quality that overrides other timbral effects; it is an aggregate of these effects.

But isn't it contradictory that, while a singer is understood by a vocal community to be simply emitting timbral evidence of his or her, say, "ethnicity," that vocal community also has the capacity to recognize that the same singer—at will and with practice—is able to perform across a wide timbral range? It is not contradictory. I understand these different listening outcomes as arising from a split in listening, with both branches emerging from the FoS listening framework. That is because, while within a Western listening context all sounds are heard through the FoS, timbre is believed to fall into two broad categories. Some aspects are understood as essential, while others are understood as acquired, performed, and somewhat open to interpretation. But those aspects considered essential are no different from those that are viewed as acquired. The validity of each rests on the naturalization of the FoS.

Through daily vocal practice, voice in its material presentation as flesh, ligaments, and tissue is encultured according to its constant comparison to the FoS. Because the voice is formed in conjunction with the body, it too broadcasts the social attitudes and values of the trained body. Every interaction, from state educational systems to the informal lessons imparted when a person receives positive or negative feedback on his or her voice, entrains (auto-)listening and vocal behavior. I believe we may take a crucial step toward untangling the "politics of frequency," to use Steven Goodman's apt term, by considering—through a systematic examination of the micropolitics of timbre—how vocality, a learned physical behavior, is trained and perceived.[33] Part of the micropolitics is to begin to render all vocal activity as learned physical behavior; through such activism, vocal timbre and any given categories of it that we know can be denaturalized.

Each and every reading carried out after a person's voice is reduced to the FoS contributes profoundly to that person's feeling of place in the world, to his or her attunement to the world and the self, and to his or her subsequent vocal exchanges. In short, informal vocal exchanges are powerful "voice lessons" that invite or discourage particular vocal practices. They are daily vocal performances that in turn are manifested in flesh, and sounded through it. Therefore, in a vocal encounter, the most productive question is not *Who is this?* Instead I propose that we ask questions such as these: On what naturalized assumptions about sound and voice are responses to the acousmatic question based? Through which unexamined assumptions are culturally created categories such as race and ethnicity upheld? In short, by turning the acousmatic question to the listener, and ultimately to ourselves, we are encouraged to denaturalize vocal timbre by asking *Who am I?* Who hears this? And how was that sound learned, and through which sets of practices, constraints, desires, and structures of power did its so-called meaning become unquestioned?

The micropolitics of listening is not only applied by others to us, or by us to others. The assumption that it is possible to know sound leads to an overarching listening stance—the acousmatic question—through which the casual listener, the teacher, and listeners listening to themselves (i.e., auto-listening) seek fidelity. When it is assumed that it is possible to know sound, the primary tenet in listening is *identification*. The basic tenet of identification is comparison with an "original," whether an actual sound or the idea of a sound in the mind's ear. The success of such listening is then dependent on the listener's ability to distinguish between similarity to or difference from the ideal. In other words, on a basic yet profound level, such listening entrains listening for sameness and difference.

As argued earlier, the sounds we ultimately produce and hear are based on enculturation; they are not merely essential qualities expressed through timbre in an unfiltered manner. To further clarify, it is because of assumptions around the FoS—for example, the assumption that sound can be identified—that we are unlikely to critically examine listening processes and the meanings they produce on a fundamental level. We thus further extend basic assessments regarding a given sound's sameness and difference from the ideal. The given categories, which offer the basis for listening for sameness and difference, are, of course, culturally dependent.

The sound categories that can be further identified include distinct pitches, adult voices (versus, say, children's voices), male versus female, "ethnic" versus "nonethnic," "authentic" versus "inauthentic." However, because the premise of *listening* is identification, we do not question the likelihood of the a priori existence of the identified categories. Thus, due to a basic belief in something as seemingly innocuous as the possibility of knowing sound, the question of whether it is possible to identify social categories via listening remains unexamined. And when listening within the ontology of the FoS, what is heard is then understood as evidencing essential and nonnegotiable traits.[34]

What takes place, then, is a curious division between the way we listen to and assess categories understood by a given society as essential, and the way we listen to those aspects of human vocal timbre that the same society understands as performed. Thus our assumptions around the "innateness" communicated and evidenced by vocal timbre arise within a triangulation between the FoS, a society's belief in certain essential categories, and listening that is entrained to detect sameness and difference. And detection of sameness and difference, in this case, is the detection of essential categories. The catch-22 is that once these essential categories are called out and grounded in FoS listening, there is no room to question them. The very premise is that they are indisputably *true*. It is such assumptions around the possibility of identifying meaning based on listening to and assessing sound in general, and voice in particular, that forms the basis of racial judgment. To combat racism through the mechanism of vocal timbre, we must examine this process in both seemingly unbiased (A-sharp) and biased ("ethnic") views of timbre.

Listening to Listening

Turn the ear to the listener and listen critically to listening, to the "listening ear" in action.[35] In carrying out an analysis that is conscious of the fact that any voice is part of the collective voice, and that listening contributes to shaping that voice, we must listen to how we listen. With the knowledge we gain from listening in this way, we can deconstruct the situations that, without such an analytical breakdown, will serve only to reinforce structures of power. By insisting on voice as event, as encultured even before birth, and as collectively projected, we can understand voice as the result of an ongoing pedagogical enterprise. This understanding, in turn, allows us to align vocal practice, listening to voice, and voice scholarship with the critical turn in pedagogy.

What I term formal and informal voice lessons are the sites where the micropolitics of timbre are played out through the fibers of the vocal folds and the habituation of the cricothyroid. These formal and informal voice lessons are the starting points of any meaning-making through voice. They are also where we can assess the process of meaning-making and present and manifest new ranges of meaning. The methodological framework of critical performance practice may already be recognized as informed by educational theorists such as Henry Giroux. As does Giroux, I want to resist the sentiment that a totalizing dominant culture merely imposes itself on students. I am inspired by the ways critical pedagogy understands resistance as enabling transformation and maintains that goals of hope and emancipation should be central to any curriculum.[36] My own resistance has taken the form of demonstrating that the practical experience of exploring more of the wide range of timbral potential inherent in each voice offers a perspective on any single timbre. In this way, it is through deconstructing basic assumptions about voice at the outset of listening, and through attending to the process within which listening takes place—through *listening to how we listen*—that the listening framework becomes apparent and that we can grasp the politics of listening.

By shifting our analytical lens from the so-called sound to observing and understanding the process of listening, we may *listen against* the FoS by hearing voices as entrained. With this shift in listening, we demonstrate that every timbral quality or meaning may be interrogated. Even timbral qualities thought to be innate can be deconstructed as reflective of ways of listening that reproduce, or return, the listener's historical, cultural, social, political, moral, ethical, academic, or any other positionality.

Then, once again, we see that there is no a priori sound (FoS) or meaning. Within a given context, there is only the triad: the consortium of sound, meaning, and listener. Moreover, within this consortium the listener is the point of origin for meaning production.[37] The point is that by understanding the relationship between the FoS and the way such general assumptions about sound are acted out within a given society's values, we may begin to grasp some of the ways in which listening is always already political. By breaking down the consequences of FoS listening, we can understand its potential power. But, more important, by enumerating the consequences of the FoS, it is once again confirmed to be false.[38] That is, since sound is not always already static and knowable, the "identified and its meaning" are listener-derived. And while the "identified and its meaning" are listener-derived, the assessments produced are assumed to be so indisputable that they are used as evidence of everyday observations and their validity is extended to the American court system.

By performing through a range of timbres and witnessing other voices doing the same, and by critically listening to listening, we can create a counterlogic to any given response to the acousmatic question. *Who is this, vocalizing?* It is President Obama, who "sounds white." By focusing our attention on that listening ear, we hear a *listener* who holds the views that Obama is a black man. Ergo, he is not a white man. Black men sound X. White men sound Y. President Obama sounds Y. Ergo, President Obama sounds like a white man. The implication is naturally that it is only worthwhile to make this observation because President Obama does not sound black. By denaturalizing the assessment that gives rise to these responses to the acousmatic question, we can counter the meanings that arise. In this way we can gain critical distance and harness powerful analytical tools by keeping the critical performative aspect of voice front and center. Consider again the 1999 ruling mentioned in the introduction to this chapter. The Kentucky Supreme Court judge decreed that since no one would find it inappropriate for an officer to identify the voice of a woman, "we perceive no reason why a witness could not likewise identify a voice as being that of a particular race or nationality, so long as the witness is personally familiar with the general characteristics, accents or speech patterns of the race or nationality in question."[39] With this pronouncement the Kentucky Supreme Court ruled that a conviction was appropriately based solely on a police officer's identification of a suspect whose voice he had heard in an audio transmission. The officer identified the suspect as a black male, testifying that during his thirteen years as a policeman he had had several conversations with black men and therefore was able to identify a black male voice. We here witness an assumption that because a voice is heard as black, it is emitted from a body that is unquestionably black.

Critical performance practice offers a path to examining assumptions such as "what you hear [i.e., blackness] is what he is."[40] In other words, while the expression of many commonly held sentiments around race (or any other category important to a given society) is often curtailed, enactments through everyday listening are carried out, reported on, and deemed sound evidence, including in the Supreme Court. Even in cases where racialized politics are not expressed by institutions, like the Supreme Court, adapting the analytical framework of critical performance practice allows for methodologies to denaturalize racialized timbre and hopefully disrupt assumptions that otherwise would slip under the radar.

Adopting the mindset that listening is always already political has the potential to put intense pressure on the positionality of the listener. That is, listeners are not let off the hook, as they otherwise would be, existing under the radar when it comes to understanding timbral meaning. Keeping in mind that listening is always already political, listeners would examine any interpretation or judgment, acknowledge that it is the process of listening and interpreting that willed that particular meaning into being, and interrogate why it was projected onto a particular vocal timbre. In other words, through such a process, listeners would know that any meaning that arises is based on their own meaning derivation.

An examination of meaning would lie not only in the "objective" sound, but also in a meeting between the sound and the listening stance of the listener who derived those meanings. And, most important, such a critical inquiry would find new sites to deconstruct the process of signification.[41] For example, how and why were aspects of vocal timbre, such as health and race, areas of signification that were understood as innate, and to which no interrogative or deconstructive pressure had been applied? For my part, uncovering the overall pedagogy of FoS listening, and understanding that it is involved in each and every act of listening, made the performativity of these areas very apparent. Therefore, while I continue to stress that each teacher (and every one of us who has made and inadvertently continues to make racial judgments based on voice) is not necessarily doing so because of overt racism, I do not suggest that this erases the violence committed through microaggressions. On the contrary, each and every one of us is still responsible for how we contribute to our collective upholding of these racialized practices. As a community member, my work is, first, to understand how I listen and, second, to gain awareness about what I *produce* through habituated listening practices.

"Questions of form and politics are frequently subsumed in criticism by racial metaphor," Jennifer Doyle writes. "The mere presence of race as an interpretative factor" often overshadows the "work's difficulty and the complexity of its relationship to its context."[42] In other words, such artists are primarily understood through racial categories. The analogue is to the singers discussed earlier, who are felt to be singing with their "true voice" when they are heard as whichever ethnic or racial category a listener understands them to inhabit. However, as this chapter has shown, form and function create one another. The form produced through loaded racial metaphors (say, *African American opera singer*) limits what and who may be allowed to inhabit and express that form. In a paradigm of naturalized vocal timbre, instead of examining vocalists in all their idiosyncrasies and the communal projects in which they have participated and of which they are a product, listeners seek to find ways to explain the category or form, such as race, that they believe to be true. However, by attending to the performed aspect of vocal timbral production, individual listeners can denaturalize vocal timbres one at a time while helping to effect a broad cultural shift. It is that shift this book hopes to inspire.

2

PHANTOM GENEALOGY

Sonic Blackness and the American Operatic Timbre

———————

The Saints were supposed to be Spaniards [wrote a *Time* reviewer about *Four Saints in Three Acts*,] but Virgil Thomson had chosen Harlem Negroes because of their diction. White singers, he feared, would act foolish and self-conscious chanting such lines as "Let Lucy Lily Lily Lucy Lucy let Lucy Lucy Lily Lily Lily Lily Lily let Lily Lucy Lucy let Lily. Let Lucy Lily."

— "Music: Saints in Cellophane," *Time*, 1934

A great diva with a long career behind her was singing Tosca at the Met in 1961. Her dresser asked her whether she had yet heard Leontyne Price, who had just made her unmatched debut as Leonora in *Il Trovatore*. "Ah, yes," purred [the diva]. "Price. A lovely voice. But the poor thing is singing the wrong repertory!" The dresser registered surprise. "What repertory," he asked, "should Price be singing?" The great diva smiled a knowing smile. "Bess," she purred. "Just Bess."

— Martin Bernheimer, "Yes, but Are We Really Colour Deaf?," 1985

On a cloudy January 7, 1955, the golden-red auditorium glowed with expectation. On the dark, gaping stage beyond the proscenium, Marian Anderson took her position as the gypsy sorceress Ulrica in Verdi's *Un Ballo in Maschera*. Anderson recalls, "The curtain rose . . . and I was there on the stage, mixing the witch's brew. I trembled, and when the audience applauded and applauded before I could sing a note I felt myself tightening into a knot . . . and things happened to my voice that should not have happened. . . . My emotions were too strong."[1]

FIGURE 2.1 Marian Anderson at the Metropolitan Opera, 1955, as Ulrica in Verdi's *Un Ballo in Maschera*. Reproduced with the permission of the Marian Anderson Collection, Rare Book and Manuscript Library, University of Pennsylvania, and CMG Worldwide.com.

The emotional power of this moment is not surprising. At the time of Anderson's debut, the Metropolitan Opera, the largest and most prestigious opera house in the United States, had been exclusively white for its entire seventy-two-year history. Despite her brief 1955 tenure (only eight performances over two seasons) Anderson's hiring was a decisive moment on the path toward desegregating classical music; it was celebrated as a new chapter in American racial relations and policies. As the *New York Times* noted, it would "open doors" for "other Negro singers."[2] In fact Anderson's triumphant debut was one of many concrete manifestations of incremental improvements for which the civil rights movement—which came to a head the same year, with Rosa Parks's activism and the Montgomery bus boycott—had fought long and hard.

Many of the conditions that Anderson had to overcome to reach this pivotal moment gradually improved for later generations of African American singers. However, while the second half of the twentieth century saw American opera houses decisively integrated, the black performer is still consistently viewed as peculiar. While descriptions of her visual appearance have been toned down over the decades, the timbre of her voice has routinely (if often admiringly) been characterized as "black." Which door (was it really the front door?) had been opened for Anderson to step through when she was only being engaged to portray the other? Case in point, only a few years later the African American soprano Camilla Williams debuted next door at the New York City Opera in the role of Madame Butterfly, the abandoned Japanese geisha. And what did that mean for subsequent generations of African American classical and opera singers, and for the filters through which they were heard? In which ways did this compromised invitation reflect the politics of the racism under which these singers and their audiences lived? While chapter 1 detailed the process of vocal timbral entrainment, this chapter shows how a given historical-political moment set the agenda for entrainment, casting into relief how figures such as Anderson were limited in artistic opportunities due to structural racism. Moreover I detail how, despite the considerable progress signaled by the Metropolitan Opera's desegregation, the old story about vocal essence is upheld today.

The year 1955 was pivotal in the path the United States took toward becoming a desegregated country. Anderson's January debut and another decisive event in American history, Parks's December arrest, bookended that year. And while the two women had different relationships to the civil rights movement and to their individual roles within it, they both emerged as major figures within the story. Anderson's appearance was the first desegregated performance on the Metropolitan Opera stage, arguably the country's loftiest music venue; Parks's resistance led to desegregating public space. Both milestones offered the promise of a society beyond race. However, in thinking about today's post–civil rights landscape, we see that the country as a whole is still acutely aware of race, acting it out sensorially, through, as we learned in the previous chapter, formal and informal pedagogies—and, more specifically, still hearing it.

A Phantom Genealogy of Timbre

The strong connotation of race associated with celebrated African American opera singers was something that took me greatly by surprise when I began spending substantial time taking voice lessons in the United States (in 1995) and subsequently moved here (in 1999). Listening within a European context, I was familiar with more general timbral brackets such as operatic timbre versus different types of popular music, and various national schools of singing, as discussed in the previous chapter. I also recognized that certain musical genres were culturally connected to particular communities and that members of a given community could hence be easily associated with a musical and timbral style. In moving to the United States from Europe, I nonetheless believed that all singers growing up in this country would come to the operatic musical tradition and most of its repertoire on an equal footing, as cultural outsiders.[3] However, I found that African American opera singers were discussed in a particular way in regard to their relationship to this tradition and repertoire.

Based on the graphic nature of historical and late twentieth-century descriptions of African American classical and operatic voices, I also expand upon the issue of acousmatic listening by attending to the question posed in the introduction: What do we name when we name voice in general, and vocal timbre specifically? I have found that the response given to the acousmatic question is not merely a consideration of the sound at hand. If assessment is not limited to aural components, then, through what associative network are African American singers' vocal timbres assessed?

This question was partly addressed in chapter 1. Some of these networks can be teacher genealogies or national schools of singing.[4] We also learned that associative listening filters can be informed by singers' visual presentation as it pertains to gender, race or ethnicity, and bodies that are considered normative. In this consideration I am indebted to scholars of avant-garde music, jazz, and literature, such as Fred Moten, who is concerned with the rematerialization of the visual through sound, and the objectification of persons based on how their visual presentation is understood.[5] Specifically, contextual information concerning the singer seems to be considered differently when comparing so-called normative and nonnormative opera singers. This is also the case when it comes to understanding African American operatic vocal timbre in a historical context. What dynamics are at play in listening to African American vocal timbre? For African American opera singers, in Kimberlé Crenshaw's formulation, what are the "multiple avenues through which racial and gender oppression" are expressed through vocal timbral assessment?[6] And how do they play a part in listeners' responses to the acousmatic question?

The dynamics of networks constitute the focal point of actor-network theory (ANT). Because mapping the effect and affect of music requires mapping across human and inanimate agents, scholars concerned with analyzing music culture are increasingly drawn to this approach. "Whatever music might be," Benjamin Piekut writes, "it clearly relies on many things that are not music, and therefore we should conceive of it as a set of relations among distinct materials and events that have been translated to work together."[7] Crossing the domains of people and things, ANT offers one approach to addressing music's human and nonhuman aspects.

In Piekut's consideration of ANT in relation to music scholarship, the potential analytical power of the *network* is often limited to "something . . . thin," which he labels "network 1." This consists of understanding music culture and mediation by identifying and narrating who is connected and what comes of these connections and actions. Piekut offers a useful schematic example: "Composer A knew violinist B, who travelled to San Francisco and met composer C, a childhood friend of writer D." However, as Piekut has identified, ANT also holds the promise of greater analytical potential if we invoke network 2, which "encompasses all the labours necessary to make network 1 actually work: things such as state regulatory agencies, maintenance equipment, corporate barons, international standards bureaus, and so on."[8] We may describe these two networks that Piekut identifies as surface dynamics and depth dynamics. Piekut suggests that, without considering the forces at work in network 2 that underpin the movement that takes place on the surface, our understanding of network 1 is superficial.

In the context of vocal timbre, network 1 could describe the genealogy of actors: teachers, vocal coaches, voice students, directors, conductors, and so on. Network 2 would identify actors such as music conservatory policies and regulations like segregation that prohibited African American singers from taking lessons with white teachers or singing in integrated contexts. While the two networks Piekut identifies could theoretically encompass everything, I have identified a third network that is at play when the vocal timbre of African American classical singers is conceptualized. Listeners, the actors in network 3, may also be analyzed within the two other networks, but, under the umbrella of network 3, they are considered specifically in terms of their capacity to listen to and name sounds, including voices and vocal timbres. Through this focus I suggest a particular path—listening to how actors listen and name—to understanding social mediation in music. Specifically, in the case of vocal timbre, conceptions about timbre and timbre itself form a never-ending spiral in which the "regimes of material-semiotic meaning that condition each sounding and make it significant" are at play.[9]

Network 3 points back to our third corrective: voice's source is not the singer; it is the listener. Here the listener—not only in the form of voice teachers but also of listening audiences—amasses an associative fabric of naturalized musical and cultural genealogy that includes voices described as "husky, musky, smoky, misty," "[retaining] much . . . original savagery," and "thrilling with their weight of sorrow."[10] Thus, connecting the identification of network 3 to my overall framework reveals how the symbolic dimension is re-created in the material—that is, in the seemingly correct response to the acousmatic question.

The key to understanding the dynamic at play around network 3 is realizing that the network that surrounds and is believed to explain a given singer's vocal timbre (as identified by the listener-actors) is not necessarily based in reality.

However, it is nonetheless acted upon and acted out. That is, listeners apply associative filters whether they are truly associated with the singer or only believed to be so by the listener as he or she prepares to respond to the acousmatic question. Moreover the narrative descriptions of voice and timbre that arise from the application of these filters then enter the realm of discourse, and thus are actors in subsequent assessments of African American opera singers.

I think of network 3 as a *phantom network* or, in the case of vocal timbre in relation to African American singers, more specifically as a *phantom genealogy*.[11] Like a phantom limb, together the listeners that make up this network materialize their conceptualization of timbre, even if it is not found in reality or even recognized by the singers involved. And, like a phantom limb—a lost limb that seems to ache but cannot be treated because it does not physically exist—a phantom genealogy's associations and their ramifications are more difficult to debunk, as they are continuously renewed through unexamined listening practice. A phantom network is one with which the person it purports to describe does not identify, nor does he or she identify with the discourse that develops from this network. For example, Anderson was explicit in asserting her identity as an artist rather than a political activist. Yet she was repeatedly framed and heard through a particular interpretive lens: as an African American singer in the context of the civil rights movement. While she understood her own artistry within the context of the operatic vocal tradition, she was often viewed as a natural singer within the genealogy of African American music.

While there are multiple streams of discussion within the humanities and social sciences regarding the question of human and/or nonhuman actors, I would like to forward the notion of a human actor who becomes an actor when naming something: when he or she names African American vocal timbre and offers an explanation for it. Hence, as stated in chapter 1, I believe that to understand the phenomenon of singers' racialized vocal timbre is to understand listening to and identifying that vocal timbre.

By paying close attention to how actors describe the voices and vocal timbres of African American classical singers, and by tracing the associative networks that influenced these descriptions, we can reveal the story of the timbral bracketing of African American classical singers. By considering the phantom network that is activated and acted upon by listeners, I identify the constructed phantom genealogy that is used as a rationale for this timbral bracketing. In short, I show that the timbral traits (real or imagined) often cited as evidence for racial essence arise from listeners' beliefs, not from the voices themselves—and thus, like a phantom limb, both material existence and effect exist only in the imagination. Specifically I posit that at the pivotal moment when Marian Anderson was invited to sing at the Metropolitan Opera, she was cast and staged in such a way that connected her to the phantom genealogy associated with earlier generations of female African American classical singers who sang during segregation. In other words, the phantom network—network 3—continued to act upon subsequent generations of African American singers.

Listening Filtered through Nonsonorous Aspects

Several opera scholars discuss the visual appearances of African American singers in terms of casting. Rosalyn Story investigates the ambiguous feelings expressed by many African American singers toward George Gershwin's black cast–only opera *Porgy and Bess* (1935) and its racial typecasting. Lisa Barg describes how the first casting of Virgil Thomson's *Four Saints in Three Acts* (1934) relied on preconceptions that tended to exoticize African American performers.[12] And Jason Oby's important bouquet of interviews reveals that it is easier for African Americans to succeed as baritones or basses because the roles written for these vocal types are typically villains.[13] George Shirley has also addressed the ways in which African American male opera singers with baritone and, especially, bass voices tend to have more successful careers than tenors.[14] The particular obstacles for African American tenors relate to the operatic tradition of assigning set character types to set *fachs*, akin to typecasting. Typically, villainous roles are composed for basses and sometimes baritones, while the hero and romantic lead characters are written for tenors. Therefore the careers of tenors like Shirley are at a double disadvantage due to the typecasting of their voice type. First, there is resistance toward casting African American tenors as romantic leads, and second, there is resistance to creating what would, in most instances, result in interracial romances portrayed on stage, as a major production would most likely not fill both feature roles with African Americans. And third, as Naomi André has noted, the black operatic protagonist as antihero can be found from Otello to Johnny and Porgy.[15]

There are both overlaps and differences in how the intersections of race and gender play out for female and male African American opera singers. The way female character types are written for vocal types, with the heroine set for the soprano, while mothers, servants, and villainous figures are set in lower voices or in extreme vocal ranges, parallels that of the relationship between male character type and pitch range. Notably some characters who are othered in terms of race and ethnicity are set for soprano, and, as we've seen, those roles often serve as an entry point or limited casting opportunity for opera singers of color. Thus while African American female singers share roles of others, villains, and tragic characters, Farah Jasmine Griffin has shown that African American women's vocality serves an additional role: they are called upon to heal the country. Anderson is used to fulfill the latter function.

However, while much research exists on racialized language perception and casting, there has been no thorough investigation of the oddly discerning listening practice that so readily identifies certain classical voices as "black" and specifically locates blackness in timbre—the aspect of the voice that remains essentialized.[16]

The identification of a person who has mastered Western classical vocal production and repertoire as black requires a very different conceptual process than does the identification of a popular-music singer as a member of a racial category.[17] In popular and vernacular music genres—say, blues or country—vernacular languages and pronunciation styles signal performers' social distinctions.[18] In other words, contextual or linguistic information is available in popular music genres that enables listeners to position the singer. The resultant identifications are not primarily about race per se; they involve, for instance, geographic and social locations, which often coincide with racial divisions. Therefore what might mistakenly be understood as vocal distinction due to race could be a correct identification of difference, but misguided in its assumption about the cause of this difference.

In contrast, when people make statements about race in relation to operatic timbre, this misunderstanding cannot be explained as a misguided statement about geographic or social location. While the singers' native languages and dialects may influence their pronunciation, there are a number of reasons why this cannot be the cause of perceived differences associated with the singers discussed in this chapter. First, all native speakers of American English come to the core repertoire of opera (Italian, German, and French) with a foreign accent. Thus if native language and dialect were the causes of the differences that are identified, all American singers would be flagged as outsiders. Second, while accents are difficult to overcome, diction in core operatic languages is a foundational aspect of training for singers who aspire to professional careers. Singers who do not gain an extremely high level of proficiency in this area are weeded out and thus do not fall within the scope of our discussion. Third, in general the aesthetic of operatic timbre rides such a narrow line that any voice that falls even slightly outside it would simply not be considered a legitimate operatic voice.

In addition, not only does classical repertoire feature narrowly defined conventions of pronunciation, timbre, and stylistic range determined by a work's historical period, geography, and composer, but the notated compositions also dictate fixed pitches and durations for syllables and pauses, which therefore must be produced in the same way by each singer.[19] Unlike in popular music genres, where individual style is encouraged, taking liberties with pronunciation is not rewarded in the classical vocal world.

It is not an exaggeration to say that adherence to these established aesthetic, technical, and stylistic conventions defines the classical singer and that instruction in these conventions results in the characteristic vocal timbre recognized as a "classical voice."[20] A singer without these vocal qualities is simply not considered a classical singer by the opera community. Hence my question: Given that American classical singers are trained in a (European) musical culture that is equally secondary to all of them, and given classical music's minimal indulgence of individual style, what singles out African American classical singers as nonetheless inhabiting a particularly "black" voice?

If we believe that the black body is intrinsically different from the white body, that the voice communicates unmediated essence, and that, even when emitting a timbre recognized as classical, the resonance of a singer's black body is evident, the "black voice" is not an unthinkable idea. We can see the reasoning that seeks to explain it along these lines. For example, reactions to recorded reproductions of the black voice frame it as distinct: "Negroes [record] better than white singers, because their voices have a certain sharpness or harshness about them that a white man has not," the trade paper *Phonogram* reported in 1891.[21] This notion of a fundamental physiological difference was clearly expressed in a 1903 *Washington Post* article: "There is a peculiar vibrating quality in the negro voice, due, perhaps, to a peculiar arrangement of the vocal chords [*sic*], which is not found in the white race."[22] However, research on vocal morphology concludes that there are no more similarities within a so-called racial group than there are differences between groups.[23] Therefore the distinction must lie beyond the sound itself, in a phantom genealogy that is often activated by nonsonorous cues.

A Phantom Genealogy of Early African American Classical Singers

In order to better understand the listening context within which Anderson's Metropolitan Opera debut took place, we must move back in time from this performance. I first call to mind earlier performance contexts that laid the foundations for the association of black voices with certain repertoires. African American singers performed classical music in the same spaces and on the same programs with the minstrel repertoire, burlesque shows, and spirituals;

thus perceptions of classical performances by African Americans became inextricably linked to these genres. Second, I engage Jon Cruz's work on how abolitionists listened to slave song, examining his notion of *ethnosympathy* to understand how provisional subjectivity was granted to slaves and what this meant to how they and subsequent African Americans were heard. Third, I revisit two American operas from the early twentieth century, *Four Saints in Three Acts* and *Porgy and Bess*, which formally reenacted prevalent white views of African American identity and performance skills. Having unpacked the cultural baggage at play in the years leading up to the pregnant moment recalled at the opening of this chapter, I return to Anderson's story. Finally, in light of the surge of African American operatic divas who entered the scene during the 1960s and 1970s, I look closely at the frayed edges and visible seams of the integrated stage. Many centuries of racial politics that were activated by listeners in the 1960s and 1970s are similarly activated today. Thus, for contemporary operatic artists such as Ryan Speedo Green, the phantom genealogy of race is acutely present and, like a phantom limb, is famously challenging to negotiate.[24]

In the nineteenth century Elizabeth Taylor Greenfield (1820s–1876) and Matilda Sissieretta Jones (1869–1933) were among the first African American singers to perform classical repertoire for large interracial audiences, winning national and international acclaim (see figures 2.2 and 2.3).[25] Their performance practices and reception by audiences—where listeners based their opinions on related artists' work and on the work of white artists in blackface—have influenced the later reception of African American classical singers.[26]

Greenfield, a freed slave, was largely an autodidact, as no voice teacher during her era would have staked his or her reputation on a black singer. A generation later, improved race relations enabled Jones to train. But beyond this, Jones's and Greenfield's experiences bore similarities, many based in hardship resulting from the racial climate and white audiences' limited perceptual frameworks. Both singers had to either perform in segregated venues, with black audience members relegated to separate balconies, or sing for all-white gatherings. The dissonance felt by many members of the public when confronted with the unfamiliar sight and sound of a black person singing classical music was too much to overcome. On the one hand, the solution for which many reached, it seems, was to categorize these performances as minstrel shows rather than artistic experiences, attempting to deny that African American voices were suitable for classical music qua classical music. On the other hand, the connection audiences made between opera and minstrel show can also be seen in one of the nicknames by which minstrelsy was known during Reconstruction: "black opera."[27]

(THE BLACK SWAN.)

MISS GREENFIELD'S
GRAND EVENING CONCERT,
In the Town Hall, Birmingham,
ON THURSDAY EVENING, JUNE 23, 1853.

PRICE SIXPENCE.

FIGURE 2.2 Poster for Elizabeth Taylor Greenfield's 1853 performance at the Birmingham, United Kingdom, Town Hall. Birmingham Archives and Heritage, Local Studies and History: LF 55.4 _F2 (8/351). Reproduced with the permission of the Library of Birmingham.

For audiences of the day, the sight of a white usher accompanying Greenfield to the stage was so jarring that, judging by their reactions, the viewers might have been watching a "carnival freak show."[28] In 1854 the *New York Herald* described one escort who "seemed afraid to touch her with even the tips of his white kids, and kept [the performer] at a respectable distance, as if she were a sort of biped hippopotamus. The audience laughed at the attitude of the gentleman usher and still applauded with all their might," treating the performance as a "super minstrel show."[29]

The public's interest in Greenfield's and Jones's physical appearance is clear from their sobriquets. Greenfield performed under the name "the Black Swan," most likely a reference to her Scandinavian vocal contemporary Jenny Lind, endearingly called "the Swedish Nightingale." Jones was dubbed "Black Patti," a play on the name of a contemporary Italian diva, Adelina Patti. Both nicknames imply that the American women were their namesakes' lesser counterparts.

FIGURE 2.3 Matilda Sissieretta Jones poster: "The Black Patti, Mme. M. Sissieretta Jones: The Greatest Singer of Her Race." New York: Metropolitan Printing Co., 1899. Library of Congress, Prints and Photographs Division, LCUSZC4-5164.

In addition to these caricatured and derogatory comparisons to renowned opera singers, music critics also applied racial epithets to Greenfield's and Jones's physical appearance, overlooking their musical abilities, including instrumental proficiency.[30] The *Cincinnati Enquirer* called Greenfield the "African Crow"; the *Detroit Daily Advertiser* described her as a "woolly headed, flat nose[d] negro woman, and no one would suppose there was any more enchantment . . . in her than a side of leather." Some critics were aware of their racist biases. An Ohio journalist wrote, "We know the natural prejudice that we all have against [Greenfield's] color . . . and it is very difficult to divest one's self entirely of them and criticize fairly and justly in such a case." In the same spirit, another critic reported, "Upon the suggestion of another . . . we listened to her without looking toward her during the entire performance of 'The Last Rose of Summer' and were at once satisfactorily convinced that her voice is capable of producing sounds right sweet."[31] Elsewhere Greenfield's voice was lauded for its "naturalness," as though it were somehow primal, primitive, untouched by cultivation.[32] Despite such self-awareness on behalf of a few reporters, when Jones was presented to the public a generation later, the singer's physique continued to fascinate white audiences. Jones's attributes were logged with the most embarrassing details. "Her teeth," a journalist reported, "would be the envy of her fairer sisters and the despair of dentistry. Her rather thin lips are fond of exposing heir [*sic*] even row of teeth."[33] Knowingly or otherwise, these journalists acknowledged that historical-cultural lenses influenced how they heard Greenfield's and Jones's voices.

Although audiences shamefully deprecated Greenfield's and Jones's visual appearance, critics could not help but be in awe of their voices. Nevertheless, much like participants in a linguistic experiment in which listeners' perceptions of a recorded voice were deeply affected by visual cues, audiences' limited exposure to the sounds of black classical singers—via performance genres and repertoire predicated on stereotypical and derogatory depictions—caused them to project their expectations of blackness onto those performers' operatic vocal timbres.[34] Again, through network 3, listeners connected African American *voices*, while the timbral phantom genealogy was based on the singers' appearance.

Greenfield's voice rivaled that of her contemporary, the world-renowned Lind, reaching to an E6. Unlike Lind, Greenfield also reached a G2 in the bass clef. In 1852 the *Toronto Globe* not only rhapsodized about "the amazing power of [Greenfield's] voice, the flexibility and the ease of execution," but also reported that the "higher passages were given with clearness and fullness, indicating a soprano of great power."[35] Although Jones was intermittently criticized for her lack of training, she was also reputed to have "great range," "power," "sweetness and smoothness" of tone, and "distinct enunciation," with compliments for the "ease and naturalness with which she handled the voice."[36] Such praise points to her excellence as a classical singer, but she was nonetheless framed as a *black* singer.

Both Greenfield and Jones performed in a wide range of genres. Although Greenfield was noted for her performances of Handel, Bellini, and Donizetti, audiences frequently requested such songs as Steven Foster's "Old Folks at Home." Jones also offered a collection of favorites from the operatic repertoire— arias from *Robert le Diable, L'Africaine, Rigoletto, La Traviata*, and more—mixed with popular ballads such as "Home Sweet Home" and "Swanee River." She also sang a "stammering" song, "Wait 'til the Clouds Roll By," and an early "coon song," Paul Allen's 1883 hit "A New Coon in Town."[37] Even though minstrel vocal style was timbrally close to bel canto style, and for the most part was given voice by white performers,[38] Greenfield's and Jones's repertoire lists conformed to white audiences' expectations of black voices.

In the nineteenth century the classical repertoire seemed an anomalous choice for black singers. Audiences' expectations posed perennial challenges to Greenfield's and Jones's obvious desire to be taken seriously as artists while also having to consider the reality of earning a living. An overbalance of classical music seemed inappropriate for, and probably unmarketable to, the burlesque venues in which African American artists were typically able to perform. Although during Jones's lifetime the African American baritone Theodore Drury headed a black opera company (with which she did not perform), there were hardly any opportunities open to black singers in the world of art music.[39] As John Graziano points out, few companies were willing to pay black artists enough to make a living.[40] Prohibited from major performance outlets, African American singers were primarily relegated to minstrel songs, popular songs, and spirituals.

In Jones's case, difficulties in finding sufficient opportunities and willing coworkers to sustain an operatic career forced her to reevaluate the direction of her line of work. In 1896 she rejoined the minstrel circuit after a hiatus as the lead singer of Black Patti's Troubadours.[41] The Troubadours offered a rousing and popular "Operatic Kaleidoscope" that included scenes from such operas as *Carmen, Faust, Il Trovatore, La Bohème,* and *Rigoletto* while conforming to the minstrel show format. Although she appreciated the Troubadours as an outlet for her operatic skill, Jones always preferred concert venues. "There are so many things in vaudeville performance to distract the attention of the audience," she said, "that they are not in a proper frame of mind to enjoy straight singing."[42] In her own way, Greenfield too was reconfined to the minstrel show, as she became the inspiration for the minstrel "wench" character Lucy Neal—implying that audiences made little distinction between a blackface performer in an Italian burlesque opera and an African American singer performing classical repertoire.[43] Even with superb reviews and calls for listening beyond racial difference, neither Greenfield nor Jones was able to shed the timbral blackness that their audiences heard in response to the acousmatic question, over and above their otherwise celebrated renditions.

In summary, nineteenth- and early twentieth-century white audiences dealt with the shocking phenomenon of black classical singers by re-relegating the singers to stereotypical black roles. Even when they were included in classical performances, these singers' vocal abilities and timbres were impossible for white audiences to assess independently of visual and other contextual information. Visual blackness was projected onto auditory timbre, resulting in the perception of sonic blackness.

Atop this identification of African American classical singers' timbral otherness lay an even more complex historical listening practice: the particular way black voices first gained a listening public as part of the shift from being regarded as subhuman, and thus justifiably enslaved, to subjects worthy of consideration as sentient human beings. Both of these strains contributed to the networks activated by those who listened to Marian Anderson on the Metropolitan stage and to her subsequent colleagues.

A Dimension of the Phantom Genealogy
Created by Early Abolitionists

In 1845 Frederick Douglass—emancipated slave, author of the first well-known ex-slave autobiography, and one of the foremost leaders of the abolitionist movement—asked his readers to pause and listen to the songs of the slaves. In their "songs of sorrow" a listener would hear "tales of woe," for "every tone was a testimony against slavery."[44] Douglass's audience did listen, and by the end of the Civil War voices and melodies once considered noise were heard as song and were used by abolitionists as symbolic weapons against slavery. The sociologist Jon Cruz describes this as a "new mode of hearing," possible only under the assumption that slaves possessed an inner life. Cruz terms this mode of reception *ethnosympathy*: a humanitarian pursuit of classifiable subjects. In this perceptual mode, the spiritual was recognized as a clear cultural expression, the form preferred for blacks by "white moral and cultural entrepreneurs." The ability of whites to hear the cries to God embedded in spirituals indicated a mature cultural interpretation of a vocal culture that, until then, had been impenetrable.[45]

Such unprecedented interest in slaves' songs constituted a break from the previous perceptual framework that classified black song as alien noise. The combination of white efforts to convert slaves to Christianity (under the assumption that blacks, like whites, were created and loved by God) and whites' growing appreciation of slaves' religious songs gradually "granted [slaves] a new subjectivity" within white discourse. It also functioned as a vehicle for sympathetic whites, particularly abolitionists, to further imagine slaves as culturally expressive subjects. "Cultural authenticity," Cruz writes, "was the key to subject authenticity." In other words, evidence that slaves were capable not only of worship but also of cultural exchange was taken as proof that they possessed agency and emotion—that they were human subjects, not mechanisms or animals. Hearing enslaved voices with ethnosympathetic ears allowed listeners to discover an "underlying authenticity of subjects through their cultural practices," a perception arguably carried over into conceptions about African Americans singing classical music.[46] Possibly ethnosympathy underlies audiences' prevailing preference for spirituals paired with classical repertoire, as well as discourse that attributes the emotional capital present in interpretations of classical music to a natural aptitude for spirituals.

In the changing perception of the slave voice, from noisy and incomprehensible to lamenting and expressive, voices become metonyms of skin and hair, often referred to by placeholder terms indicating exceptional emotional expressivity. When the Fisk Jubilee Singers introduced spirituals to the concert circuit in the 1870s, the performers' vocal presentations were praised as "plaintive and touching," "thrilling with their weight of sorrow," and having "an indescribable pathos."[47] An anonymous reviewer described the voices as being "so full of character and so full of color, and so little originality is met with these days that their strangeness is agreeable."[48] As Julia Chybowski observes, this language echoes that of the abolitionists, especially that of Harriet Beecher Stowe, who sponsored many of Greenfield's British appearances. Greenfield's reception in America and Britain would influence that of the Fisk Jubilee Singers. For her British listeners, Greenfield embodied American slave culture. Audiences were "charmed by her perceived musical humanity" and "[Anglo-European] musical achievement."[49] A review of Jones echoes both abolitionist accounts of slaves' voices and reviewers' sketches of the Fisk Jubilee Singers:

> In every note Mrs. Jones sang in her concerts here that one quality was unfailingly present. In the arias, in the ballads comic or sentimental, it was noticeable, and it soon became evident that it was the most individualizing element in the voice, and that no amount of schooling or training could create it. Not that one would desire to have it eradicated. It is the heritage the singer has received from her race, and it alone tells not only of the sorrows of a single life but the cruelly sad story of a whole people.... The tones of the negro voice are totally devoid of the humorous quality. The song that is sung may be comic but the voice itself never ceases to be plaintive. This is true of Mrs. Jones, and is it not equally true of every negro singer in every place and under every condition?[50]

In the *Washington Post*'s 1903 consideration of the "Negro voice," the author made associations between sentiments and language resonating with earlier descriptions of slaves; African Americans, such as Greenfield and Jones, who tried their luck as concert singers; and later the Fisk Jubilee Singers. In the *Post*'s account, the voice is "absolutely unique and indescribable," with a "remarkable quality" that would be "lessened by cultivation": "This unique quality arises from a music almost as old as the world, for it has been chanted in the wilds of Africa to the accompaniment of rude drum and punctured reed ever since human beings could articulate. It still retains much of its original savagery, and when sung with the peculiar timbre which is the especial attribute of the negro's voice it produces an effect which sets the nerves tingling."[51]

Just as the perceptual filter of ethnosympathy changed the way abolitionists heard slaves' voices, we can see that the modern assumption of sound as stable and knowable leads to readings of blackness as essence rather than as stylistic expertise. Such selective listening offers African Americans a place in this normative cultural space while maintaining their difference. Might the persistent association of black classical singers' voices with the sound of the spiritual be an updated form of ethnosympathy? And is this ethnosympathy derived from a phantom network that attributes the Fisk Jubilee Singers' artistry to voices that "[retain] much . . . original savagery" instead of to their daily rehearsals, visionary director, and discipline?

The phantom genealogy of operatic timbral blackness arose from several historical and cultural turns. White audiences first perceived the black body in performance as enslaved and subhuman through distorted, derogatory images brought to life by, among other cultural-social forces, minstrel performances. Because of how such imagery colored whites' perceptions of the first African American classical performers, it was difficult, if not impossible, for those performers to advance their careers without reinforcing stereotypes, as Jones's return to the minstrel stage attests. Even when black voices won the ethnosympathy of white listeners, their acceptance as subjects was contingent on blacks' distinctiveness from other members of society.

Along with its complex history, the belief in the existence of timbral blackness has significantly influenced the trajectory of subsequent African American singers' careers, including Anderson's, as well as characterizations and vocal writing in original American opera. I suggest that this particular trajectory, which also played a role in how Anderson developed vocally, has proved difficult for subsequent African American singers to escape. It is to that story, and to an exploration of how American opera deals with the idea of blackness, that I now turn, considering the ways in which sentiments about race have been written into the American operatic repertoire and its casting practices. In this inscription we see the phantom network—the association created between African American singers and othered vocal timbre as evidencing essential difference—as an actor in the formation of American operatic repertoire and practices.

How Phantom Genealogy Filters Racial Sentiments in All-Black Casting

Characterization and vocal writing in early American opera were not far removed from African American performers' burdensome roles in burlesque, vaudeville, and minstrel shows. As such, associations with African American singers built up around burlesque, vaudeville, and minstrel shows were not disengaged from the first castings of African Americans in opera. For example, Thomson's opera *Four Saints in Three Acts*, which premiered in 1934 with an all-black cast, is described by Barg as rehearsing "romantic racialist discourse on black sound."[52] There are a few explanations of Thomson's casting choice in circulation. Carl Van Vechten quoted the composer on tone quality: "[Negro singers] alone possess the dignity and the poise, the lack of self-consciousness that proper interpretation of the opera demands. They have the rich, resonant voices essential to the singing of my music and the clear enunciation required to deliver Gertrude [Stein]'s text."[53] In an interview he shared that they had a "more direct and unself-conscious approach to religious fantasy."[54] Thomson also related that the idea for an all-black cast came to him in 1932–33, after he attended a Harlem performance featuring Jimmy Daniels as host and entertainer. "I turned to Russell [the architectural historian Henry-Russell Hitchcock], realizing the impeccable enunciation of Jimmy's speech-in-song, and said, 'I think I'll have my opera sung by Negroes.' The idea seemed to be a brilliant one; Russell, less impressed, suggested I sleep on it. But next morning I was sure, remembering how proudly the Negroes enunciate and how the whites just hate to move their lips."[55]

Here it seems Thomson was attracted to what he viewed as the "racial qualities" of Daniels's voice. Yet another story relays how he conceived the idea for an all-black cast while attending DuBose and Dorothy Heyward's play *Porgy* in Princeton.[56] Whichever inspirational moment came first, these tales convey Thomson's fascination with the black voice and body, his recognition of and pleasure in the "grain" of the black voice.[57] But he expressed his approval in patronizingly loud praise that, to Barg, masks a "deeper racial logic, one with considerable historical precedence in cultural commentary about black singing."[58]

The material from which this "racial logic" was bred is also evident in the public discourse surrounding *Four Saints*. After opining that the conceptual strength of Thomson's opera consisted in its resistance to traditional "reason and logic," one critic observed, "[It] is doubtful if white singers could have given the core, with its strange alternation of comedy and exaltations, the flavor it requires."[59] Another review found that "the players from Harlem . . . speak their lines without spoofing them, and lend a poignant dignity to even some of the most absurd moments of the text."[60] W. J. Henderson agreed that the "spell" of the production was "to be found in the natural talent of Negroes for playing seriously like a lot of children." The cast, he wrote, "knelt and rolled their eyes toward stage heaven, genuflected, saint before saint with the deepest gravity, and sang their nonsense syllables with as much faith and devotion as they might have sung, 'It's me, Lord, standin' in the need of prayer.'" He added, "[Ma]ybe it was meant to be a burlesque on 'grand opera.' If so, it is a gorgeous success."[61]

One contemporary humorist mocked the opera by writing a parody of a spiritual: "Nobody knows the opera I seen; nobody knows but Gertrude."[62] Additionally commentators ran with the idea that Gertrude Stein's libretto played with racialized speech. Stein's nonsensical use of the name Lucy does indeed carry references to two minstrel songs, one of which features a Lucy, the ur-wench of minstrelsy.

Let Lucy Lily Lily Lucy Lucy let Lucy Lucy Lily Lily
Lily Lily Lily let Lily Lucy Lucy let Lily. Let Lucy Lily.[63]

At least two of the most popular songs in minstrel repertoire referred to this stock character. "Miss Lucy Long" was a love song with a twist of humor, while "Miss Lucy Neal" was a sentimental "plantation song" with a tragic ending. And if indeed Greenfield was the inspiration for the character of Lucy Neal, the idea that an early African American singing classical repertoire was perceived as burlesquing opera is also invoked here. Over and over, in the conception and production of *Four Saints in Three Acts* and in the discourse surrounding the opera, we observe a multitude of preconceived tropes of blackness. Tropes of blackness were freely reimagined in the musical references to minstrelsy and the spiritual, the staging of the voice and body, as well as the parodying of black language and pronunciation.

Premiering one year after *Four Saints*, *Porgy and Bess* stipulated a similar cast. Gershwin's folk opera in three acts (with a libretto by DuBose Heyward and lyrics by Heyward and Ira Gershwin) has been a mixed blessing for African American singers ever since. "Thank God, I never had to sing Bess," the Metropolitan Opera soloist and longtime executive director of the Harlem School of the Arts Betty Allen said. She continued, "I never had to sing Aida. I was really against the typical casting that had nothing to do with your voice, or your type, but just to do with your dark skin. What's that?"[64] Allen's sigh indicates relief at avoiding what some African American singers call the "Porgy and Bess curse" and also points to the larger issue of racialized casting in opera.[65] In 1985, when the Metropolitan Opera mounted a fiftieth-anniversary production of *Porgy and Bess*, the employment rate of African American singers rose to 25 percent, compared with only 2 percent in the 1970–71 opera season. In 1989, when *Porgy and Bess* was not produced, the employment rate dropped to 14 percent.[66] These statistics show that there is a decent amount of work for African American opera singers only when *Porgy and Bess* is mounted. Regarding the depiction of African Americans in *Porgy*, Edward Said declared, "It is so condescending. These are not real characters. These are folklore characters, harmless in some ways, distant. . . . A natural sense of rhythm; they eat watermelon—all the cli-chés that go back to Al Jolson."[67]

Overall, while operas such as *Four Saints in Three Acts* and its contemporary *Porgy and Bess* help launch careers and secure work for African American singers, they are double-edged swords, working against efforts to integrate American opera in earnest. These operas reproduce stereotypical ideas about African American culture, music, and voice and oblige African American performers to be molded into "natural" portraits of the stereotypes, which the performers themselves thereby unwillingly reinforce. Since American opera (and not only minstrel, vaudeville, burlesque, or spiritual concert performances) presented African American singers in what may be described as compromising roles, the question becomes whether African Americans *could* be cast and perceived beyond such stereotypes in opera and classical performance.

The phantom genealogy through which African American classical singers were heard was constructed around othered visual traits and caricatured character associations. As we saw with *Four Saints*, connections that were transposed to the realm of opera and cemented there included stereotypes about African Americans: how their enunciation reflected a lack of reason and a childlike attitude to life, that their musical gifts were born of the spiritual tradition, and that they were heavily associated with burlesque and minstrelsy. Anderson—who, as we will see, was subjected to many of the same challenges as Greenfield and Jones—did break through the barrier, appearing on the most important opera stage in the United States. But did this new platform break or retain the association of African American singers with the phantom genealogy?

Overlapping twenty-one and twenty-eight years with Greenfield's and Jones's respective life spans, Anderson (1897–1993), the granddaughter of a freed slave, was born into a working-class Philadelphia family. Biographies of her early life tell of a young girl feverishly absorbing music with the help of communities that recognized and supported her talent and dedication.[68] Her church community, the Union Baptist Church in Philadelphia, embraced and supported her vocal talent, inviting her to sing solos during services. But racism and financial difficulties obstructed her efforts to obtain musical training. Even when the congregation offered to pay for her tuition at a local music school, she was turned away: the school "[didn't] take colored."[69] It proved impossible for Anderson to study with a white teacher who would have had the necessary performing experience and professional connections to offer. Years went by with help from various black teachers and choir directors, but it was not until 1919 that she found her first long-term instructor, one who possessed the competence she deserved. He was the Russian Jewish Philadelphian Giuseppe Boghetti (born Joe Bogash), graduate of the Royal Conservatory in Milan, a mentor with whom Anderson maintained contact throughout her life. With Boghetti she expanded her vocal technique and repertoire and developed the desire to perform opera.[70]

During the initial phase of her career (1915–27) Anderson toured the American South. But growing steadily impatient with the restrictions imposed on black traveling musicians by Jim Crow laws, and with an increasing desire to delve deeply into the German lieder repertoire, she set out in 1927 for London and a year later had her London debut.[71] Despite her recent training with some of the foremost European vocal pedagogues, critics in London were far from impressed. Although her "warm and rich tone" is mentioned by one reporter, others noticed a certain "naive appeal in her readings that compensated for occasional lack of subtlety." One wrote, "Her voice has the peculiar timbre common to colored vocalists." Another opined more harshly, "The 'scoop' is evidently a racial fault, for it fell into place as the natural thing in some Negro spirituals."[72] These journalists questioned her delivery of classical repertoire while noting that what they heard as vocal flaws in that genre seemed to suit her realization of spirituals.

Like American reviewers, London critics typically insisted on a connection between African American timbres and spirituals, questioning any black singer's choice to attempt anything but the latter. Before Anderson, the African American tenor Roland Hayes experienced considerable resistance to his performance of lieder. And years after Anderson's debut the Paris critic Mercer

Cook dryly wrote, regarding a skimpily attended American performance of *Four Saints in Three Acts*, that had it offered a program of spirituals, "the theater would have been packed for months."[73]

Vincent Sheean's reception of Anderson's performance of spirituals in Salzburg is not unusual and echoes the London critics' sentiments:

> In the last group she sang a spiritual, "They crucified my Lord, and he never said a mumblin' word." Hardly anybody in the audience understood English well enough to follow what she was saying, and yet the immense sorrow—something more than the sorrow of a single person—that weighted her tones and lay over her dusky, angular face was enough. At the end of this spiritual there was no applause at all—a silence instinctive, natural and intense, so that you were afraid to breathe. What Anderson had done was something outside the limits of classical or romantic music: she frightened us with the conception, in musical terms of course, but outside the normal limits, of a mighty suffering.[74]

Recalling the "collective sorrow" that reviewers heard in Jones's voice, Sheean evokes the same sentiment for which abolitionists reached as, for the first time, they grasped the humanity and subjectivity of slaves. But even Sheean's favorable review insists on the spiritual as the root of African American expressivity. Anderson's attitude toward repertoire was very open and exploratory. Her repertoire encompassed all of the major arias suitable for her *fach*, including some for soprano.[75] She went on to develop programs of Finnish, French, German, Italian, Norwegian, Spanish, and Swedish art and folk songs, always ensuring that she would sing something by a national composer in her concerts throughout Europe. When she was invited to sing a recital at the White House, she was asked to sing only spirituals, but, characteristically, she insisted on including a few pieces by Franz Schubert.[76]

Although she was arguably one of the most gifted singers of the twentieth century—of whom Arturo Toscanini said, "What I heard today one is privileged to hear only in a hundred years"—in the public's mind Anderson's artistic career was often overshadowed by her assigned role as a "tattered social symbol."[77] While her appearance at the 1939 Lincoln Memorial on Easter morning, where she sang for over seventy-five thousand people, including President Franklin Delano and Eleanor Roosevelt, became an iconic moment for the civil rights movement, her symbolic role in the movement ran counter to her own intention to be a classical musician. It is likely that listeners who had also associated blackness with singers such as Greenfield and Jones, had seen the racialized casting of African American singers in *Four Saints*, and had heard Anderson within the context of the spiritual were unable to shake such associations when Anderson was finally hired by the most prominent opera company in the United States. By casting her as a gypsy sorceress, the Metropolitan Opera arguably intensified and further propagated this association. Considering the long associative chain invoked when African American singers are heard in terms of race rather than style and technique, which door did this pivotal moment open for Anderson and subsequent African American opera singers?

Racialized Casting

After Anderson's debut at the Metropolitan Opera, a relatively large number of African Americans won operatic roles. Dorothy Maynor, Leontyne Price, Martina Arroyo, Grace Bumbry, and Shirley Verrett triumphantly sang on both American and European stages. However, the majority of the roles they were asked to sing perpetuated the association of their voices with othered, racialized characters, and as much as they were recognized as divas, attitudes toward color always haunted them. For example, critics credited Price's voice with "an unmistakably individual fragrance—husky, musky, smoky, misty (on a bad day foggy!)—and palpitating pagan sexiness. It is not the voice of a good girl."[78] Like Anderson, Price ultimately lamented, "Whenever there was any copy about me, what I was as an artist, what I had as ability, got shoveled under because all the attention was on racial connotations."[79] Robert McFerrin Sr., who appeared at the Metropolitan three weeks after Anderson in the role of the Ethiopian king Amonasro, the protagonist's father in Verdi's *Aida*, shared, "I had been [at the Met] for three years and had done only three roles, which averaged out to a role a year." Observing that this rate was much lower than that of comparable white colleagues, he reflected, "I did not want to continue the uncertainty of my future of whether or not I would progress beyond the status of singing the role of a brother or father." Instead, he confessed, "I wanted to sing Wotan or Count di Luna or a romantic lead. I guess this would have created too much controversy. Therefore, I simply chose to resign my position on the Met roster and take my chances in Hollywood."[80] While these artists were hired alongside whites, their color and its intersectionality with gender (which led to differing problematics for female and male opera singers) was a novelty factor that diverted attention away from their vocal ability. Besides the basic challenges involved in just being hired, the considerable professional strain led artists like McFerrin to leave the opera industry altogether.

We have seen that African American operatic singers had limited performance opportunities. While it would seem that shattering the operatic glass

ceiling would eliminate these obstacles, and while opera companies now offered these singers opportunities beyond characters that parodied black speech
and sound, a curious pattern also emerged. The term *typecasting* refers to an
actor's strong association with a character he or she has played, with a certain
type of character, or with the idea that his or her personal appearance and demeanor lend themselves to a particular kind of role. In regard to female African
American opera singers, Rosalyn Story refers to the "maid/slave-girl/gypsy syndrome" as a form of racialized typecasting.[81] As I have shown, the black body
in opera has been so consistently associated with certain categories of roles that
this association amounts to a typecasting of African Americans in the role of
the other: Japanese war bride slowly going insane, enslaved Ethiopian princess,
gypsy seductress, the cripple (a liminal figure), and so on. For example, with
her 1946 debut at the New York City Opera, Camilla Williams was the first
African American woman to receive a contract with a major American opera
company. (While she preceded Anderson, Anderson's debut eclipsed hers in
symbolic importance.) Williams was hired to sing the title role, a Japanese war
bride, in *Madame Butterfly*. One year earlier Robert Todd Duncan became
the first African American member of the New York City Opera, signed as the
hunchback Tonio in Leoncavallo's *I Pagliacci*. Price, who might be considered
the first African American operatic diva after debuting in the role of St. Ceci-
lia in the premier of Thomson's *Four Saints in Three Acts*, went on to sing the
role of Bess. However, her versions of the black characters Aida and Cleopatra
(the latter role written for her by Samuel Barber) are the interpretations with
which her audience came to identify her most strongly. Duncan's assignment
as a duplicitous character with physical limitations and Price's regal characters
reflect the different ways in which race intersected with gender for female and
male African American singers. What Duncan, Price, and most of their African American opera-singing colleagues have shared is the experience of being
plugged into the standard repertoire's liminal roles.

As African American singers were integrated into the standard repertoire,
their visual appearance underwent debate. This is, of course, noteworthy precisely because the world of opera is, in general, a world of suspended belief. The
critic Bernard H. Haggins recounts a 1974 performance of *Don Giovanni* at the
Met, describing "Price's superb singing as Donna Anna up to the concluding
florid last [*sic*] passages of 'Non mi dir,' which she managed in a sort of vocal
shorthand that implied the notes she didn't sing." Haggin continues, "Price
presented with her Donna Anna the same obtrusive incongruity as previously
with her Leonora in *Il Trovatore* and her Pamina in the *Magic Flute* but not
with her Aida. When I look at what is happening on stage my imagination

still cannot accommodate itself to a black in the role of a white."[82] And, as I have indicated, one white diva imagined Price, despite her celebrated voice, to be appropriate only for the role of Bess. While we know that realism in terms of age and body size is routinely violated in opera, a so-called realistic hue of skin was apparently a crucial point on which many audiences were unable to suspend disbelief.

Although he has sung at major opera houses across the world, one of the most celebrated African American baritones, Simon Estes, has encountered obstacles throughout his career because of the practice of racialized casting. At Bayreuth, Estes sung the title role of the *Flying Dutchman* (1978) with great success, as well as Amfortas in *Parsifal* (1982). However, when Sir Georg Solti and Sir Peter Hall assembled their new *Ring* (1983), Estes's audition for the role of Wotan was rejected. Stephen Fay writes that Hall "might indeed have been troubled by the idea of a black Wotan surrounded by a large family of white singers. . . . He did not object in principle to a black Wotan, as long as there were black singers among his daughters, but he felt that Estes' audition had relieved him of the need to make such a choice." Despite denials by Hall and Solti, who claimed that the decision was based purely on his vocal abilities, Estes publicly claimed that the unfavorable casting decision was racially based.[83] The implication is that racial conflicts that, in late twentieth-century culture, were unable to be tackled head-on could be freely discussed under the auspices of vocal aptitude.[84]

For a Glyndebourne Festival production of *Don Giovanni*, Director Sir Peter Hall ignored suggestions that he hire Leona Mitchell for the role of the Spanish aristocrat, Donna Anna. Her presence, he said, would "ruin the realism and social structure which were to form the very heart of the production."[85] In opera, then, even many insiders seemingly suspend disbelief in all aspects but race. The stories are mythical and fantastical; plots turn on devices such as a man's inability to recognize his wife because she has donned another's clothes; and narrative flow is suspended in time by arias that meditate on a singular feeling over improbably long stretches of time. Yet when it comes to the question of integrated racial hiring, a production calling for demographic "authenticity" is often a key objective. Might directors be wary of the influence of a visually raced body on the way audiences will hear the voices in the production?[86]

While the suspension of disbelief around many aspects of operatic performance—most notably those having to do with the bodies of singers—is an established part of the tradition, critics and audiences have often failed in this imaginative activity when faced with significant incongruities, such as differences in weight and age, between the visual image and the specified character.

However, African American singers' presence on the stage represented a new level of incongruity, one that largely white audiences were less prepared to assimilate. In other words, this new incongruity brought social issues outside of opera into play, while previous incongruities had not. Mitchell responded, "You'd think people wouldn't even consider all that any more. They just shouldn't be saying that somebody doesn't look the part when certain singers are 350 pounds fat. Now are they gonna play a nice young Donna Anna?" Cynthia Clarey was turned down for a role when a director claimed he wanted to do an "authentic" production of a particular opera. "If the director feels that way, fine," said Clarey. "I don't like it—it's a job that I could have had. But if he really feels that way, I think I'd be a lot happier not doing it." Such subtler forms of discrimination are difficult to pinpoint. "Opera is such a subjective art," said Mitchell, that "they can always hide behind words like 'She's just not my type.'"[87]

In more recent opera journals and reviews there seem to be fewer public conflicts of this nature, but there are also considerably fewer major black opera stars today than there were in the golden age, beginning with Price and continuing through the 1980s.[88] The latest highly exposed and publicly debated incident of which this author is aware is Hope Briggs's 2007 dismissal from the San Francisco opera.[89]

Racialized casting is yet another materialization of the phantom genealogy, a phenomenon that arises through omission. This omission takes place when performers who appear to be white are cast in most operatic roles, especially as prestigious characters. The phantom genealogy also arises when African Americans are cast in othered roles, not only reflecting the current state of society but also amplifying this type of framing. Network 3 listeners project their listening schema through casting, by naming a given timbre as an appropriate representation of their idea of a particular character. Through the continuous alignment of black bodies with certain characters, a connection between these bodies and these characters is made, not through the voices alone but through consistent association.

Listening through Phantom Genealogy

The listener who assesses voices based on a set of associations that are not connected to the vocal education of the singer in question is an actor within the undulating dynamic that determines perceptions of African American classical voices in the United States. That listener takes part in manifesting and perpetuating a particular image of African American classical singers, an image that, in turn, shapes how other African American singers are understood. Hence, through an activated phantom genealogy, listeners understand vocal performance as race instead of hard-earned style.

A popular narrative attests that African American singers arrive at a distinctly "black" version of the classical timbre by first working with spirituals. Simon Estes and the celebrated soprano Barbara Hendricks do indeed cite their experience with spirituals as influential in their growth as classical singers. Specifically Hendricks attributes her ability to express suffering in Mozart arias to her embodied understanding of spirituals. In contrast, the first African American Metropolitan Opera coach, Sylvia Lee, hired in 1950, bemoaned African American soprano Martina Arroyo's attempts at spirituals. Lee claimed that she had never heard such white spirituals in her life.[90] Lee subsequently coached Arroyo in that repertoire in the same way she coached diction and phrasing in German lieder.[91] Thus while some singers acknowledge spiritual singing (or any other musical genre, for that matter) as an important stage in their artistic development, others not brought up with the spiritual were in fact "illiterate" in the idiom and had to learn it in the same way as any other vocal style—as part of a professional repertoire. Nonetheless the claim that a distinguishable African American operatic vocal timbre is conditioned by singing spirituals is relentless. Based on the studies mentioned earlier, one may suspect that this narrative's persistence stems from unspoken beliefs about a uniform black culture, as well as the belief that the black body is distinct from the white body and thus possesses a different vocal timbre.[92] Within such a narrow understanding of the black body and voice, an *either/or* dynamic dominates. Sufficient space to hold *both/and*—a space that can contain different situations simultaneously—is not facilitated. Instead within the either/or model, any such richness is interpreted along the lines of deviance or incoherence. That is, black cultural life is not granted complexity and depth.

As Arroyo's "white-sounding" spirituals demonstrate, the African American vocal apparatus possesses no physical features that would account for the perception of its "black" vocal timbre.[93] Nor do socialization and acculturation quite make sense as explanations for lingering dialects or accents vis-à-vis vocal virtuosi who routinely sing in languages of which they are not native speakers. Moreover listeners have been known to misjudge singers' or actresses' races—Marilyn Horne as black, Arroyo as white.

While Arroyo grew attuned to the interpretation of the spiritual genre through careful coaching in vocal and musical style, listeners naturalized the performative effect as arising from her blackness. The actor who articulates the sentiments and ideas that the dominant discourse will perpetuate is the audience member who knows nothing about the beautifully stylized spiritual acquired in a practice room as standard preparation for a scheduled concert. This listener's response to the acousmatic question is related to essentialized notions of vocal timbre. Thus this listener-actor will be moved by the exquisite performance and will attribute its effect to an assumed network or a phantom genealogy.

If, as Piekut explains, action is a kind of translation, listeners' articulation of an association constitutes action.[94] Through this limited and highly interpretive mode of listening, the hearing and articulation of blackness act upon the narrative through which the voices are subsequently heard. These articulated listenings also act as translators or as particular "responses" to the acousmatic question. In reply to the question *What is this?*, a given listener musters his or her intellectual and associative resources and responds, *I hear a singer whose voice expresses the suffering of all black people through the essential blackness of his or her body*. We know, however, that the answer could instead be *I hear a singer who, through careful coaching by a person who understands the stylistic aspects of this genre, is able to perform this genre with stylistic fidelity and thus express the cultural, affective, and social sentiments from which the music arises*. And as captured by the both/and model, a singer can, of course, sing a spiritual perfectly as the result of absorbing the repertoire and stylistic grammar from cradle to adulthood, but this is also a learned style.

My point is that in each of these scenarios style is learned. But while style is acquired through social and cultural contexts, the learning process remains unacknowledged; it is explained instead as naturalized essential timbre, with a phantom genealogy erected around it, affecting all perceptions. In the alternative scenario, learning is acknowledged, as are the singer's aesthetic, social, and cultural locations. The difference is that, in the latter scenario, cultural heritage is understood as such rather than reduced to racial essence.[95]

In choosing Anderson, years beyond her vocal prime, to break the color barrier, the Metropolitan Opera presented a figure who symbolized quiet perseverance and patience. Listeners could therefore hear Anderson through the "new mode of hearing," *ethnosympathy*.[96] Although Patricia Turner lauds the Metropolitan Opera director Rudolf Bing for his astuteness in casting Anderson as Ulrica, a role that did not require a young, fresh-sounding voice, it was, to one reporter, a "tardy tribute to [Anderson's] rank and achievement as an artist of international fame."[97] Moreover the gypsy role reaffirmed the hearing of Anderson's voice as other. Finally, the year—1955—coincided with the decade in which amateur minstrel performers finally put down their cork and with the Montgomery bus boycott.[98] I wonder if this role—like Jones's and Greenfield's often compromised performance opportunities—led audiences to again connect the voice of Anderson with the sight, and therefore with the sound, of the other, thus confirming the otherness of blackness. Would "the door," as the *New York Times* dubbed Anderson's Met debut, open only for those who could credibly be heard through a phantom genealogy that helps to explain and justify listeners as actors by reaffirming timbral blackness in response to the acousmatic question?

Because of the politics of pervasive racism under which opera desegregation was defined, the appearance of the first African American female performer at the Metropolitan Opera failed to disrupt the phantom genealogy. We feel pain in a phantom limb long after the actual limb is gone, but because that limb is no longer connected to the body, traditional treatments cannot be applied. With Anderson's debut, the segregated state of major American opera stages was cut off, like an amputated limb. It might seem, then, that the problem of inequality had been dealt with, like a body freed from infection with the severing of a limb. But, as with a phantom limb, it has been difficult to pinpoint and treat the persistent pain of the marker of difference. Deep-seated assumptions about difference that listeners projected onto African American voices have affected the way subsequent African American voices—even those lauded by Metropolitan Opera audiences—are heard. African American singers and their audiences are still affected by the impact of the phantom limb, by desegregation as a veneer only. Even Ryan Speedo Green, the 2011 Metropolitan Opera competition winner, has experienced repeated typecasting through requests that he sing "Ol' Man River."

Addressing the emotional, economic, and social afflictions that arise through being marked as an outsider in relation to a repertoire or vocal practice is as challenging as prescribing a cure for phantom limb pain, as in each case the cause of the pain is no longer present. To cure phantom pains in an amputated arm, a mirror may allow the amputee to come to grips with the limb's absence. To cure the pain of being reduced to the sum of a phantom genealogy constructed within a racist history, we may also hold up a mirror. However, since the phantom genealogy is not materialized by the singer, but is instead located within the listener, the mirror should reflect not the singer, but the listener.

The mirror shows this: listeners not only categorize voices but also construct a genealogy around voices that serves to support racial sentiments. Such erroneous historiography contributes to the rationalization of the naming. And the cure we can apply with the tool the mirror allows is deconstructing such listening. In deconstructing listening, and in devising new listening heuristics, we can attend to the phantom genealogy—the collective conception that voices and difference are essential, stable, and knowable—and enrich and complicate listeners' responses to the acousmatic question.

3

FAMILIARITY AS STRANGENESS

Jimmy Scott and the Question of Black Timbral Masculinity

What are the hallmarks of vocal masculinity? Or, more accurately, how do we recognize culturally coded signals of masculinity in a person's voice? Most people would say the determining factor is *pitch*; they would report that a feminine voice is higher in pitch than a masculine voice. In addition some would report that they find deeper male voices attractive and higher-pitched male voices less attractive. These sentiments are reproduced in everyday practice in various ways. For example, in schematic terms, composers of four-part choir music arrange voices vertically, starting at the bottom with male basses and moving upward to male tenors, female altos, and female sopranos.[1] Scientific literature concurs with this notion of the masculine voice. It explains masculine signaling in evolutionary terms, detailing how a deep voice can indicate reproductive fitness, authority, social dominance, and intelligence, ultimately serving a key function in terms of reproducibility.[2] Both the cultural and the evolutionary explanations often focus on one aspect of voice: pitch. Through a close reading of Jimmy Scott's voice and self-identification, as well as audiences' and producers' ideas about and presentations of him, this chapter complicates assumptions about the relationship between pitch and gender, pointing to another potent but undertheorized factor in gendered (and other) readings of voices: timbre.

Whereas the previous chapters showed that all voices are entrained within a given set of values, this chapter expands upon the idea that play, and the practices in which vocalizers engage, can overcome even such gravitational forces. Specifically I show that vocalizers can use entrainment as a starting point to fashion expressions beyond dominant cultural cues. Furthermore, whereas Marian Anderson and her predecessors' stories exposed dynamics of racial listening and the segregated society within which female African American opera singers and their audiences were entrained, in considering Scott's story we gain more insight into the ways in which blackness is configured in gendered terms in a musical-cultural context where "blackness was a powerful symbol of the masculine."[3] On the one hand, studying Scott confirms that this black masculinity is highly constructed and limited compared to the range of experiences of the black men who had to perform these aesthetics. On the other hand, Scott exemplifies a vocalizer who refined techniques and attitudes in order to resist labels.

I see Scott as a musician-activist who carries out the micropolitics of voice by bringing unexpected timbral content (non-falsetto) to a form (black masculinity), thereby challenging that form's very definition. Through Scott's critical performance practice, the limits of essence and meaning-making and the utility of entrainment and culturally constructed presentations of black heterosexual masculinity are contested and subverted. Though it may be uplifting in its utility as an academic case study, it should not be forgotten that Scott's story also exemplifies the hardships artists and vocalizers at large experience when listeners are challenged by the way they choose to define their vocal art and, indeed, themselves.

While Scott's biography was uniquely determined by his physical condition, the dynamics that shaped his career involved conceptions of timbre, gender, and sexuality that determined a culturally and historically situated idea of the African American male jazz artist—a model Scott did not fit. Artists who fail to fit neatly into a recognizable social category tend to disappear into obscurity, and for several decades this seemed to be Scott's fate. But the sheer strength of his voice and artistry, combined with a long-overdue turn in his luck, led to sounds so compelling that, against all odds, audiences did engage. However, to make sense of Scott as a male African American jazz singer, listeners needed to devise ways to engage with his voice. This chapter considers how timbral listening and practices of consumption around Scott fall into a limited number of discrete social categories. In order to manage these categories, listeners participated in the interactive co-creation of Scott's voice and overall gender identity by projecting familiar stereotypes onto a complex artist.

This study shows that Scott, whose physical development made his voice similar to that of a castrato, transcended gender distinction, thus becoming uncanny, transgressive, and ripe for projection, misidentification, and dismissal as theater or play. What I wish to draw out in this chapter is the way that cultural constructions of timbre are gendered, as well as addressing how issues around masculinity are complex and sometimes unexpected when intersecting with issues of race and with particular music repertoires. In the previous chapter I discussed issues of race and gender in the context of opera; these dynamics were played out in the realm of opera vocal character types and social relationships. In popular music genres, however, where male and female singers share much of the same vocal range, a large part of the concern regards signaling masculinity. The complex reception of Scott shows that this reading is less about the pitches men or women can sing than about *how* these pitches are sung and timbrally mediated. What follows are some examples of this process and its multifarious results.

Introducing Jimmy Scott

June 12, 2014, was the last day of Scott's extraordinary life. Major newspapers and media outlets, including the *New York Times*, the *Guardian*, and the *Washington Post*, marked the occasion with admiring and beautiful obituaries that outlined the life and professional story of Jimmy Scott, an artist whose "star," as the *Times* put it, "rose late."[4] Noting "the triumph of Jimmy Scott (1925–2014)," *Rolling Stone* made a similar implication.[5] After a long life and a career that saw early success followed by seemingly endless, hopeless oblivion and at long last by recognition from the music world and its audiences, Scott died at the age of eighty-eight. While his long eclipse was due partly to shaky business deals, the sonic particularities of his life and career are interesting and complex.[6]

Known for most of his career as "Little Jimmy Scott," the jazz singer James Victor Scott was born with Kallmann syndrome, a hormonal condition that prevented his voice from changing at puberty.[7] Both Scott's life and his career were shaped by his congenital medical condition, which kept his voice higher in tessitura than that of a man who had gone through the hormonally induced vocal changes that typically take place during puberty. The condition also stopped Scott's body from growing after the age of twelve.[8] He lacked some adult traits, such as facial hair, and he failed to go through other, more significant physical changes that visually mark the transformation from boy to man. Although people mistook Scott for a masculine woman, an effeminate man, a homosexual, or a transsexual throughout his life, the singer consistently described himself as a "regular guy," maintaining that the most unusual thing about him was his "obsession" with music.[9]

Scott's intense interest in music led him to keep up with the new popular vocal repertoire while, from the age of sixteen, he spent most of his time working odd jobs. He first tried to obtain a position that would allow him to hear live music and meet musicians, and in 1942 took a job as usher at the Metropolitan Theater in Cleveland. The Metropolitan Theater featured movie musicals as openers for the era's major jazz acts, including Ella Johnson, Cab Calloway, Duke Ellington, Count Basie, and Erskine Hawkins. Working at this job allowed Scott access to live music that he could not otherwise afford to hear. He developed a side hustle offering extra dressing room preparation services to artists. Scott's "janitorial service," as he called it, allowed him to get close to artists. This ultimately led to an offer to join tap dancers Lem Neal and Dickie Sims on tour as a traveling valet, or what we would refer to today as a "personal assistant."[10]

Scott's first public performance opportunity took place at the age of eighteen, during his second month touring with Neal and Sims. In Meadville, Pennsylvania, Neal and Sims shared a weekend bill with a group that included Ben Webster and Lester Young. So moved was he by the music, Scott managed to convince the musicians to let him sit in on a few pieces. Shortly after he began to sing, he recalled, the audience stopped dancing and gathered around the stage to listen—and then, out of the blue, he heard someone call out, "That boy sounds like a grown woman."[11] This performance, framed by that comment, began his career. Due to his small stature and ambiguously gendered voice, Scott was initially booked as a teenage novelty act. He worked as a freelancer around Cleveland for some years before Caldonia (Estella Young), a contortionist, invited him to join her tour in 1945.

Touring with Caldonia brought Scott to New York City, where his career began in earnest at Harlem's Baby Grand. There he impressed Billie Holiday and Doc Pomus, whose early interest foreshadowed the role Scott would play as a "singer's singer." Although Scott's career as a professional singer spanned about six decades—from the mid-1940s until his death in 2014—it was only during a short period in the late 1980s that he managed to achieve mainstream commercial success. He had been on the brink of large-scale fame a number of times, but something—family issues, trouble with contracts, producers pulling out because they were afraid that Scott was too different—always interfered with the breakthrough one might expect from an artist of his caliber and continued exposure.

Scott's 1962 album, *Falling in Love Is Wonderful*, seemed, at the time, like it might be his big break. Produced by Ray Charles for Tangerine Records, it marked a pivotal career point for Scott. But his former label, Savoy Records, refused to release him from his contract, and the album was withdrawn, as was his subsequent album, *The Source* (Atlantic, 1969).[12] Scott then fell off the music world's radar and turned to nonmusical work. Decades later, in 1984, live appearances on Newark's WBGO put him back on the map.

In 1988 Jimmy McDonough published a piece about Scott in the *Village Voice*. This article reached a different, hip, urban audience. It coincided with a chance appearance at the Blue Note: Scott happened to be in the audience for the eighth anniversary celebration in honor of Cab Calloway and was asked to sing. These two events led to renewed interest, culminating in Scott's appearance on the twenty-ninth episode of the television series *Twin Peaks*, "Beyond Life and Death." Director David Lynch said he was drawn to Scott's energy and gave him the uncanny role of Death. A few artists who had their first major successes in the 1980s also used Scott to underline some element of uncanniness. Madonna used him in her "Secret" video (1993), and Lou Reed took Scott along as the opening act on his *Magic and Loss* European tour (1992). Scott's otherness is manifest in the strong emotions he triggers: "Jimmy Scott's voice," Madonna said, "makes me weep," and Reed testified, "He has the voice of an angel and can break your heart."[13] Five years after the WBGO appearances, his 1991 performance at Doc Pomus's funeral led to a contract with Warner Brothers. The resulting album, *All the Way* (1992), earned a Grammy nomination.

After that release Scott maintained an international profile, re-releasing old albums and recording new works: *Dream* (1994), *Heaven* (1996), *Holding Back the Years* (1998), and *But Beautiful* (2002). As a singer Scott has been celebrated not only by the hipster fringe but by the jazz establishment, receiving the National Endowment of the Arts' Jazz Master award (2007), the Kennedy Center "Jazz in Our Time" Living Legend Award (2007), NABOB's Pioneer Award (2007), the Lifetime Achievement Award from the Jazz Foundation of America (2010), and the R&B Hall of Fame Induction Award (2013). Having attained a cult following for his one-of-a-kind voice, Scott scored TV and film appearances and, as the obits show, was celebrated at his death.[14]

"That Boy's Alto Voice"

Arguably because Scott's self-described identity as a heterosexual male vocalist evaded basic recognition, his career went through a number of distinct phases that included framings and presentations that he himself did not perform in private life.[15] In other words, manifestations of measurable and symbolic aspects of masculinity, conveyed through visual representations and discursive descriptions of Scott, were defined by the cultural and historical context within which his career took place and reflected the limited performative roles available. Hence in his journey from obscure newbie to established National

Endowment of the Arts honoree, Scott, who insisted on his heterosexuality and normativity, was never presented as such. Instead, over the length of his career we find three general methods of presentation. He was first hired as a novelty act, or as a singer marked by difference. He was then recorded as an unnamed vocalist, sometimes paired with images of other people, which suggested gender ambiguity. Finally, he was framed by identities reaching beyond the human. Even after his comeback, when he was presented under his own name and image, his identity was entangled with and made potent by previous complex representations.

Scott's first and only chart hit was recorded during a session with Lionel Hampton in January 1950.[16] Of the four songs released, "Everybody's Somebody's Fool" remained on *Billboard* magazine's rhythm and blues charts for six weeks, reaching number 6. While this success might have brought Scott's name to audiences' radar, the cut was labeled simply "Lionel Hampton, Vocalist with Orchestra."[17] This mode of presentation exemplifies the first stage of the way Scott was presented—namely, as an unnamed and unidentified singer. A 1988 reissue did not rectify the error but amplified it, crediting one of Hampton's female vocalists, Irma Curry.[18]

During the same period, Scott also recorded for Charlie Parker. His recording of "Embraceable You" (1950) exemplifies the first and second patterns symptomatic of the neglect he suffered throughout his career. Scott's biographer, David Ritz, retells the story of the singer's missing credits on this record. Initially, bootleg versions were distributed without a vocalist credited. In 1977 Columbia Records commissioned the critic Gary Giddins to annotate a reissue of *One Night in Birdland* and hired Dan Morgenstern, the director of Rutgers University's Institute of Jazz, to write the liner notes. In these notes Morgenstern misidentified the voice on "Embraceable You" as female vocalist Chubby Newsome. Ritz called both Giddins and Morgenstern decades after the reissue; Morgenstern was already aware of the error and "graciously acknowledged his mistake." Giddins, however, was made aware only through Ritz's phone call. Scott's biographer reports that Giddins listened to the recording again and agreed that the vocalist had to be Jimmy Scott. Furthermore Giddins was "amazed" that the error had gone undetected for so long. For Ritz, the fact that two experts had mistaken the singer and even his gender was symptomatic of the misunderstanding and neglect Scott suffered. Ritz's indignation over the situation leaps off the page, and he ends with the report that a 1990s CD reissue, *New Bird*, included the track, but that Scott was *still* unnamed.[19] Whether due to deliberate action or sloppy oversight, the implication in each of these two scenarios is that Scott was not seen and treated as an artist worth crediting.

FIGURE 3.1 Jimmy Scott, *The Source*, Atlantic Records, 1969.

So far we've seen that Scott's recordings were, at times, uncredited. At other times credit was mistakenly given to other vocalists, almost always to women. Ironically, when Scott was finally able to record under his own (masculine) name, he himself was not associated with it. That is, while his name was indeed used, Scott himself was still not identified or identifiable. For example, the headshot on the cover of the album *The Source* features a young, beautiful woman with a large Afro—a model (see figure 3.1). On *Falling in Love Is Wonderful* a photo of a man and a woman, presumably two lovers, graces the cover (see figure 3.2).[20] "I understood what they wanted," Scott says about the photo for *The Source*. "Naturally I would have preferred to see myself somewhere on the cover, but if they thought that would help sell the thing, I could only hope they were right." Describing his reaction on seeing the cover of *Falling in Love Is Wonderful*, he says, "[Of] course it hurt. . . . It's your record and you want to see your picture."[21]

In designing the record sleeve for *The Source*, Atlantic Records' marketing team responded to, and played directly into, the perception of Scott's voice as female, setting up a feedback loop between listeners and the way an imagined identity or image is reproduced, elaborated, and strengthened. Joel Dorn, producer of *The Source*, confirmed that after seeing the record packaging featuring the female model's photo, most listeners believed Scott to be a woman with a man's name.[22] Thus the packaging for *The Source* suggested two possible readings of Scott's voice and (presented) look: "Jimmy Scott" might be a man mak-

FIGURE 3.2 Jimmy
Scott, *Falling in Love Is
Wonderful*, Tangerine
Records, 1962. (Reissue
by Rhino, 2002.)

ing his voice sound female and dressing in drag, or "Jimmy Scott" might be a
woman with a man's name. Jimmy Scott did not identify with either of these
powerful presentations.

With *Falling in Love Is Wonderful* the imposture only deepens. The cover
art depicts a man and a woman—both unrelated to the recording—in a stereotypical romantic encounter. Both could pass as either white or black.[23] In other
words, the cover can be read as an attempt by the producers to sidestep any (gender) confusion and avoid the resulting distress and disengagement. By implying
a drag performance on the cover of *The Source* and a performance featuring a
possibly mixed-race couple who conform to essentialist heterosexual roles on
the cover of *Falling in Love Is Wonderful*, Scott's record label preempted audience recoil from his idiosyncratic performance of heterosexual masculinity. Listeners are thus free to hear Scott's voice as either man or woman, black or white.

Moreover the photo of a couple embracing on the floor could also suggest
that the voice singing was detached from any particular gendered body. That is,
perhaps Jimmy Scott is not cast as the guy with the movie-star looks seated on
the floor. Perhaps he is not cast as the man for whom the woman in the picture
fell. And perhaps Scott is also not cast as the woman, lying on the floor, arms
stretched out and above her head in a position that suggests surrender. Instead
the cover suggests a scenario during which the music within might be played.
Center stage, two glasses of wine are half full, and the woman's gold slippers lie
nonchalantly next to the Ray Charles LPs scattered across the floor. The fire

is roaring, creating heat behind the two people; it probably accompanies the sound of their voices engaged in romantic murmuring. Does the cover image suggest that Jimmy Scott might be the presence *not shown* in the image, a voice we assume is playing as background music to the scene—a "neutered" voice that does not represent a threat to the image's male protagonist?

It was Ray Charles's manager, Joe Adams, who conceived of the cover photo with the Cesar Romero look-alike and his female counterpart in front of the roaring fire.[24] If he wanted *Falling in Love Is Wonderful* to be a record guys could put on when they were with a girl—one they could make out to—it might it be the case that the man in the cover photo does not replace Scott but instead represents what men might be empowered to carry out in Scott's *presence*. Is Scott's voice so genderless, and therefore so unchallenging to another man—either as competitor or distraction—that it is deemed unintimidating company in such situations? Does Scott's voice offer a perverse intimacy due to the very difficulty of locating it in terms of gender? Does Scott, in this album cover scenario, partake of both sexes because of his ambiguously gendered sound? Or is his uncanny voice that of *la petit mort*, the mutual orgasmic peaks toward which the evening's play is bent?

Sex and death are states that, in the words of Bonnie Gordon, "involv[e] a physical transformation and flux that threaten[s] the unity of the body," and both have occupied a space of liminality since early modern times.[25] Sex, or the question of sex—in terms of both sexual organs and the sexual act—tends to be at the forefront of people's minds when encountering any sexuality not directly linked to the possibility of fertilization. Seventeenth- and eighteenth-century castrato singers, with their inability to inseminate, exerted a tremendous sexual draw on female (and male) audiences.[26] While the ability to have sex without insemination does not itself threaten patriarchal control in the way it did before the advent of birth control, and though Scott very openly talked about the infertility linked to Kallmann syndrome, a eunuch's mystique still surrounded his sexual abilities (or disabilities).

This potential analogy between the voice of orgasm and of death was realized later in Scott's career. Indeed, after his resuscitation it was the character in which he was most frequently cast. These topics—curiosity and mystery around and suspicion and fear of sexual life, death, and also contagion—come together in the 1993 movie *Philadelphia*.[27] In "Streets of Philadelphia," the main single from the film's soundtrack, Bruce Springsteen recorded Scott's voice as a cry-like song.[28] The soaring voice resembles lyrical moaning, set within the confines of defined pitches. It is a cry that is uttered when the main character, a homosexual lawyer named Andrew Beckett (played by Tom Hanks), is wrongfully fired for having contracted HIV/AIDS. Here Scott's voice is cast to express the inexpressible: a feeling of betrayal and loss resulting in vulnerability and, ultimately, for Beckett, death. For Beckett, being asked to leave the company represents more than being fired from a job, for this was a firm in which he had been groomed to become a partner in the near future. At a pivotal moment he steps out on the street after having been rejected by the lawyer he had asked to take his unlawful termination case. As the camera moves into a close-up of Beckett's face, Scott's voice accompanies his despair, drawing the range of human emotions into an uncanny sonic space that signifies extreme emotional range, the dark tenor of Beckett's affective state, and the fragility of both human relationships and human life.

In the last episode of season 2 of the television series *Twin Peaks*, created by Mark Foster and David Lynch, Scott is again cast as a liminal figure from the beyond. His is the plangent voice heard in the Red Room, located within the Black Lodge, an extradimensional place that materializes in dreams and (perhaps) in reality. The main character, FBI Special Agent Dale Cooper, walks through a maze walled by red curtains. The heavy fabric and the deep color allude to the brothel Cooper thinks he is about to enter; it is also material that would muffle any potential cries for help and can signify royalty as well as blood. A chair appears through a curtain opening, and a dwarf with a twisted body begins to dance around Cooper. Scott's voice is at first nondiegetic, seeming like any mood-creating television music. Then the camera pans out and Scott appears, dancing a lonely dance against a red-curtain backdrop while singing Lynch's composition "Under the Sycamore Tree," which refers to twelve sycamore trees that hold clues about the murder that drives the plot of the series. The episode ends here, in limbo, where the dwarf and Scott signify, or even *are*, death. Scott provides the ominous music about which the dwarf says, "Where we come from, there is always music in the air."[29]

Recall that, from the beginning of his career, Scott struggled simply for appearances and credits under his own name. Ironically, later in life, when he finally reached the point where he did appear under his own name, his unique identity was doubled by identities and significations not his own. In a strange way, then, Scott has sometimes been presented under his own name and sometimes with his own image—but, as if in a kaleidoscope, both name and visual representation have consistently been twisted or morphed into something that does not connect to the identity by which Scott knew himself.

What caused this incoherent experience for audiences and producers? What underpinned listeners' projections of their own social categories onto Scott?

These manifestations—such as, for instance, labeling him a "boy" performing as a "grown woman"—can be understood as a kind of *audience drag performance*. Unlike, for example, the vaudeville star Frankie "Half-Pint" Jaxon, who in the 1920s and 1930s relied explicitly on vocal drag and female impersonation as part of a "novelty" act, Scott merely performed what he understood to be his real-world identity: a heterosexual male jazz singer with an unusual voice. Why, then, did record companies and other promoters repeatedly present Scott's voice within gendered performances with which he himself did not identify? In short, why did listeners find Scott's voice incoherent in relation to social and cultural expectations of normative masculinity and, specifically, of normative black masculinity?

This Is a Man's Voice

"For many of us," the sociologist Herman Grey writes, "jazz men articulated a different way of knowing ourselves and seeing the world through very different 'structures of feeling' they assumed, articulated and enacted." Despite their very different view and treatment of the women in their lives, the two iconic figures to which Grey points, Miles Davis and John Coltrane, played public roles of unambiguous masculinity and heterosexuality. Grey argues that Davis's and Coltrane's "black masculinity . . . not only challenged whiteness but exiled it to the (cultural) margins of blackness—i.e., in their hands blackness was a powerful symbol of the masculine."[30]

Not only did such popular contemporary jazz figures, who were Scott's own acknowledged heroes, provide powerful models for heterosexual men; they also offered African American men a space that turned blackness into hypermasculinity. In this environment, where "black masculinity is figured in the popular imagination as the basis of masculine hero worship," it is "the same black body . . . onto which competing and conflicting claims about (and for) black masculinity are waged."[31]

Within such a framework, what do we require to arrive at the affirmation *It is a man* as a response to the acousmatic question? How is the thick event that is voice sliced and framed so that we recognize it within the societal and cultural norms that guide us to hear a masculine voice, or a man's voice, or a masculine man's voice? In Scott's presentation as an artist, he was recognized neither as masculine (whether as a masculine female or a masculine male) nor as a man. Besides his smaller body frame and potentially shortened vocal tract caused by his small stature, in which ways may Scott's voice have differed? And how did a given listener's response to the acousmatic question *Who is speaking?* yield these extreme pairings of images and identities with Scott's voice?

As I mentioned at the outset, it is easy to jump to the conclusion that these rewritings—for example, Scott's presentation as a "female voice"—were due to a high vocal range that signaled femininity. When the acousmatic question was posed about Scott's voice, audiences answered that they heard a "feminine [vocal] range."[32] Listening for queerness, Judith Halberstam notes that Scott "is a male vocalist whose high countertenor voice causes him to be heard as female" and that "Scott has a high voice for a man."[33]

It is true that when voices are discussed in terms of gender, one of the concrete factors presented is pitch. It is standard in any text, from vocal pedagogical and performance resources to music theory and instrumentation references, to show the difference between genders by plotting their pitch range (see musical example 3.1). While the pitches given can vary slightly, they tend to fall within the same general ranges:[34]

Soprano C4 to A5
Mezzo soprano A3 to F#5
Alto G3 to E5
Tenor roughly C3 to A4
Baritone A2 to F4
Basses E2 to C4

These indications are given in order to stress difference between the voices. According to the chart, male voices occupy the first octave and two notes (E2–F3), then for another octave and two notes (10 semitones) (G3–A4) male and female singers occupy a range together. This is followed by an octave (A3–A2) that is indicated as the female range. These guidelines highlight differences, showing the parts of the vocal range that are occupied purely by males or by females. There is an overlap of 10 semitones, or about one third of the overall human vocal range, between men and women. In short, while these indications of vocal ranges are undoubtedly accurate, they stress divergence rather than commonality. We therefore cannot say that pitch is an absolute defining factor in gender signaling.

By way of trying to solve the question of pitch, I compared Scott's vocal range with those of a number of his contemporaries. In musical example 3.2, I show the results of comparing three of Scott's biggest hits with comparable artists performing around the same period. The list shows the entire range used in the songs, from the lowest to the highest note.[35]

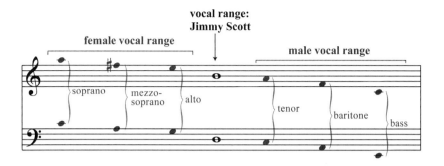

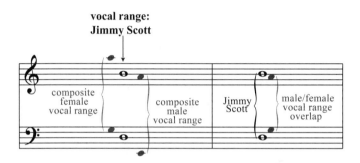

Jimmy Scott, *The Source* (B3 – D4)

James Brown, "I Feel Good" (G3 – D5)

Sam Cooke, "A Change Is Gonna Come" (F3 – B♭4)

Marvin Gaye, "Trouble Man" (A3 – D5)

Smokey Robinson and the Miracles, "Ooo Baby Baby" (A3 – G5)

Smokey Robinson and the Miracles, "I Second That Emotion" (B3 – D5)

Otis Rush, "I Can't Stop Baby" (E3 – G5)

Swan Silvertones, "Brighter Day Ahead" (A3 – C5)

The Temptations, "Get Ready" (A3 – D5)

Frankie Valli, "Big Girls Don't Cry" (D3 – E5)

Stevie Wonder, "Uptight" (B3 – D♭5)

Stevie Wonder, "For Once in My Life" (G3 – F#5)

The simplest interpretation of Scott's slow career start is that against the backdrop of performers who fell into recognizable (African American) male categories, his high tessitura—not the complete range of the voice but the part of the vocal range that is most comfortable and most *utilized*—was so high that

EXAMPLE 3.2 Comparison of vocal ranges between Jimmy Scott and some of his contemporaries.

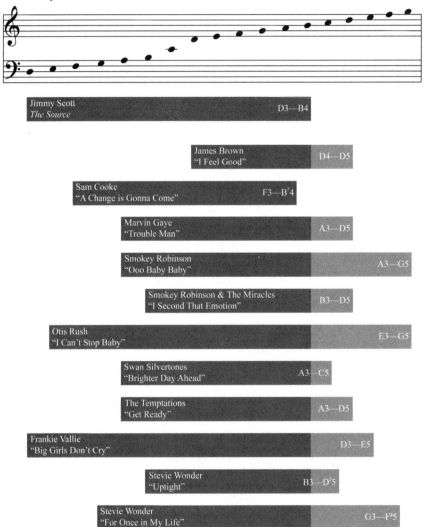

he sounded like a woman and thus was difficult to market as himself. However, as we see, Scott's higher range is not much higher than his colleagues'. In fact Scott's highest note is B4, which is seven and eight semitones below Stevie Wonder's F#5 and Smokey Robinson's G5, respectively. Scott occupies the same range as the tenor vocal range specified in *Grove Music Online*: his top note is B4, while *Grove* indicates that tenors go to A4. That is, Scott's pitch range—one note above the average tenor voice—is not the main distinguishing factor between him and his contemporaries.

A closer analysis of the mean F0 (the vocal sound's fundamental frequency) of Scott and three of the singers from the list, Marvin Gaye, Smokey Robinson, and Frankie Valli, yield surprising results.[36]

Mean F0:
Marvin Gaye, "Trouble Man," 382.62 Hz
Smokey Robinson, "Ooo Baby Baby," 412.44 Hz
Frankie Valli, "Big Girls Don't Cry," 416.19 Hz
Jimmy Scott, "On Broadway," 263.77 Hz
Jimmy Scott, "I Wish I Knew," 248.18 Hz
Jimmy Scott, "This Love of Mine," 325.48 Hz[37]

This comparison shows that Scott's mean F0 average is significantly lower than that of the three other artists. Gaye's, Robinson's, and Valli's mean frequencies are similar to each other.[38] For our case, then, Scott is neither higher in the overall pitch range or frequency range nor in mean frequency compared to key colleagues who were read as masculine. What, then, contributed to the reading of Scott as nonmasculine while his colleagues were read as masculine? I'd like to consider the question of audiences' readings of Scott in a roundabout way.

Signaling Vocal Masculinity with Timbral Scare Quotes

How is gender signaled vocally? For most people who fall within traditional gender norms, this question does not require attention. Vocal norms are naturalized. However, the question of gender signaling is an urgent one for transgender individuals, a population that deals with this issue on a very practical level. First, pitch is considered in terms of the physical vocal apparatus and hormonal state. From an anatomical point of view, vocal range is tied to the length of the vocal folds: longer folds yield a deeper pitch, and shorter folds yield a higher pitch. However, a body's hormonal environment can also greatly modify the voice and lower pitch while maintaining the same vocal fold length. Therefore, for female-to-male transition, steroid treatment is often used successfully to lower vocal pitch.[39] For male-to-female conversions, hormone therapy does not alter pitch.[40] Instead surgical interventions are used, but they pose risks, and their success varies.[41] Second, research on the perception of transgender voices shows that FO is only one of many cues on which speakers and listeners rely.[42] In fact even a voice with a very high FO can be perceived as male or masculine if other aspects of the thick vocal event signal male parameters. To adopt Jody Kreiman and Diana Sidtis's terminology, the voices of some male-to-female transgender individuals are interpreted as "unambiguously male" even if pitched within a stereotypically "female range."[43]

Third, besides pitch, a number of additional vocal characteristics contribute to the signaling of masculinity and femininity, a fact that many transgender individuals use to their advantage. Parameters and characteristics that have been identified as gendered markers include word choice, precise articulation (clearly pronounced consonants and endings of words), uptalk (ending declarative sentences with a rising intonation, or a pitch contour associated with a question), more upward shifts in FO, fewer downward shifts in FO, variable intonation contours, and longer word durations.[44] In singing, during which many of these variables are not engaged, feminine vocality can be signaled with increased breathiness, a limited dynamic range, a less dynamic variable, particular articulation, and vocal timbral manipulation.[45] For example, when Deborah Gunzberger compared the female and male voices of six transgender people, she observed that, when speaking in their female voice, most speakers increased the mean FO, the overall range of FO, and the time durations of each increase. In moves relevant to singing, most of the speakers retracted the corners of their lips (as in a smile) and/or raised their larynges, shortening the vocal tract.[46] These two relatively simple movements drastically raise the formant frequency, which signals femininity.[47] However, Gunzberger also reported that, while one of the speaker's utterances was not differentiated in FO and dynamic patterns were coded neither male nor female, the speaker was still classified correctly 74 percent of the time. The overwhelmingly correct classifications were based on listeners' ability to compensate for a lack of FO signaling and misleading intensity cues by focusing on articulation and resonance cues.[48]

In short, scholarship from music, the sciences, and medicine confirms that there is significant overlap between male and female voices as we interpret them, but that timbre is also a strong factor that can override even pitch information in pointing unambiguously in a single direction. While music literature stresses the divergences between male and female pitch areas, if we read the data we can easily and accurately stress the overlap. However, we also know that human identification of gender based on voice patterns tends to be fairly accurate. In the words of Kreiman and Sidtis, "These patterns confirm that a male or female voice quality depends on a constellation of static and dynamic cues, and not simply on mean FO." Moreover a "female voice cannot be created by simply scaling up male vocal parameters, because culture-, accent-, and dialect-dependent cues to a speaker's sex can be essential to a successful transformation."[49] Thinking back to work around the transgender voice, we recall that while men may speak in a pitch range that is marked female, they still may not be read as female.[50]

What, then, was the strong differentiating factor between Scott and his contemporaries? Remember, Scott's contemporaries vocalized in pitches associated with women but were read as male or even hypermasculine. Yet Scott, who vocalized in a range that is within the traditional male vocal spectrum, was read as ambiguous in gendered terms. In terms of cues that are often used in gendered signaling, such as pronunciation, Scott does not offer apparent gendered cues. Overall Scott's pronunciation is clear, while, specifically, the endings of his words are less clear. The male singers listed earlier also have very clear pronunciation.

However, one differentiating factor is the use of what I call timbral scare quotes—the use of a portion of the voice that is set apart timbrally from what the singer deems to be the normative part of his or her voice. The specific vocal technique used by Scott's contemporaries to create a different timbre was *falsetto*.[51] By enlisting falsetto, a vocal technique and recognizable timbral shift, male performers can utilize larger portions of their voices while maintaining an image of masculinity. Indeed, the most recognized and recognizable African American male vocalists of the 1960s, the decade that could have included Scott's mainstream breakthrough, made liberal use of falsetto technique as timbral mediation.[52] Applying this particular technique and timbre to a high vocal range signaled hypermasculinity.

While falsetto can indicate both a vocal function and a technique, most people experience or know it through timbre. A strong *timbral* shift marks its separation from the vocalizer's "natural" voice. Falsetto occurs when the vocal muscle relaxes, and the cricothyroid muscle is able to create further longitudinal tension upon the vocal ligaments. By increasing this tension, the pitch can be raised beyond the vocal cords' maximum possible length. This takes place in a process of thinning the vocal cords, so that the vibration is located almost entirely in the ligaments (akin to thinner strings on a stringed instrument).[53]

Thus male singers can engage the upper vocal register while holding that part of their voice at arm's length.[54] Even Prince, in his carefully crafted gender-ambiguous presentation, marks off some of his falsetto singing, performances that are pitch-shifted even higher by speeding up the tape. He identifies this type of vocal performance with a different name: Camille.[55] In effect, by timbrally marking the otherness of this vocal range in relation to their so-called true voices, male singers' masculine personae are held intact while singing high notes. Accessing that part of their vocal range through falsetto marks off the area in a form of timbral scare quotes. Therefore, contra the commonly held belief, it is not pitch that is the distinguishing factor of Scott's voice, but rather timbre.[56] And it is a specific timbral expression that serves as the comparison to normative masculine vocal performance against which Scott is measured.

While, as I explained, a clear set of parameters are performed during speech, timbral scare quotes can take different forms in the singing voice. For example, those who exhibit what is experienced as gender-ambiguous vocal presentation can deflect the gender-ambiguousness of a sung performance through their spoken presentation. Putting timbral scare quotes around a high vocal range may also take place outside the act of singing. Alisha Jones has reported that countertenors—male singers who sing entire repertoires in falsetto—within the black church negotiate what could be understood as queerness by framing their sung vocal performances, which are understood as feminine or queer, with strong masculine cues in their *spoken* interactions. Jones considers male singers with conservatory training as they sing countertenor repertoire within the context of the black church service, and addresses the pressure they experience to conform to "longstanding heteronormative constructs in gospel" and "the socio-cultural anxieties" around gender. Discussing this practice through a sensitive ethnography with the singer Patrick Dailey, Jones draws a distinction between these countertenors and singers who sing in noticeable falsetto, describing the countertenors and their style as "singing high."[57] Jones and I both look to draw this distinction as a sign that falsetto is marked as outside the normative voice.

As did Scott, the countertenor Dailey maintains an integral voice throughout the vocal registers. Daily's timbral integration of the falsetto with his rare use of the lower part of the vocal register sets him apart from soul and gospel performers, who use falsetto in the upper range of the voice and modal voice in the medium and lower ranges. However, while Daily generally sings in a higher vocal range than male soul and gospel singers, and maintains falsetto throughout, he puts scare quotes around the entire range with spoken framing that performs traditional male masculinity.[58] Dailey pitches his speaking voice slightly lower than his singing voice, a strategy that he believes establishes an "aural baseline" and demonstrates what he refers to as "neutral," that is, a voice that offers the cues expected from a male singer. In his words, in order to

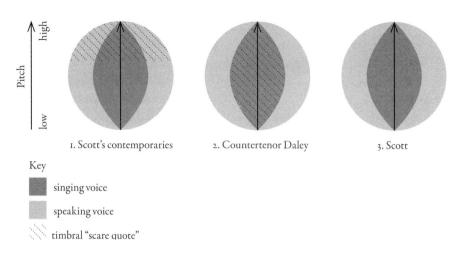

Pitch high low

1. Scott's contemporaries   2. Countertenor Daley   3. Scott

Key

singing voice

speaking voice

timbral "scare quote"

FIGURE 3.3 Timbral scare quotes. 1: Jimmy Scott's contemporaries, who sing in falsetto and perform hypersexuality; 2: countertenor Patrick Dailey, who sings in falsetto but marks with speech; 3: Scott, no marking.

stave off "professional hassles" because his musical performance is not "consistent with hegemonic perceptions of ideal masculinity," Dailey carefully frames his singing voice by demonstrating "competency" and "'ideal' black Christian manhood" within the church service context. This includes maintaining strict protocol around formal salutations.[59] Dailey believes it is absolutely necessary to take such measures to "frame his masculinity," saying he is "keenly aware that black congregations deplore effeminacy in black men and easily become suspicious of mannerisms that fall outside of a heteronormative ideal."[60]

Figure 3.3 illustrates the ways in which nonnormative vocal timbre is bracketed. Soul and gospel singers bracket off the higher part of the range by singing it in a different timbre, namely falsetto. Countertenors such as Dailey bracket off the entire performance by speaking in a low voice and performing other masculine ideals when not singing. Scott, on the other hand, sings in a consistent timbre throughout his musical numbers, and this timbre does not change when he is speaking.

Scott's assertion of agency was performed through a precise, microscopic arrangement of overtones; while the beauty of his artistry was his smooth and seamless transition from top to bottom, it was precisely his avoidance of falsetto and his refusal to bracket off parts of his voice that yielded timbral consistency throughout the vocal registers, marking him as different. In other words, Scott was othered not because of his higher voice but because of his consistent timbre, evidencing his inability or unwillingness to delineate a so-called real masculine vocal range from its so-called false upper extension. Moreover he maintained this consistency in his spoken voice, not only sonically but also in his assertion that this was his voice. This consistency, and the lack of scare quotes around any parts of his voice, disqualified Scott from the category of male jazz singer and also from the category of female jazz singer; his timbral evenness across vocal registers and his self-presentation together created a significant timbral ambiguity. It was that ambiguity, which did not lend itself to easy gender categorization, that opened a space within which, instead of dealing directly with the complexity of Scott's voice, we take an easier route, projecting onto it the representations we want to hear.

Timbral Performance as Radical Resistance

Within this construction of black vocal masculinity how—if at all—may Scott negotiate his desired identification as a black heterosexual man? What did the acousmatic question yield in our engagement with Scott? Within this timbral framework, is Scott simply read as female, or beyond-human, while men using falsetto or framing their singing voice in masculine-timbral code are read as masculine men? Did the acousmatic question tell us only that each timbral performance begins and ends with listeners' projections—addressing my third corrective to misconceptions about voice (voice's source is not the singer; it is the listener)? And that these projections, materialized through imagery, descriptions, characters, and the female voice, are the legacy associated with Scott? I'd like to push the reading of Scott's case further.

José Esteban Muñoz, a theorist of queer performance, suggests that there is at least one additional layer to the observations that can be made by listening to listening—that is, by paying attention to various groups' interactions with and responses to the acousmatic question. Muñoz's concept of *disidentification* provides a useful framework through which to deal with the complex dynamic arising between an artist's positionality and the material performed. Especially poignant is the play between audiences' preconceived notions of a character and the way such notions are castrated through juxtaposition with unlikely material. In this way the very success of the performance depends on the dynamic between a commonly held notion and the revelation that results when a character is presented in a new context. What these performances highlight, Muñoz notes, is "the fiction of identity." The "cultural performers" he considers "negotiate between a fixed identity disposition and the socially encoded roles that are available for such subjects."[61] By identifying disidentification as a positionality,

Muñoz recognizes that performance need not only consist of identifying with or reinscribing existing essentialized roles (including guerrilla fighter and drag queen) but that creative play with social roles, and even essential identities, can prove politically and semiotically productive.

While Scott insisted on heterosexuality and normalcy, he also availed himself of career opportunities that compromised that gender identity—yet he filled those feminine, queer, or beyond-human roles with his heterosexual identity. Like the performers Muñoz discusses—who show layers of identity rather than perfectly passing from one normative identity to another (say, from male to female, as in the case of the drag performer Vaginal Creme Davis)[62]—Scott neither militantly insisted on a masculine identity nor catered to the alternative identities fashioned for him by producers and audiences.

While they differ on the surface, there are strong resonances between Scott's power and the power of political drag found in the performance of the theater group the Mirabelles, whom Muñoz describes to flesh out his explanation of disidentification:

> The Mirabelles are experimenting with a new type of militant theater, a theater separate from an explanatory language. . . . They resort to drag, song, mime, dance, etc., not as different ways of illustrating a theme, to "change the ideas" of spectators, but in order to trouble them, to stir up uncertain desire-zones that they always more or less refuse to explore. The question is no longer whether one will play feminine against masculine or the reverse, but to make bodies, all bodies, break away from the representations and restraints on the "social body."[63]

While Scott, in contrast to the Mirabelles, does not himself "resort to drag," an audience that cannot make sense of him has done so, over and over again.

Each listener responds to slightly different aspects of performance and, reifying his or her own listening experience, adds another layer of meaning to the sound. Using his or her own set of experiences, each listener makes sense of the singer's voice. This process is not static; individuals define the meanings of things through interactions.[64] Therefore the listener's *impressions* of the singer's voice and identity are formed through the listener's own active contribution. Each audience member is deeply involved in the formation of what he or she perceives to be the singer's voice.[65] Thus it was his audience, rather than Scott himself, who actively produced the drag performance. And what seemed like quiet acceptance on his part may also be understood as an extraordinary pedagogical move. In Scott's words, "I saw my suffering as my salvation. Once

I knew that, I understood God had put me in this strange little package for a reason. All I needed was the courage to be me. That courage took a lifetime to develop."[66]

Scott's act of disidentification took place by simply not fighting audiences' and producers' projected and manifested drag performances. "For a long time," one of his colleagues said, "the joke was that Jimmy wasn't a fag, he was a lesbian." Another colleague remembers, "People were harsh with Jimmy. You'd go to his show and hear someone yell out, 'He sounds like a freak, he looks a freak, he *is* a freak.' But Jimmy was a gentleman. He just stood there and took it." In contrast, Scott recalls from this period, "Funny, but I saw myself as a normal guy looking for normal happiness. A home. A wife. A nice income."[67] The performance setting, and existing ideas of physical and vocal masculinity and femininity, defined Scott's performance work as liminal and drag.

It is precisely his calm self-representational insistence on normalcy that challenges producers and audiences alike. Scott performed disidentification. His performance, which largely rolled with other people's ideas about gender while maintaining a steadfast assertion of agency through timbral performance, exhibiting a solid self-identity throughout, constitutes a kind of haphazard beauty that is true to most people's lives: a continuous negotiation between what others project onto our voices and the strength to counter it, more or less, with our own ideas. To me, Scott's lifework exemplifies the type of critical performance that I took as inspiration for this book's methodological approach. This theoretical and performative strategy, which I call critical performance practice methodology, can help articulate the polyphony of what can sometimes seem to be the oxymoronic modalities of race, gender, and sexuality at work within any identity.

Despite his "unusual voice" and ambiguous gender identity making him a "hero for the margin" and "a cult figure only," I suggest that Scott's performance offers radical resistance on a much deeper epistemological level. Scott shows us what cannot be subsumed within the current "mainstream" paradigm of vocal timbre, hence exposing the paradigm itself.[68] That is, if we listen to our own listening to Scott, he offers us the opportunity to confront the *habitus* of that listening, that choir of voices to which we compare every new voice. He does this by sonically foregrounding a truism: that existing language cannot capture the voice *itself* beyond clichéd categories into which it is forced and with which it re-creates timbral meaning. Rather than hearing Scott's voice and (fooling myself into believing that I am) forming a description of that voice only, I hear it through and toward the traces of not-quite-erased voices and the socially mediated ways I categorize them. In fact it is through Scott's continued quiet activism in performance, which seems to fold into hegemonic projections, that he shows us the scare quotes around other male singers' timbral signaling. In this instance the politics of listening require that we listen beyond pitch and that we carefully attend to the multivalent capacity of timbre.

The lesson of Jimmy Scott is not unlike one taught by John Cage. In his infamous piece *4′33″*, Cage instructed a pianist to sit silently in front of an open piano for the given duration, teaching audiences that whatever they listened to *as* music indeed *became* music for them. By allowing the full range of interpretations of his sexual and gender identity to flourish, and by doing nothing to accommodate or frame them, Scott shows us that while every listener brings historically and culturally situated conventions to an instance of listening, the artist invents with that very material. Thus, while not operating within and being interpreted independent of his given context, Scott nonetheless disrupts easy readings and conclusions by playing and creating, as an autonomous artist, with the techniques made available to him through enculturation. Scott's challenging career exemplifies that audiences create whatever meaning they please and that the artist can make his own meaning. While Scott (like all of us) is entrained through informal lessons that seek to pin him down in terms of the intersection of gender and race, as well as through more formal lessons as a working musician, he composes something new and different out of this entrainment.[69] In other words, even though audiences hold on to entrainment and its limited meanings, for himself Scott is able to escape the static meaning to which most of the world around him clings.

4

RACE AS ZEROS AND ONES

Vocaloid Refused, Reimagined, and Repurposed

—————

Thus far I have considered a number of ways in which formal and informal pedagogies shape human bodies and vocal practices, focusing on timbre. First, considering classical vocal pedagogy, I showed that vocal timbre does not exist a priori but is shaped by cultural forces. I discussed that the available imagery and language are saturated with race- and gender-related power structures, thus presenting a challenge in themselves to combating such wrongs. Second, examining Marian Anderson's opera career, I discussed how female African American opera singers are perceived through racialized layers generated by listeners, and how the segregation that ended by law decades ago is still activated by listening practices, fueled by phantoms instead of facts. Third, I examined the tension between Jimmy Scott, his self-presentation, and how his listeners perceived him. As with Anderson, this case showed that listeners took little care to understand Scott's self-identification, instead projecting their own interpretations onto him. I noted in Scott a deliberate resistance to certain aspects of encultured projections. In all of these cases, the materials I dealt with are the sounds of, bodies of, discourses around, and visual representations of singing bodies. While most of these representations are wildly off base, they at least purport to refer to the human body.

In this chapter I turn to a different type of archive and show that gravitation toward racializing voice is not reserved for the human voice. Examining the vocal synthesis software Vocaloid shows that popular discourse around timbre, race, and racialized timbre is equally present in the technological realm.

The second iteration of the voice synthesis software program gained international fame with Hatsune Miku, the blue 3D-animated anime performer who has been presented at arena-size concerts in Asia, Europe, and North America. Examining this phenomenon throws into sharper relief the central role played by audiences in the production of voices. Thus while previous chapters investigated various ways in which audiences' listening and listening pedagogies affect singers' entraining bodies, this chapter shows a complete production of raced voices through a technology-enabled loop that audiences and producers feed into.

While the reader may still be somewhat hesitant about accepting my argument that race, as thought to be heard in vocal timbre, has no essential origin, this chapter shows that even when assembling zeros and ones, listeners continue to produce and reify notions of racialized vocal timbre. The figure of sound, then, is truly a symbolic concept that travels with listeners who are invested in (vocal) stereotypes. Thus the various iterations of Vocaloid can be understood as crowdsourced articulations of the response that arises when the acousmatic question *Who is this?* is applied to an open-ended potential. For many of the Vocaloid voices, although a possible response to this question is not even linked to an existing voice or image of a vocalizer, societies and cultural productions built on the economy and value tied to racial difference still serve as a gravitational force. In the wide-open digital realm, as though listeners have pulled out the same measuring tapes and templates used to form the voices discussed in chapters 1–3, opportunity and promise are eschewed in favor of the familiar, producing stylized articulations of stereotypical raced and gendered typology.[1]

The hologram phenomenon Hatsune Miku, which made its way from Japan to the United States and beyond as a YouTube meme, was voiced by a Vocaloid voice bank and reached a mass audience by performing on *The David Letterman Show*.[2] Hatsune Miku illustrates how audiences project varied physical attributes onto voices.[3] This projection is not unlike what took place in the reception of Jimmy Scott; however, Scott's insistence on his own identity offered a counterweight to the multiple personae fashioned by audiences for him. Theoretically producers and audiences have an open field when listening to a voice and conjuring up a corporeal idea of the singer.

When I first learned and wrote about the ways in which Vocaloid fans had initially rejected the blackface imagery and racialized discourse around the Vocaloid synthesis software versions LOLA and LEON, I thought this could be an opportunity to study a community that rejected such crude depictions.[4] But in revisiting the software nearly a decade later, instead of learning about a group that functioned outside of the vocal engagements I knew very well, I saw a community that grappled with the same issues, even when the voice in question was vocal synthesis software. This shows us that the acousmatic question does not point to a knowable voice but rather to the listener—the one who silently poses the question—and this brings up the third corrective. In other words, the response to the acousmatic question follows the same pattern whether the voice is human or synthesized. We listen in the ways that we have learned to pay attention, so any answer to the acousmatic question points to the listener himself or herself.

Shifting to a different type of archive compared to the book's other chapters has allowed me to ask a number of questions: What could these very rapid cycles of producing, publishing, and reacting to listeners' responses tell us about the production of voice, and about underlying assumptions around epistemologies and ontologies of voice? Did the fact that this vocal technology was digital, and that many of the social practices surrounding the voices and their music were carried out using a digital platform, imply an ontology and an epistemology different from those underpinning analog practices? How might listeners' conceptions be affected by a singer who provides the initial sounds for the synthesis and who is a strong advocate of his or her own ethnicity? Engaging with synthesized voices and with their user- and fan-based practices offers a unique opportunity to observe audiences' articulated manifestations of the figure of sound. Therefore the Vocaloid phenomenon provides a unique window into many listeners' engagement with and responses to the acousmatic question. Precisely because the concept and naturalized practices of voice are so deeply infused with notions of the essential, it is almost too complex a task to listen and assess while remaining divorced from those ideas. In examining the ways in which synthesized vocal fonts serve as a vehicle for a seemingly endless stream of projections about voice we may be able to understand more about how, in our encounters with voice, we formulate our responses to the acousmatic question.

Vocaloid

The commercially available vocal synthesis software Vocaloid was first introduced to the American market in 2004 at the National Association of Music Merchants (NAMM) event in Anaheim, California, one of the most important annual music industry tradeshows.[5] The application received enormous attention, garnering awards from several music and technology journals. A *New York Times* review published after the 2003 European release in anticipation of the NAMM show hailed the Yamaha synthesis method as a "quantum leap" in hu-

FIGURE 4.1 Vocaloid 1 screenshot.

man voice modeling.[6] The attention and praise Vocaloid received from industry professionals and journalists was, for a time, consistently high.

While Vocaloid is far from the first voice synthesis program, it was the first specifically created as a commercial, consumer-oriented music product. Vocaloid is described by its developer, the British music technology company Zero-G, as a "vocal-synthesizing software that enables songwriters to generate authentic-sounding singing . . . by simply typing in the lyrics and music notes of their compositions."[7] Zero-G invites users to imagine the different voices as a "library" of "vocal fonts" (see figure 4.1). The user enters pitches and durations on conventional staff paper in one application setting, and through a piano interface or connected midi device in another. The user can type in lyrics that correspond with the notes, and melody and words are then sung back by the voice the user selects. This process is roughly comparable to typing words into a text document and having them read back by text-reader software; however, unlike a conventional text file reader, Vocaloid assigns pitch and duration to each word based on user input. Also, each pitch-duration-word compound may be treated with added vibrato, envelope, attack, dynamics, and so on. In the same way that a few mouse clicks will change the font type in a word document, a Vocaloid song may be sung back by any of the available voices.[8]

Each Vocaloid voice is made up of thousands of samples recorded by a single singer.[9] Together the samples represent about 3,800 of the possible vowel and consonant combinations found in the English language. Each original singer

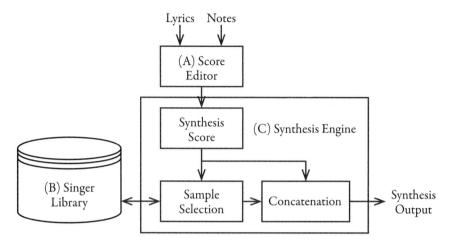

Lyrics Notes

(A) Score Editor

Synthesis Score   (C) Synthesis Engine

(B) Singer Library

Sample Selection

Concatenation

Synthesis Output

FIGURE 4.2 System diagram of Vocaloid, adapted from Hideki Kenmochi, "Singing Synthesis as a New Musical Instrument," in *Proceedings of the International Conference on Acoustics, Speech and Signal Processing (ICASSP) 2012* (Piscataway, NJ: IEEE, 2012), 5385.

recorded sixty pages of scripted articulations (e.g., [pel, pep, lep]) on three different pitches, which were then manually trimmed into precise samples.[10] The fact that this process required eight hours of recording per day for five days may offer an idea of the sheer volume of these combinations.

The synthesis procedures used in Vocaloid were developed through a collaboration between Pompeu Fabra University (Barcelona) and Yamaha. Using the system described above, Vocaloid's synthesis combines the recorded phoneme samples into a seamless string of notes sounding words in melodic sequences.[11] In electroacoustic music terms, Vocaloid may be considered a "hybrid vocal synthesis" in that it uses basic sonic material from the phoneme recordings, whereas "complete sound synthesis" does not use sound samples. Vocaloid relies on synthesis techniques in order to combine and alter the sounds of the samples.[12] Within the Vocaloid system there are three major areas: (1) the score editor, (2) a singer database, and (3) the synthesis engine (see figure 4.2). The user inputs lyrics, notes, adjustments, and musical expressions into the score editor; based on this information, the prerecorded diphones and sustained vowels are pulled from the singer database. Finally, the synthesis engine concatenates them.

To clarify, the term "Vocaloid" refers to the technical protocol regarding the translation from spelled words and given pitches to the actual emitted sound. "Vocaloid" is also used to refer to all the commercial technology that is created based on the Vocaloid synthesis protocol. Companies utilize the Vocaloid protocol to create the voices, or vocal fonts. Each of these is given a name that refers to both the specific vocal font and the attending character, envisioned as a singer, that is part of the marketing and packaging of the vocal font.

One of the main challenges in creating software that sings words is the translation between the *spelled word* entered by the user and the actual *sounded phoneme*. For example, the word "Philadelphia" begins with a phoneme similar to that beginning the word spelled "fish." One of Vocaloid's tasks is therefore to choose the recorded phoneme that corresponds to the written word; in this example both words, although spelled differently (*ph* and *f*), begin with the same sounded phoneme. Due to the spelling-to-phonation relationship and for other technical reasons, a given synthesis system is created with specific language capabilities.[13] If we think about this from the point of view of the figure of sound, the goal of these iterations is to make the vocal synthesis as close to the user's figure of sound as possible. The test of success is whether the software is recognizable as what it presents itself to be. At this point, Vocaloid can sing in English, Spanish, Japanese, Korean, Mandarin, Spanish, and Catalan.[14] The Vocaloid 1 engine was created for English and Japanese. Further generations of the synthesis system were developed for the following languages: Vocaloid 2 (Japanese and English); Vocaloid 3 and 4 (Japanese, English, Spanish, and Catalan [the latter two using very similar phoneme sets], Korean, and Mandarin Chinese). Some of the voice banks (Megurine Luka [v2, v4], Yohioloid [v3], Kaito [v3], Meiko [v3], Hatsune Miku [v3], Gumi [v3]) are bilingual. From the first two voice banks to the subsequent proliferation of languages and companies producing Vocaloid, market intentions for this cohort of voices clearly moved beyond the originally targeted language groups and, in the process, pushed the technology's development.

Not Software, but Singers

Prior to Vocaloid, vocal synthesis applications were described in terms of their technological advances and their advantages as powerful sound synthesis tools. In contrast, Zero-G has framed each vocal font not merely as a synthesis application but as a *singer*. Different versions have been marketed in varying degrees of detail, but all have been given Christian names. For example, the first two voices to be released were given the names LOLA and LEON. A third edition was called MIRIAM, the name of the South African–born British singer Miriam Stockley, who provided the voice samples for the synthesis.[15] (At the time of this writing, summer 2015, just two Vocaloid voice banks described solely in gender terms have been released: VY2 [male voice] and VY1 [female voice].[16])

Zero-G compares Vocaloid's quality and advantages to singers rather than to other pieces of technology, and does not brag about the tool's power as *software*; for example, the marketing materials emphasize the convenience of recording a voice without waiting for a singer to arrive. However, they rarely discuss the vocal fonts' human-like qualities, as is common in the discourse around speech-to-speech technology or fantasies such as the iPhone's Siri application and the voice in the 2013 movie *Her*.[17]

Besides names, the Vocaloid applications were each assigned a personal profile, which ranged from the specific (identification with a particular singer, such as Miriam Stockley) to more general categorizations in terms of, for instance, genre and gender. LOLA and LEON were marketed in the latter manner: Zero-G describes them as "the world's first virtual" male and female "soul vocalists," highlighting the gender, genre, and possible applications of each voice. In contrast, MIRIAM is described in personal and concrete terms, such as "based on British singer Miriam Stockley's voice."[18] Rather than closely identifying the MIRIAM voice with a genre, an emphasis is placed on the notion that "[her] voice is pure and suitable for the current synthesis engine" and that she is a "virtual vocalist."[19]

Presentation of the profiles as singers rather than as software was also carried out through their packaging. While the highly problematic images on the boxes containing LOLA, LEON, and MIRIAM (figures 4.3–4.5) depict, to varying degrees, a person, the packaging of Cantor, an older synthesis software (figure 4.6), highlights the technical aspect with sound waves and an anatomical drawing of the vocal tract.[20] Cantor's packaging is rather generic.

The packaging of LOLA and LEON is unambiguous in its portrayal of the intended racial profile of these voices. Unlike Cantor, LOLA and LEON are portrayed as full lipped, with lips protruding, offering up a voice (or perhaps a body) and cropped very close in order to eliminate any association with a specific person. These voices are wrapped in imagery that plays on blackface iconography. Like a stock figure returning in minstrel repertoire, the picture used for both LOLA and LEON is the same. For LOLA, the designer simply mirrored the blue-tinted image of LEON and colored it red.

While LOLA and LEON were seemingly created with an image of anonymous backing vocalists in mind—an image that was, itself, recycled, retinted, and reversed—MIRIAM originated in the idea that the user could be offered access to the familiar face and voice of a popular singer. At the time of the MIRIAM application's creation, Miriam Stockley was known to a broad audience through U.K. chart placement with the 1991 song "Only You" and the 1995 Karl Jenkins project "Adiemus," recorded for a Delta Airlines commercial.

FIGURE 4.3 LOLA,
software box artwork.

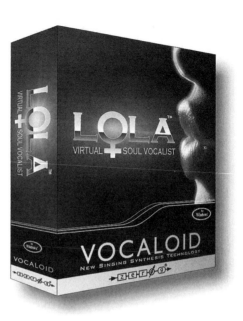

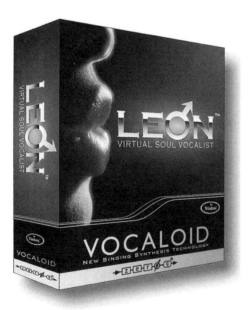

FIGURE 4.4 LEON,
software box artwork.

FIGURE 4.5 MIRIAM, software box artwork.

FIGURE 4.6 Cantor, software box artwork.

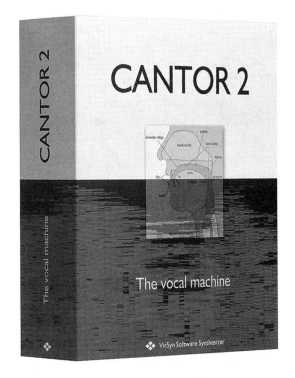

"Adiemus" was so popular that it was released on the London Philharmonic Orchestra album *Song of Sanctuary* and has subsequently been used in movie soundtracks (e.g., *Invisible Children*) and in several other commercials.[21] Rather than representing a *genre* (as in the case of LOLA and LEON), it is the voice of an individual artist that gives the MIRIAM Vocaloid singer its sonic identity.[22]

Users' Perceptions of LOLA

Despite Zero-G's comprehensive efforts to present a black soul singer, many of LOLA's users did not hear her voice as a soul voice and/or as black. User Robot-Archie wrote on Zero-G's Internet message board, "Do we have a British soul singer with a Japanese accent who lisps like a Spaniard? Eesa makea me tho unhappy."[23] Heatviper chimes in, "Hello . . . I think LOLA works great for mondo/mournful/giallo morricone style tracks using vowels. . . . Wordless soulful vowels are nice."[24] Jogomus asks for advice: "My LOLA sounds a little bit like a 'big Ma'—what can I do, [so] that she sounds a little bit neutral?" hk suggests lowering the "Gender Factor" value.[25]

In addition to comments such as these, users reported that an unexpected and problematic accent emerged during their implementations of LOLA's voice, an accent that became difficult for Vocaloid programmers to explain. The head programmer reported subsequent online exchanges with users wherein he, with convoluted technical explanations of the synthesis method, tried to obfuscate the fact that some users found the performer's pronunciation strange or unexpected in relation to the anticipated black soul singer's voice.

Despite the initial glowing reviews and awards, the Vocaloid user forum reveals that general reception was less uncritically accepting. User discussion centered on the appropriate genre in which to use the software, precisely the aspect of the product that Zero-G had worked most diligently at defining. Whereas the *New York Times* reviewer was interested in Vocaloid's potential to revive the voices of famous singers (such as Elvis) by extracting existing sound samples from recordings and patching them together with the new synthesis method, users of the software took a more practical approach.[26] They listened to the applications and thought about what these voices sounded like—and they discovered that the sound failed to match their conceptions of a black soul singer's sound and the product advertised by Zero-G.

Because the sound of a standard vocalist within the soul genre is well-defined, it is safe to assume that both Zero-G and Vocaloid's users possessed reasonably similar ideas about how a soul singer's voice should sound. However, an apparent gap emerged between the product Zero-G wished to sell and what its users, or at least those who participated in the user forum, experienced. This gap was articulated by the differences between the vocal font profile created by Zero-G—a composite of sound, visual representation, textual description, and genre reference—and the experiences about which LOLA's users write. It is this gap between the expected and actual experiences of hearing LOLA that points to a nonessential and constructed relationship between vocal timbre and identity.

The gap was essentially caused by mistaking race for the style and aesthetic of spoken and sung vocalization. In essence Zero-G's producers conflated blackness and soul. The two singers who provided the source sounds for LOLA and LEON worked in the United Kingdom, were black, and did some work in the soul genre.[27] The male singer was British and spoke with a British accent; the female singer was Jamaican and spoke with a Jamaican accent. As professional musicians they would sing in any genre, including soul. In the same way that the Beatles and the Rolling Stones performed rock'n'roll with American accents but spoke with their British accents, when LOLA's and LEON's source singers sang soul, they sang with American English pronunciation.

Providing source material for the Vocaloid voice banks, however, does not take place within the context of a musical genre. As mentioned earlier, the source sound is a careful recording that forms the sonorous basis for pronouncing the 3,800 possible vowel and consonant combinations. In other words, the syllables are recorded out of context. Within the conventions of soul singing, the syllable *ma*, as part of the word *man*, would be pronounced with short *a* sound compared to American or British English. Outside a soul context, native speakers of British, Jamaican, and American English would sing the syllable *ma* differently. This means that every voicing takes place within what we may think of, albeit in a simplified way, as an aesthetic genre. Such an aesthetic genre can be chosen, and is very likely to be chosen, when singing within the context of a vocal musical genre, such as soul.

The same processes took place with the singers who provided the source sounds for LOLA and LEON. When they sang within a given musical genre, they pronounced the words in a manner consistent with that genre. Here, in contrast, the singers recorded lists of syllables for the voice bank. In vocal production outside the context of a specific aesthetic scheme, such as the soul genre, people tend to revert to their native language. This is especially true when producing nonverbal vocalizations, such as "ah," "eh?," "oh," and other filler-sound exclamations. Thus when pronouncing syllables divorced from context, vocalizers commonly revert to the subtle details and timbres of their primary accent. Hence LOLA's and LEON's source sounds were infused with British- and

Jamaican-accented aesthetics. These British- and Jamaican-accented syllables were not saturated with the soul aesthetic; instead they were filled with the style of each source voice's primary pronunciation scheme.

With LOLA and LEON, then, it seems that genre, style, and technique were confused with a belief about essence: that the style, genre, and aesthetics of soul were conflated with blackness. The result, we recall, was described as "a British soul singer with a Japanese accent" who "lisps like a Spaniard." LOLA and LEON seemed to be heard in three different ways, which may be connected to the vocal synthesis technology's development in Spain and Japan and the recording studio's location and the software company's origin in the United Kingdom. The choice of the singers had been made through an erroneous conflation of professional knowledge about a musical genre with the assumption that blackness infuses the voice throughout all vocal circumstances.[28]

LOLA and LEON: Soul Singers?

Eventually, after the hype and promise of technology that would insert real singers and the belief that virtual vocalists such as LOLA and LEON would be heavily used as backup singers, the voices failed to generate large sales and were not actually employed as the advertised "soul singers." In fact besides the demos provided by Zero-G, I have not been able to locate a single example of their use that falls even remotely under the soul genre, or indeed has any affinities with soul. The two original demos that were used in the release campaign—"LOLA Is Here" and "Check It Out," with music and lyrics by Andy Powers and Joe Hogan, respectively—seem to be the only available musical tidbits that flirt with soul. Therefore, while the samples in the voice bank are quite static, in that they are always the same every day and for every user, the reactions toward them are not universal. In fact, as we will see, the reactions are dramatically split. These mixed reactions tell us that when things that are objectively the same (voice samples) are met with such radically different interpretations and ideas about appropriate musical contexts, the differentiating factor is the listener, here in the form of the software user. Ironically, while the use of LOLA and LEON proved diverse, it was ultimately limited and fell outside soul.

Strictly speaking, even the introductory demo "LOLA Is Here" uses LOLA only for limited vocals and lyrics. Therefore the only piece I have been able to locate within what I hear as a hybrid soul, funk, and electronica genre mainly communicates its genre characteristics through the music rather than through extensive vocalization. The lyrics are "LOLA is here for you"; "LOLA, I love you," and the vocalises are sung on the syllables "sha," "yeah," "ah," and "oooh." The

FIGURE 4.7 Screenshot of "LOLA Is Here" melisma.

vocal track has been treated with vibrato through the expressions menu, and some of the pitches have been edited. When entering a pitch on the score or through MIDI input, the pitches fall within a tempered scale, and the pitch-editing mode can alter the actual pitch in relative relation to it (i.e., the user can make it higher or lower). The composer, Powers, sequenced the voice and added multiple notes, a technique that creates smooth vocal runs on long notes (see figure 4.7). There are also a few layered harmony tracks and some ambient reverb effects added to the main vocal line.

The LEON voice introducing the software demo, "Check It Out," sings "LEON and LOLA, check it out," "Come on," "Sing to me baby, yeah (yeah, yeah, yeah)" alongside some short vocalises on the syllable "yeah." The 33-second nugget makes use of generous pitch, portamento, and vibrato tuning to add expression to the voice that fits the style of the music, including a very small spoken section ("Sing a little song for me"). Additionally the vocal scatting sounds like it must have required custom phoneme input. Vocaloid uses the Extended Speech Assessment Methods Phonetic Alphabet (X-SAMPA), designed to simplify the more complex character set used in the standard phonetic notation system, the International Phonetic Alphabet (IPA), by adhering to today's more typical Latin letters, such as those used in English. When typing in a word—for example, "baby"—Vocaloid's default system, X-SAMPA, translates the typed

FIGURE 4.8 Screenshot of "Check It Out" custom phoneme input.

word into pronunciation. Each character-to-sound translation is based on a database wherein the programmer provided the relationship between the typed
word and its sounded pronunciation. While some of these default phonations
work well, the creator of the song may wish to override the default pronunciation to accommodate changes that occur when a word is sung within a string
of words in a phrase, with a particular accent, or otherwise, in a manner that
requires other vowel-consonant combinations and transitions. In the example,
the creator of the vocals works within the phoneme box and inputs custom
phonemes (see figure 4.8).[29] That is, the vocal would have needed quite a lot of
treatment to sound even somewhat related to a vocal from a soul-related genre.
Overall, however, it is the demo's composition and instrumentation, rather than
the voice, that enabled these samples to be interpreted as funk, which is not
unrelated to soul.

As mentioned, beyond the demos issued as part of their release, I have not
been able to find published uses of LOLA and LEON that allude to soul. In general, while LOLA and LEON did not turn out to be very popular Vocaloid fonts,
some of the published work does evidence a wide range of imagination. For
example, LEON was used in a version of "The World Tonight," which could be
said to fall broadly within electronic/pop music. Here LEON's phonemes have

been edited away from their inbuilt defaults for clearer pronunciation, but this has also given him a bit more of an Americanized accent—in contrast to, for example, the fan cover "Obsoletion→Retirement" [sic] created by graceinlife.[30] Technically the function called "gender factor" has been lowered to make a deeper, rounder, arguably more mature-sounding voice. There is also heavy use of autotune on the voice to flatten it out, which is noticeable in the pitch shifts. It is especially audible in the text "show me how right now." The autotune, choppy sound, and repeated vocals accentuate LEON's robotic voice.

An example of creative use of LOLA can be found in "Light Comes My Way," which sounds more like a mixture of electronic and pop genres rather than soul, as the software designers intended.[31] Much like the demo, this song features repeated vocal phrases: "The light comes my way / Feeling this." LOLA's voice is used simply to render basic notes and words with no pitch or expression tuning applied. The LOLA producer has also applied many effects, including reverb, delay, and chorus. Additionally it sounds as though the user may have increased the voice's brightness, and perhaps the parameter termed "noise" in Vocaloid 1 (renamed "breathiness" in Vocaloid 2).

When the Vocaloid 1 synthesis system was upgraded to Vocaloid 2—a process referred to as the "retiring" of Vocaloid 1—fans began making art in response. The Vocaloid community treated the obsolescence of LEON and LOLA as a kind of "passing on." Some of the videos expressed strong emotional responses by, for example, pairing Vocaloid-created music with a string of videos of building demolitions.[32] Agatechlo posted "The Disappearance of LEON," which sets the voice bank to a very high tempo that rises above the understandable and more natural-sounding voice.[33] The song is in Japanese, thus the producer also had to translate English phonemes to Japanese phonemes. The Vocaloid community therefore understands making LEON, whose language is set to English, sing at an extremely high speed in pseudo-Japanese as an exciting and challenging exercise. Part of the overall complexity of vocal synthesis is the actual time the software needs to calculate and pronounce a string of phonemes. Each voice bank's tempo that will render ideal singing results as imagined by the manufacturer is noted on its featured specifications. In a way, though, the choppiness—resulting from both the speed and the setting in a language for which the synthesis is not intended—accentuates the artificial-sounding qualities of the voice. Furthermore the strategy of not trying to make the synthesis sound human, but rather of accentuating its artificiality and nonhumanness, also gravitates away from its designated soul genre. Along the same lines, a British electropop musician uses LOLA's voice under the handle anaROBIK. Here the

Vocaloid font fuels an entirely different character or personality from Zero-G's soul singer or the more standard fan imagery of LOLA that has come from the Vocaloid community.[34]

While LOLA's and LEON's voices have been used in genres other than soul, users have also envisioned different *visual characters* for them. See, for example, the fan art in figure 4.9.[35] This fan worked with the five voice banks that had been issued by Zero-G and created five corresponding characters. MIRIAM, PRIMA, and SONIKA have the same coloring as in the official Vocaloid visual art. The vocal font MIRIAM, as previously mentioned, was based on the voice of the South African singer Miriam Stockley, and a photo of Stockley is shown on the software package. The voice of PRIMA has not been released, but the software package is decorated with a photo of a silhouetted woman with brown hair and green eyes, her hair slicked back (see figure 4.10). The font is curvy, perhaps alluding to a time when the art of cursive writing was valued and opera was the popular music of the day. The fan art of this opera-singer character retains the white skin, brown hair, and deep pink accent color of the original packaging, but her hair is now curly and is adorned with a red rose, while the color scheme of the eyes and accent colors follow the original cover art's color palette. The original SONIKA art is a drawing of a young rock princess with a microphone stand placed diagonally across her body. She has green hair and eyes, navel piercings, and wears fingerless gloves, jeans, and a top that reveals a large rose tattoo extending from her right breast to her shoulder. The fan-drawn version of the character keeps the green color accents but sports anime style with a yellow top and a green tweed-patterned skirt.

LOLA and LEON are completely transformed in fan representations. Recall that, in the artwork featured on the original box, they were shown only in close-up profile in a style that echoed blackface-coded visual representations, with dark-hued skin and full dark red lips. The new LOLA is drawn in anime style, with big green eyes, a tiny mouth, and full blonde hair, her youthful bangs cast to the left side. LEON wears a harlequin costume consisting of red pants, pink, pointy shoes, and a white shirt with red hearts forming the chest pockets and a tall oversized collar framing his head. The image shows LEON removing a mask that depicts a black man with a buzz cut, sideburns, and wide open mouth. Behind the mask, LEON sports shoulder-length blond hair and has large blue eyes.

Another piece of fan art develops yet another blond character for LEON, in imagery is echoed throughout the fan world. Here he has the same green eyes and a shoulder-length elfin hairstyle. In this materialization LEON's rose is displaced from his blue shirt into his hand, as he takes in its scent. This artwork's

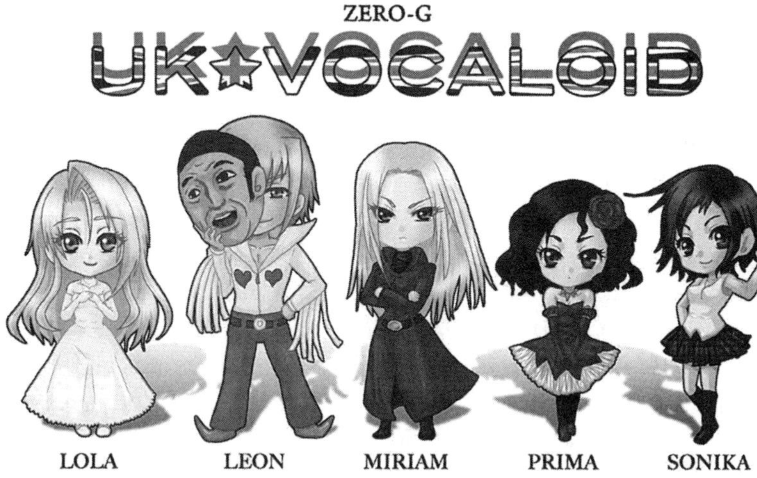

ZERO-G

UK★VOCALOID

LOLA   LEON   MIRIAM   PRIMA   SONIKA

FIGURE 4.9 Fan art of the English-language voice fonts created by Zero-G.

FIGURE 4.10 PRIMA,
software box artwork.

overall aesthetic also conforms to anime style. As is common practice among the anime community, cosplay, or dressing up as a character, was performed using this version of LEON and posted online by Leon Cosplay, a German, and the Americans Leon and Lola Cosplay (see figures 4.11–4.12).

Overall LOLA and LEON were unsuccessful from a commercial point of view. They were not engaged as originally intended and often were discovered by users only after the users had already committed to other Vocaloid voice banks. Rather than engaging directly with the original LOLA and LEON identities, users would look them up secondarily, spurred by a general interest in Vocaloid. One user's commentary on this lack of engagement with LEON came, unsurprisingly, in the form of a song uploaded to YouTube called "[LEON] I'll Quit Singing [VOCALOID]."[36]

A December 26, 2013, press release announced, "Zero-G Vocaloid 1 products LEON, LOLA and Miriam will be discontinuing soon," and "on 1 January they will finally be 'retired' to that great Vocaloid playground in the sky."[37] Naturally the song "Disappearance of LEON" was covered and posted as a response.[38] Thus the so-called soul singers that weren't used as such were officially retired. Users had clearly not heard ear-to-ear with Zero-G. But while the discontinuation of LOLA and LEON was a concrete acknowledgment of this disconnect, Vocaloid voice bank–producing companies had already begun changing their marketing strategies five years previously. Both Zero-G's creation and users' reactions were based on their figures of sound. Moving away from delivering vocal synthesis-based singers with a single fixed identity (like Miriam Stockley and the tongue-in-cheek request for the resurrection of Elvis through Vocaloid),[39] the developers had intentionally left room for interpretation.

Fanbase-Created Vocaloid Personalities

Long before LOLA's and LEON's retirement, various companies that issued Vocaloid voice banks tried different marketing and packaging approaches in response to the lukewarm response the pair received. With Japanese media company Crypton Future Media's August 2007 release of Hatsune Miku, the first Japanese Vocaloid 2 product,[40] a new era was ushered in for Vocaloid. Hatsune Miku's name is translated as "the sound of the future," and her voice bank was recorded by the Japanese voice actress Saki Fujita.[41] With a broader audience base for the voice bank spurred by the popularity of Hatsune Miku in Japan, the user base shifted toward fans of the characters and the music produced with the Vocaloid voice banks. In response to the similarly poor sales of Meiko, the first Japanese Vocaloid creation, Crypton's CEO, Hiroyuki Ito, created their

FIGURE 4.11 Leon Cosplay.

FIGURE 4.12 Leon and Lola Cosplay.

next Vocaloid voice bank as an *aidoru*, derived from the English word "idol." Aidoru can range from human celebrities to imaginary characters such as Hello Kitty.[42] This tactic worked: in an industry where 1,000 units sold means the program is a hit, the sale of 100,000 copies of the Hatsune Miku software was unprecedented.[43]

With the ensuing popularity of the idol character, a sixteen-year-old girl who was five feet two and weighed ninety-two pounds, many users bought the Vocaloid fonts in the same way that they would purchase a musical toy or an anime collectible. Many would use it to play around without making any songs or tracks or to create covers of existing songs—mostly songs sung by other Vocaloids!—rather than producing original music. A bidirectional flow of interaction arose, with Vocaloid listeners becoming Vocaloid producers and vice versa. In an interview with *Wired* magazine, Ito says that no backstory had been created for the idol beyond "just age, height, weight—and outfits." Tapping into the phenomenon of *niji sousaku* (secondary creativity), he knew that if Hatsune Miku became the phenomenon he hoped for, fans would rush to fill in her life story.[44]

A music technology that was intended for a market consisting primarily of music producers in Japan and beyond, Hatsune Miku became a breakout success with "otaku" culture, the umbrella term for general geek culture that includes both anime fans and fans of idol groups.[45] Crypton's marketing of Hatsune Miku as an "idol that you can produce," with accompanying anime-styled artwork, hit a nerve. The company was also able to tap into the otaku "doujin music" crowd, which usually refers to fan creations that are sold at conventions but sometimes refers simply to independent music or art.[46] For example, a Google Chrome ad shows Hatsune Miku's old website where she is announced as the "idol anyone can produce."[47] Ian Condry has identified Hatsune Miku's character "as a platform people can build on. She becomes a tool of connection who, through people's participation, comes alive."[48] Due in part to such engagement, Hatsune Miku's songs are regularly at the top of Japan's most-requested karaoke list.[49]

With this change users began playing with the vocal fonts in their own ways, undermining the issuing company's initial efforts toward vocal specificity.[50] There are many different interesting and creative examples. Users proved so powerful that many of the Vocaloid companies adjusted their marketing strategies accordingly. For some voice bank releases, a large part of the marketing campaign consisted of artwork for the Vocaloid character (e.g., Vocaloids Sonika [2009], Aoki Lapis [2012], Merli [2013], and Luo Tianyi [Mandarin, 2012]) that was fan-created—from name to design to voice—and drawn from user competitions.[51] Arguably even the competitions that created massive controversy because the winner's artwork was not used as the official character provided buzz and user engagement.

One competition arose as a response to negative user feedback on the artwork released with the initial demos of a voice bank. Created by the Swedish company PowerFX, Big Al was an intended partner for the 2007 voice bank Sweet Ann.[52] Responding to a question regarding the "monster theme" PowerFX had used with their Vocaloid products, CEO Bil Bryant observed, "The first Vocaloids were marketed as 'replacement singers' or 'a vocalist in a box,' and this was not the case and a lot of professionals and journalists in western media did not review the first versions of Vocaloid very well."[53] In an effort to minimize the comparison between Vocaloid and "real singers," Bryant explained, "We wanted to make it quite clear that Vocaloid is an evolving technology and is a fun and creative product." The first iteration of Big Al echoed an old monster movie poster (see figure 4.13) and was intended to accompany the movie theme begun with Sweet Ann (see figure 4.14).

The original Big Al voicer was an Elvis impersonator named Michael King.[54] Numerous rumors circulated regarding the continued development of the character, which included recording a new voicer, Frank Sanderson. The complete voice bank was finally released in 2009, two years after the original announcement, with new character artwork that responded to the Vocaloid fans' sentiments.[55] This version became an instant hit among Vocaloid fans. The Vocaloid wiki page features Big Al portrayed as a human singer or athlete, his vitals listed next to his image: "Gender: male; age: 25; height: 6'4"/193cm; weight: 190lbs/86kg."[56] When Big Al was released in Taiwan, his design was radically reenvisioned for that market (see figure 4.15).

While the Big Al vocal font was revamped for the Asian market, within the Western producer community only a few breakout voice banks have become hits among both English-language and Japanese Vocaloid fans. However, within the Japanese Vocaloid fandom and user community, those voices are so prevalent that since 2008, users' compositions already divide into four musical phases, ranging chronologically from mechanically paced music to fast-tempo rock, story songs, and very fast electronic.[57]

The character accompanying the vocal font was materialized most notably in Hatsune Miku. However, this character was not limited to an image gracing a software box, but also bloomed into other expressions, such as the hologram based on graphics created by James Cameron's Digital Domain, which uses the rear-projection technique (see figure 4.16). The first official SEGA- and Crypton-produced concert, in Tokyo in August 2009, featured a hologram based on the

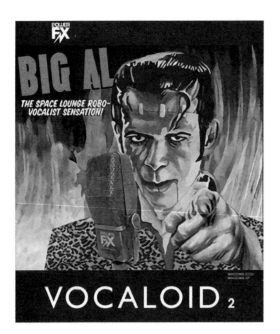

FIGURE 4.13 First box art of Big Al.

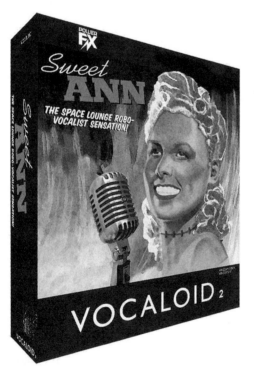

FIGURE 4.14 Sweet Ann, software box artwork.

FIGURE 4.15 Big Al, Taiwan release's software box artwork.

graphic novelist Kei's long-legged, blue-ponytailed version of the character.[58] In the same year Hatsune Miku's hologram performed at Singapore's Anime Festival Asia, her first concert outside Japan, and in 2010 she was joined by three additional Vocaloid voices—Luka, Len, and Rin—as part of the promotion for the first Project Diva video game.[59] After a second Hatsune Miku–centered SEGA/Crypton concert series, Mikupa (Hatsune Miku Live Party) kicked off in Odaiba, Tokyo.[60] In summer 2011 Hatsune Miku was hosted at the first live U.S. Crypton Vocaloid concert, Mikunopolis, at the Los Angeles Nokia Theater during the annual Anime Expo.[61] And *aidoru*, idol culture, met mass American culture when Toyota debuted a series of Corolla ads featuring Hatsune Miku as part of a cross-promotion for the Mikunopolis concert in Los Angeles.[62] In spring 2014 Hatsune Miku opened for Lady Gaga's ARTPOP/ARTRAVE tour, starting in Atlanta, Georgia.[63] Later Pharrell Williams remixed her in "Last Night, Good Night (Re:Dialed)" (see figure 4.17).[64]

While all of these Hatsune Miku mass audience events were produced using the peppy, cheerful J-pop teenager image and musical style (see figure 4.17), several other qualities have evolved around this voice bank. Music created with Vocaloid is generally referred to as Vocalo-music, while the software users and music creators are called Vocalo-P, referring to "producer."[65] For example, "Thoughtful Zombie" by Vocalo-P FICUSEL is a softer song with a jazz-lounge feel and almost nonsensical lyrics. The voice is edited to be choppy and very artificial sounding, each syllable fading out in an odd metallic way.[66] "Hibi-kase" is a song by GigaP, a producer known for making his Vocaloid vocals very staccato and autotuned to match the feel of his electronic music.[67] The video

FIGURE 4.16 Hologram of Hatsune Miku at concert.

FIGURE 4.17 Screenshot of "Last Night, Good Night (Re:Dialed)" remix, by Pharrell Williams.

shows an artificial-looking Hatsune Miku behind screens, but the lyrics of the song imply her desire to escape virtuality. "Mikusabbath" by UtsuP, a well-known composer of Vocametal, metal music with vocal tracks rendered with Vocaloid technology, exhibits a voice that is extremely dramatically tuned, with "scream" vocals created by reducing the Vocaloid synthesis to render only white noise.[68] In the listener comments, many insist this is Hagane Miku. *Hagane* (steel sound) is a suite of fan-made characters related to Hatsune Miku, Rin, and Len. The name Hagane was commonly applied when the voice banks were used to create heavy rock and metal. In contrast, in "Nyanyanyanyanyanyanya!" by daniwellP, Hatsune Miku is featured as a cat, limiting her vocabulary to the repetitive "nya"![69] Finally, the dance track "Drag the Ground" by Camellia was the 2013 anthem of Goodsmile Racing. Goodsmile is a company that produces collectible figurines, and Hatsune Miku is considered one of their mascots.[70] They've sponsored a Hatsune Miku car in Japanese motor racing for the past few years.[71] The race car is decorated with a version of Hatsune Miku (see figure 4.18); the race team dons her color palette and poses in front of her image (see figure 4.19); and the official Race Queens (akin to cheerleaders) are dressed as Hatsune Miku.

Hatsune Miku becomes the vehicle for any projection—from humorous or annoying mewing kitten to race car mascot, from dance goddess to computer game avatar, and more. But whether they are visualized as androids, cyborgs, machines, teen girls, or gender-bending young people, do perceptions and performances of Vocaloid voices move beyond essentialized notions of voice? After Hatsune Miku, other Vocaloids and their many iterations have taken the world by storm. Through interactions with various Vocaloids, listeners from Europe, Asia, and the United States have, through critical performance practice, shown that connections between race and timbre are cultural constructs and practices. Since my initial critique of Zero-G as reproducing an idea of blackness was published in 2009, users have much more effectively illuminated Zero-G's essentialized notions of race in their artistic work.[72]

#SaveRuby

As I was editing these pages, the annual Anime 2015 Expo took place in Los Angeles.[73] There Ruby (see figure 4.20), a new voice bank, was presented by PowerFX, the audio company behind Vocaloids Big Al and Sweet Ann, providing me a new opportunity to consider the question of voice as essential to a person. During the week after the unveiling, the Vocaloid community was in an uproar over the artwork for several reasons. Ruby had begun her virtual life

FIGURE 4.18 Hatsune Miku car used by the Goodsmile Racing team.

FIGURE 4.19 Hatsune Miku car and the Goodsmile Racing team and Race Queens.

FIGURE 4.20 Ruby, first box art design by Zero-G.

under a different name, and her voice was provided by a Latina woman who goes by the artist name Misha. According to information shared in the Vocaloid community, the creator and voicer of Ruby were allegedly promised control over the design as they worked with PowerFX's team. However, beyond non-disclosure agreements, it seems that no legally binding contracts over artistic control in fact exist between PowerFX and Ruby's voicer and creator. In short, at the unveiling of the new Vocaloid voice, Misha expected an animated version of herself, and instead she stood on the podium next to the poster of a character she and her fans believe is modeled on a blonde pop star.

What we will see in the #SaveRuby case is not unlike other instances where indexes of subjectivity are connected to notions of unique self-expression, which, in turn, is sometimes connected to race, ethnicity, or other categories that hold potency in a given time and place. In short, after not accepting the LEON image as an accurate representation of the voice they heard, the same general fan and user base insist upon a racially congruent image in Ruby's case. Despite having dispensed with the prepackaged visual representation of a given Vocaloid voice, they demanded visual representation that clarified the source voice's ethnicity.

The original team had been working for a year on a design in collaboration with Natasha Allegri, a well-known animator who has worked for Cartoon Network. Her original design was based on the person who provided the voice bank sample, and was intended to be a Latina with darker skin (see figure 4.21).[74] Whether or not the intricate dispute that has been chronicled online is factual, what is important about the fan base's recounting of this story is that they are invested in the race and/or ethnicity of the voice populating the database. Some think it is important to have a diversity of artwork and identities for Vocaloid voice banks, showing a diversity of people, while others stress an essential link to the voicer, Misha, who is Latina.[75]

According to the story I am able to pull together from social media, wiki sites, and reports from Anime Expo 2015,[76] the source vocalist for Ruby flew to Los Angeles from New York to be present during the July 4th reveal of the new voice. There she and the development team were shocked to learn that, unbeknownst to them, PowerFX had commissioned a different artist to produce the artwork. The developer and source singer had already worked with Allegri and had allegedly provided the artwork for the presentation themselves. We can follow Misha's excited tweets from New York City as she prepares to board the plane for the Anime Expo reveal with a live television broadcast and interviews (figure 4.22). Her disappointed postevent report reads, "Tbh you guys could only imagine how I felt standing next to that ugly design at AX. On TV. In front of people."[77]

Early in the process, Misha discussed her vision for the design, her desire to show her Latina heritage, and the color differentiation between her skin and the character's pinkish-red hair with her collaborator Syo (who created the script for the synthesis and the Ruby voice bank), the artist Artemi, and Allegri (see figure 4.23). In a Tumblr post, Misha shares her reflections on the connection between voice and identity: "im half hispanic (dominican: my mother was born there) and then a quarter ukrainian and assyrian (my dad)! . . . I wanted Ruby to be close to my mothers skin tone, specifically. . . . ruby being able to represent her, me, and my family, was very important to me."[78] Support flooded in, an uproar ensued among Vocaloid fans, and social media flared up. There were discussions about campaigns boycotting Ruby, and the Twitter hashtag #saveruby was created immediately. The fans created their own artwork in response. As Allegri's artwork had been released via social media, the version of Ruby that Misha had endorsed proliferated to the extent that it dominated Google image search results (see figures 4.24–4.26).[79]

Six days later Bil Bryant, the CEO of PowerFX, replied to one of the fans. In the publicly released email, Bryant explains that the company was trying to open up the market to DJs and "bedroom producers" who did not, at this stage, use Vocaloid along with their VSTi's (virtual studio technology instruments). Based on market surveys PowerFX determined that they would move away from the anime-based design. Bryant tried to resolve the difference of opinion, sharing that "PowerFX['s] stance is there is one official artwork we put on the

FIGURE 4.21 Design sheet of Ruby based on Misha's ideas.

FIGURE 4.22 Misha at Anime Expo 2015 at the Ruby unveiling.

FIGURE 4.23 Suggestion for box art design by the designer Misha worked with, Natasha Allegri.

FIGURE 4.24 Ruby fan art by Lena Chen.

FIGURE 4.25 Ruby fan art by Rob Gilliam.

FIGURE 4.26
Ruby fan art by
@Vanmak3D.

product but we allow anyone to interpret it the way they want—just look at all the Sweet Ann & Big Al versions about.... We will release the product soon so we will find out if this was a good move or not."[80]

At this point it is challenging to verify the stories circulating on social media. Whether or not some of the reported twists and turns in the tale really happened, I retell the story as I can stitch it together. I do this because the story is based on the very material the community currently believes in and keeps alive. The dispute is about the relationship between the software-based characters and the genres and identities given to them by the artwork adorning the software bundle. The story turns on disagreements about the relationship between the character presented as the Vocaloid voice, the person whose voice is used, and the genre for which the company has assumed the voice will be used or is most appropriate. We have—perhaps surprisingly—returned to the same questions explored in the disputes over or affirmations of vocal authenticity and essence in chapters 1–4. Similar to multiple generations of artists past and present, Misha and her fans asserted their desire to self-represent on their own terms. In 2015 those terms included a specific visual and textual presentation that signaled the contemporary political, ethnic, and cultural category *Latina*.

That "Jap Effect": A Public Articulation of the Response to the Acousmatic Question

Within the story I have recounted of the Vocaloid world, we can see the entire cycle of essentializing, reproducing, redefining, and re-creating the connection between voice and identity within short timeframes, while in the previous chapters we observed the same process over generations and entire careers. LOLA and LEON were the results of the numeric reduction of the concept of black soul singers' voices into the zeros and ones of a vocal synthesis process. Users, listeners, and broader audiences did not accept, or indeed hear the quantification of race that was presented to them. Moreover, as the second corrective reminds us, because voice takes place within a collective process, LOLA and LEON did not take hold according to Zero-G's intention. Only the demos approximated their alleged identity as soul singers. Instead users used these voices in other ways—and the voices we hear around us multiply because they are engaged by the collective.

While LOLA and LEON, the initial Vocaloid voice banks, were rejected because they didn't sound like their assigned characters, I do not read this reaction as coming from a rejection of vocal essence. Heated discussions regarding voice banks such as Big Al and Ruby arise precisely from a commitment to vocal essence. In those conversations, issues about the voice provider's connection to the voice bank and the voice bank's character identity as embodied by the artwork boiled down to a discussion about vocal essence. Different participants in the conflict could ascribe that essence to different aspects of the vocal synthesis project—say, the idea of the vocal synthesis script, the geographic and cultural origins of the technology, or the voice provider—but all parties shared a commitment to vocal essence.

When it comes to voice, the notion of essence is understood very similarly to how the Vocaloid vocal synthesis system is understood in relation to human vocalizers. Users and listeners try to hear the technical or algebraic origin of the voices, a technology developed by Yamaha. For example, robotarchie asks in the Vocaloid Forum, "Consider LOLA ... is it just me?—or does she have an audible Japanese twang/vibe going on there somewhere within the formants? Am I imagining this? Is it a leftover from her earlier Japanese roots or is it an embedded trait in the (Yamaha) controlling software perhaps? Anyone else hear this quality?"[81] After responding positively to an initial question about whether people think Vocaloid is "any good," Quetzalcoatl writes:

> I have noticed [the Japanese twang] and commented about it elsewhere. I am convinced that Vocaloid still sounds "closed-mouthed," and I think that the reason for this, is that the Japanese language is much more closed-mouthed than European languages. Watch the mouths of Oriental people when they speak, they hardly open their mouths, or at least the lips are not flapping and stretching (for want of a better description) to achieve the same sort of pronunciations as Europeans. Oriental languages are just that way, almost ventriloquist style. I think that for this reason, Yamaha thought that Vocaloid was ready for the Oriental market, and it probably is. But European pronunciations and mouth movements in speech are much more aggressive, and in short ... they need to open Vocaloid's mouth.[82]

It is common knowledge that the source singers were recorded in the United Kingdom. Roba observes, "Given the remarks about closed-mouth singing, it had occurred to me that maybe the live singers were required to sing in a particular fashion, according to the taste of the recording engineers. So I visualized LOLA and LEON (even if in a Zero-G studio in England) being told, 'No! No! Don't sing with your mouth so wide open!' by Japanese technicians."[83] Andromeda concurs: "I've just listened to a LOLA track I recorded about 3 weeks ago and not listened to since. I have to admit that it does sound very 'closed mouth.' I'm not sure it's a 'Japanese Effect' but may be something to do with the original sampling. I'm sure the solution is to adjust some of the parameters in the resonance section but there are so many and time is so precious."[84] "I think we could do with having some technical detail from Zero-G on the source of this 'Jap effect' thing," robotarchie responds. "They must admit something is causing this peculiar tonality."[85]

In all these instances the "peculiar tonality" is ascribed to racial, ethnic, or language assessments based on the synthesis technology's association with Yamaha, a Japanese company. While the discussion is about vocal fonts and its technological aspects, it resembles those around classical voice students' voices. The outbursts are reactions to breaks in the expected sound according to the listeners' figure of sound. However, what was conceived as a quest for and an ideology of vocal authenticity and health in voice students is here phrased in terms of technological efficiency and quality of vocal synthesis.

What is striking in conversations among Vocaloid users is the frank discussion of the voice, the character, and the fans' own contributions to the conversation in the form of music, character visualizations, and more. We are not left to wonder what a Vocaloid fan's answer to the silent acousmatic question is. In online forums users were quick to point out what they heard, and the acousmatic question was not typically met with an unspoken or unconscious response. Instead the response was frequently very concrete, in the form of sounds, lyrics, descriptions, and images. Users' answers to the acousmatic question are materialized when they create and listen to songs, videos, games, and other creative or commercial articulations of Vocaloid characters.

The distinction between how audiences interact with Vocaloid and how they relate to human singers is not primarily based on considerations of Vocaloid as a technologized cyborg voice. The distinction is simply that the nature of voice in the form of software allows and affords a sonorous and visual materialization of a singer. That is, the response to the acousmatic question is worked out in public and shared via easily accessible forums. While Vocaloid is vocal synthesis rather than a live human singer, the process undertaken by listeners and audiences is not dissimilar to listener and audience interactions and manifestations discussed in relation to vocal phenomena in the previous chapters.

In moving through the complex and ongoing story of the different Vocaloid voices, we not only see that vocal timbre and race are not essential, but we access the process by which timbre, visual imagery, text, and listening are tied together into a narrative about race—a dismantling at one point (as with LOLA and LEON) and a construction at another point (as with Ruby). At first the story of Vocaloid seemed to be one of rejecting the connection between race and vocal timbre, a demonstration of listeners' understanding of the nonessential and performed nature of a voice. However, by following Vocaloid's various iterations and fans' and users' interactions with the different voices and characters, we see that the unfolding story of Vocaloid voices and the visual creations related to those voices reify the common misperceptions that race is essentially expressed through the body and that this racialized body is audible through vocal timbre.

What we see are two opposing cases of the same logic. First, in the case of LEON and LOLA, the vocal synthesis producers began with the unexamined assumption that race makes body, body makes vocal timbre, and vocal timbre then represents race. Here the unexpected issue that arose to disrupt this assumption was that people heard blackness in neither LEON nor LOLA; they heard Japanese and other. While I thought for a while that this reaction would provide sufficient impetus for people to move away from the assumption that voice exhibits race as essence, it proved to be only a temporary step along a path toward restoring that assumption.

The logic that seems to be underpinning the acousmatic question in certain rare instances holds that the visual representation does not match a response to the acousmatic question. And, on some rare occasions, this mismatch between the visual representation and the timbral expectation causes the questioner to reexamine his or her answer to the acousmatic question, essentially asking, "Which source (visual or auditory) is true?" In this case, when the alignment of visual and textual representation seems wrong, the listener creates the context to re-present an alignment that satisfies his or her expectation. The success of this logic rehabilitates the idea of essentialized voice from being a myth and reinstates a new status quo. The second case does the same thing, but instead of a blank slate in terms of the source voice, as was the case with LOLA and LEON, Ruby's source voice represented a particular person at the launch and in continuous interactions with the idea of Ruby. The source singer maintained that her vocal essence was imprinted in Ruby and campaigned for her own visual self-representation to accompany the voice.

Together these two cases show us that, when confronted with the dissonance of noncongruent visual and vocal representations of an identity, listeners' (learned) reaction is to replace one of those representations with something that restores congruence according to particular cultural ideals. Instead of open-ended exploration, such as that seen at some stages of Vocaloid's development, most listeners revert to the referential frame where they can achieve sociocultural consonance between voice and representation. Faced with uncertainty regarding sociocultural consonance, listeners tend to reinscribe new categories, categories that are nonetheless generated from the same value set. Studying the various stages of Vocaloid's development shows that even when dipping into an archive where both sounds and images are assembled digitally, listeners (in the form of producers and audiences) reach for the same measuring tools that they apply to human singers. Thus Vocaloid is an extreme example of my conception of voice as audiences' articulation of the collective's cultural value system. Given this rather bleak picture, is there any space for or way to play with agency, on behalf of both singer and listener?

5

BIFURCATED LISTENING

The Inimitable, Imitated Billie Holiday

I cued the slideshow for my presentation and clicked "play." The projection displayed a classic image of Billie Holiday, cigarette in hand (see figure 5.1). To the right of the image quotes described Holiday's unique and inimitable voice. I played a few verses and choruses of "Gloomy Sunday" and saw the symposium's participants sink into the experience of listening to the luscious, rich, and profound vocal sound. Before the song ended, I peeled away the archival image of Holiday and showed them an image of the person behind the voice we had savored together. It was seven-year-old Angelina Jordan from Norway, singing on the television variety show *Norske Talenter* (Norway's Got Talent) (see figure 5.2). The segment was excerpted from her first appearance on the show, the first time she sang for the judges and the national audience.[1] During the four-and-a-half-minute segment, the television camera moved from the girl's deeply concentrated, calm, and unfazed demeanor to the judges' surprised looks and gestures of disbelief. Here was a combination of a child's body and the sound of an iconic singer, whose mythologized life story is imbricated with, and is used to explain, the sound of her voice. The television judges' and audience's facial and verbal expressions of disbelief (see figure 5.3), the symposium participants' reactions, and my own sense of surprise when I first saw and heard this clip were all produced under the condition of listening within the figure of sound, outlined in the introductory chapter and chapter 1 and discussed throughout the book.

Holiday's imitators show a mélange of admiration and appropriation, entrainment, and artistic agency. Imitators' performances are the explicit result of

FIGURE 5.1 Billie Holiday, New York City, 1957. Reproduced with the
permission of Don Hunstein / Sony Music Entertainment. Hunstein
Artist Services.

FIGURE 5.2 Angelina Jordan's first performance on *Norske Talenter*, 2014.

FIGURE 5.3 *Norske Talenter* judge Lisa Tønne, 2014.

the conceptual and perceptual work undertaken in order to uphold the concept of vocal essence and, by extension, racial essence. Up to this point in the book I have tracked the ways in which voice is entrained through formal and informal pedagogies and is integrated when the expected racialized framework is present or artificially projected onto it; I have witnessed audiences' projection of various categories onto Jimmy Scott, an artist who defied categorization; and I have examined listeners' creation of racialized singers in the digital realm through the Vocaloid engine. In this chapter I further map the ways in which audiences project not only racialized and gendered identities but also age-related markers. And, finally, I will show that autobiography and collective identity can be causes of both voluntary and involuntary entrainment, and at the same time can be a source from which artistic expression is drawn. That is, building on the argument forwarded by examining Jimmy Scott in chapter 3, I wish to clarify that entrainment and artistic agency are not necessarily at odds with each other.

I would like to preface the following discussion by returning to the overarching thesis of *The Race of Sound*: not only is the timbral identification of race not a direct result of racist views, but, if we work under such an assumption, we will ultimately fail to address and deconstruct racialized vocal timbre. The perpetuation of racialized timbre goes much deeper and is based on fundamental beliefs about sound. As long as we believe in knowable, stable sound, we are compelled to identify sound and to believe that identification to constitute essence. And whatever we believe to be a person's essence—from despairing or ecstatic to white or black—is employed in the interpretation and assessment of the voice.

Therefore, in the case of Angelina Jordan and other Billie Holiday impersonators, I will not discuss the complex politics arising from her impersonators' various racialized dynamics.[2] Instead, in considering these impersonations, I take a different analytical approach. While I fully acknowledge the importance of the detailed work involved in enumerating the specifics of performances of blackface, cultural imperialism, and exploitation in these impersonations, here I concentrate on the more general performative and perceptual moves that take place.

When voice is essentialized, any interpretive story about it—for instance, hearing a vocal timbre as though it summarizes a person's life story—always already follows a naturalized storyline. That is, the interpretive story is understood as the a priori nature of that voice (and that person) rather than as an interpretation that is dependent on a given context. That is how interpretive categories such as race can remain unexamined for centuries. I posit that the practice of essentializing vocal timbre is the unexamined foundation upon which racialized vocal timbre is maintained. Therefore, if we wish to correct this situation, we must direct our attention to the essentialized voice and must enumerate the errors that occur during the process of its formation. If the myth of essential vocal timbre is debunked, voices become immune to racialization. In contrast, if we limit ourselves to pointing out the inconsistencies in situations involving the racialized voice, but persist in essentializing timbre, we continue to naturalize all related aspects of voice. In other words, as long as we understand voice as essence, our propensity to naturalize any descriptions of and stories about it remains. By examining the naturalization of Billie Holiday's voice and considering its imitations, this chapter seeks to acknowledge Holiday's artistry as critical performance practice and, via that route, to denaturalize voice as essence.

"Billie Holiday's Burned Voice"

The classic story about Billie Holiday is summarized succinctly by John M. Carvalho: "Raped as a child and institutionalized as a consequence of it, Holiday turned to prostitution as a teenager, profiting others (and to a lesser extent herself) from an obsessive and ultimately futile search for a man who would love and protect her. She also suffered from the use and abuse of alcohol and drugs, from the questionable company she kept, and from the special attention, from the police and other authorities, her notoriety brought her."[3] While Holiday was admired as a singer, she failed to produce a significant hit recording. Her adult life presented a variety of challenges that may have prevented some of her development and productivity as a musician. The portions of her story that received much media attention were her struggle with drug addiction and related run-ins with the law. Capped by a premature death at forty-four, these tragedies clustered around themes of turbulent romantic life and loss, substance abuse, and hypersexuality. These stories make up the filters and guiding principles through which listeners hear her voice and through which reporters, writers, and audiences have sought to make sense of it.

For example, Matthew Sutton writes, "The cracks in Holiday's weathered voice, magnified by her band's deliberate, if not sluggish, tempos, speak of a life marked by abandonment, drug abuse, and romantic turmoil."[4] This description is echoed in a *Time* report that depicts Holiday's voice as "a petulant, sex-edged moan."[5] Along the same lines, the musicologist Mervyn Cooke describes her voice as "a unique blend of vulnerability, innocence and sexuality, attributes which won her a popular following."[6] In an especially dramatic interpretation, Sutton, in a discussion of Holiday's particular rendition of "Please Don't Talk about Me When I'm Gone," pins his explanation to these themes: "Even normally up-tempo songs . . . are essayed with a sense of sorrow and resignation, as if the lyric's sentiment is already being expressed from beyond the grave."[7]

In examining much of the vast amount of printed material describing Holiday, I have found that ideas about the genesis of her particular vocal sound fall into three dominant patterns. Two of these are closely related, and all three often overlap. Further, all of these patterns overlap with and act in the same way as the phantom genealogy did for Marian Anderson's audiences. In fact I see them as subcategories of the broader phantom genealogy framework, the name of which highlights its fictional character. The first pattern, which I call *auto-biographical voice*, relates to the notion that timbral meaning is stable and possible to know. Under this interpretation the specific meaning derived from the voice depends on alignment between autobiography and timbre. While there is no doubt that the physical voice is affected by material and emotional life circumstances, the stance I identify is a direct projection of particular kinds of circumstances—"abandonment, drug abuse, and romantic turmoil," for example—onto vocal timbre. The second pattern, which I call *channeling the ancestors*, returns all explanations of the timbre of a voice to an ancestral narrative and explanation. Clearly singers and artists may feel called upon, and choose to heed the call, to enact a metaphorical voice that they feel expresses their ancestors' history. However, the pattern I wish to point out is one in which no artistic license is perceived and any artistic merit is understood as a projection of the ancestral spirit. The third pattern, which I call *biological determinism*, rests on the assumption that, independent of a given vocalist's artistry, voice is an unmediated expression of the essence of a person. This aligns with the voice-as-essence fallacy, and the foundational ontological orientation toward Holiday's voice sits atop this assumption. For example, both voice as an unmediated expression of a singer's autobiography and voice as *involuntarily* channeling the ancestors depend on a basic understanding of voice as essence.

The perceptual framework that gives rise to Holiday's perceived *autobiographical* rendition is crystallized in this assessment: "When she was introduced to the song, she had already lived a hard life."[8] In other words, any vocal turn is reduced to her autobiography. Multiple writers have remarked on the way Holiday's autobiography illuminates the content and message of a given song lyric. For example, in discussing the poetry of "Strange Fruit," Janell Hobson describes the capacity of Holiday's "embodied knowledge to bring alive the poem's ironic edge by invoking the cynicism and despair that elevated the song from sentimentality to poignancy."[9] Along these lines, Sara Ramshaw writes that, in Holiday's case, "lyrical content had become fused with the singer's personality and her much-publicized personal life." In these observations the common explanatory thread is that the artist's skill is reduced to an expression of biographical circumstances.

This continued in the broader cause-and-effect explanation of channeling the ancestors. As Farah Jasmine Griffin observes, Holiday's "is a voice capable of casting spells. It is certainly a voice concerned with its connection to the world of the spirit, its ability to evoke the presence of the divine. So the sound heard as 'other,' as in 'foreign,' is also a sound that is 'other' like the mystery that is God."[10] Here Griffin echoes Eileen Southern, who describes the "strange effect that [the] sound [of black singing] had on listeners." Southern writes, "American literature contains numerous references to female slaves of colonial times who kept young audiences spellbound, and adults too with their ancient tales."[11] Along the same lines, Carvalho notes that audiences came to Café Society "in part, at least, to hear Holiday sing ['Strange Fruit']. They were largely hip and cool or imagined themselves to be enlightened enough to hear the pain and suffering inflicted on black people by those they thought less noble (or gallant) than themselves."[12] Angela Davis offers a reading of the universal communicative power of Holiday's voice and evokes the sentiments of those who felt that Holiday's particular gift to audiences was her capacity to infuse sometimes sub-par lyrics with autobiographical meaning: "In the timbre of her voice," Davis writes, "the social roots of pain and despair in women's emotional lives are given a lyrical legibility."[13]

The commonality between the patterns of autobiography and channeling the ancestors, then, is the assumption of a heavy sense of inevitability and lack of choice and of seemingly no technical or artistic skill on the part of the singer—that is, the assumption of voice as essence, which in turn is rooted in a sense of biological determinism that is audible in vocal timbre. The quotes above express sentiments connected to the assumption that it is possible to know sound and voice, and thus that they have stable meanings. Combined with a belief in indisputable personal essence, the meaning thus conceived is then aligned with whatever is believed or emphasized about a given person. For example, a sonorous quality that Sutton identifies as "cracks" is, through such assumptions, interpreted uncritically as a "weathered voice"—a voice whose blemishes were caused by "a life marked by abandonment, drug abuse, and romantic turmoil."[14]

"She didn't sing anything unless she had lived it," Tony Bennett observes. "When you listen to her, it's almost like an audio tape of her autobiography."[15] Holiday's voice is understood by many as a "metaphor for her entire life"; and this practice of reading into her voice burgeoned after her public trial and incarceration.[16] Her biographer Stuart Nicholson notes, "Now it was *what* she sang, the *authenticity* of her voice and the way her audience attributed special significance to it, that mattered. Billie's real-life story had become the source of meaningfulness in her voice."[17] "She really was happy only when she sang," Ralph J. Gleason once wrote. "The rest of the time she was a sort of living lyric to the song 'Strange Fruit,' hanging, not on a poplar tree, but on the limbs of life itself."[18] However, Gleason simply exemplifies one of the prominent trends in describing Holiday's voice and life through her repertoire. Nicholson's observations about *Lady in Satin* also follow this trend: "As a bona fide jazz classic, an understanding of Holiday's real-life history helps give this album context and adds both meaning and depth. As one half of the mind struggles and reacts to the boozy huskiness in her voice and shaky intonation, the other half listens, searching for meaning in both voice and lyrics. This disjunction produces an uncomfortable listening experience. Yet here is the unification of the singer's history and art, unified as a single self that is infinite and total, a bonding that enables *Lady in Satin* to realise its full meaning."[19]

In the same vein, audiences who were affected by Holiday interpreted their own reactions to her as projections of her qualities. For example, Ray Ellis shared, "I was in love with Billie. Not necessarily Billie, but . . . I heard her voice, I dug it. It turned me on, and maybe I was in love with that voice and I was picturing a very evil, sensuous, sultry, very evil . . . probably one of the most evil voices I've heard in my life." "Let me tell you something," he pontificates, "music relates to sex. It always did and it always will. Anything she sang that meant anything had to do with sex."[20]

This is not to say that Holiday was not a savvy businesswoman; she knew how to play into branding for her own benefit, and took direct and immediate advantage of audiences' tendency to listen acousmatically for essence. Robert O'Meally, for example, suggests that Holiday well understood audiences' "powerful urge to treat performance as a form of autobiography." "Since most love songs, in particular, are part of a long chain of melancholy," he muses, "they are often interpreted as expressions of pain by the singer in question. Even when the same song is sung by dozens of different performers, one of them is usually singled out as the most authentic, often the one who is believed to have lived the song most fully." "Holiday," he asserts, "understood this inclination better than others, and as she grew older, she seemed consciously to choose songs that underlined what she had become for many: 'Our Lady of Sorrows.'"[21]

Not only is Holiday's voice understood as channeling the ancestors, but it has also been imbued with a collective ethos. Through this process her voice becomes a type of cultural property, made to stand in for any collective experience for which black female voices are typically invoked, including motherhood, sorrow, grief, and limitless and selfless love of people and nations.[22] As Griffin says of the well-known stories from Holiday's private life, "The stories of her arrests and drug addiction joined with her stage persona of the torch singer to create a new image, that of the tragic, ever-suffering black woman singer who simply stands center stage and naturally sings her words."[23] The figure of the "black woman vocalist" is both "hypervisible and hyperaudible." The black woman's voice, Griffin concludes, is a "quintessential American voice. . . . It is one of its founding sounds, and the singing black woman is one of its founding spectacles."[24]

Interpretations that on the surface seem to be polar opposites—reduction to autobiography and generalization to "the founding spectacles"—take on the same type of cultural and social work. Both interpretations ignore internal heterogeneities and contradictions in order to utilize voice as a vehicle for archetypes. These repeated reductions naturalize Holiday's voice. And, rather than acknowledge her multifaceted and complex life and rich, carefully assembled sonic archive, these interpretations link her person to stereotypes about the tragic lives of black women.[25] Reducing Holiday's voice to an a priori—that is, limiting perspectives on her voice to the projection of an idea of her life—reduces her subjectivity and artistic agency to the oft-narrated arc of her biography. In turn, this narrative both naturalizes and obscures the active work—on the part of listeners—involved in subsequent interpretations of her voice.

Lady Day Impersonations

We also see the collective projection of the naturalized idea of Holiday and her voice in numerous vocal imitations and impersonations. The many and different renditions range from deeply sincere to parodic to pyrotechnic. The seven-year-old Norwegian girl defies age expectations. The author and radio personality David Sedaris and the drag artist Joey Arias cross gender lines. Peggy Lee's well-known Holiday medley, the Quebecois singer Véronique's "Voices" Las Vegas show, and amateur singers such as Nikki Yanofsky, who garner applause for caricatured signature phrasings and pronunciations, transport Holiday's repertoire and signature style into different venues and to audiences that may not be susceptible to Holiday herself.[26] The sincere performances seem to stem from a wish to profit from Holiday's artistic position and recognizability or from a desire to celebrate her. The parody receives its fuel, and its reward, from the gap between the person who is impersonating and the person being impersonated.

Joey Arias not only vocally imitates Holiday; he echoes her fashion and uses items that once belonged to her as props. In Arias's act there are obvious differences between imitator and imitated in terms of general appearance (Arias is taller and slimmer than Holiday), age (Arias was sixty-five at the centennial tribute; Holiday passed away at forty-four), gender identification (Holiday identified as a woman and Arias performs in drag), and life story. Despite these differences, Arias's centennial tribute concert to Holiday was lauded by the *New York Times* as "incarnating" her.[27] This term follows Arias's own descriptions of the process involved in singing Holiday's repertoire, which he describes as a type of incarnation (see figure 5.4). The review goes on to explain that Arias "has long been admired for his ability to 'channel' Holiday—there is no other ap-

FIGURE 5.4 Joey Arias as Billie Holiday in the Lincoln Center's American Songbook series, February 25, 2015. Photo by Kevin Yatarola.

propriate word." The *San Francisco Gate* also makes use of the word "channels," reporting, "The language that drag performer Joey Arias uses is less musical and more supernatural. Words like 'summon,' 'channel' and discussion of Holiday's 'vibrations' permeate the conversation like ectoplasm hanging over a seance." While discussing his San Francisco Centennial concert at the Great American Music Hall with a reporter, Arias proudly recalls that audiences who had actually heard Holiday during her lifetime tell him, "'If I closed my eyes . . .'" Recalling the memory, Arias muses, "What a compliment."[28]

Another cross-gender performance was shared on an episode of the radio program *This American Life*.[29] On the episode with the theme "Music Lessons," David Sedaris, who was forced by his jazz-loving nonmusician father to take guitar lessons as a child, muses about his childhood fantasy of singing commercial jingles in Billie Holiday's voice. In a public taping of the show, Sedaris sings the Oscar Mayer theme song à la Billie Holiday. As one commentator put it, "Did you know that David Sedaris . . . does a wicked impression of Billie Holiday?" The question was followed by the suggestion that "Sedaris has added 'potential jazz legend' to his usual repertoire of wry observations from his painfully funny diaries."[30] In an earlier music episode, Sedaris offers the first few phrases of the Christmas carol "Away in a Manger" in Holiday's voice. As Sedaris notes, "I sang it the way Billie Holiday might have sang if she'd put out a Christmas album." Again there are a number of differences between Sedaris and Holiday that make this imitation interesting as a form of entertainment: first, there is surprise that the writer can sing, and sings publicly; second, his speaking voice is distinctive and could not be mistaken for Holiday's; and third, in terms of life story, Sedaris frequently draws anecdotes from his more than twenty-year relationship with his partner, Hugh Hamrick, while Holiday was married twice and had a number of other relationships with both men and women.

The Holiday imitation performed by Audra McDonald contrasts with those of Arias and Sedaris. Embraced by the musical and cultural establishments, McDonald is an award-winning singer with a huge platform, frequenting Broadway stages and the Metropolitan Opera and working as a soloist with all of the major American orchestras. The recent centennial celebration, which ushered in entire plays dedicated to retelling the story of Holiday's life, gave McDonald yet another performance opportunity (see figure 5.5). Part of the awe around her rendition of Holiday, as part of the revived evening-long play *Lady Day at Emerson's Bar and Grill*, is the difference between McDonald's voice and Holiday's.

The *New York Times* asserts that McDonald "scaled down" her "plush, classically trained soprano" to jazz-soloist size. And although she "tamped down the lush bloom" of her highly educated voice "to suggest the withered state of Holiday's instrument during the last years of her career . . . the sound remains tangy, expressive and rich." The review further notes disjunctions between Holiday and McDonald, such as McDonald's "five Tonys at just 43, when Holiday was nearing her end," and attests that McDonald presented a "ghostly image of an artist."[31]

Seasoned artists such as McDonald are not the only singers who have impressed with their Holiday impersonations. While Angelina Jordan won the *Norske Talenter* competition with George Gershwin's "Summertime,"[32] it was her first performance on the show that was shared globally and made headlines across Europe, the United States, and Australia. We see the language in headlines—such as Gawker's "Norwegian Seven-Year-Old Has the Voice and Soul of Billie Holiday"[33]—reproducing assumptions about voice as essence. While Gawker is not considered a respectable news source, here it channels traditional language about voice, to the effect that to have a voice is to have a soul, and to

FIGURE 5.5 Audra McDonald as Billie Holiday in the play *Lady Day at Emerson's Bar and Grill*, 2014. Photo by Sara Krulwich for *The New York Times*/Redux.

hear a voice is to access the soul. According to the reporter, Jordan's "uncanny ability to sound like the tragic jazz singer brought tears to at least one judge's eyes."[34] Another writer observes that Jordan's rendition of "Billy Holiday's I'm a Fool to Love You is incredible." The same writer continues, "She's a little bit spooky. . . . She appears to be channelling the dead as I have no other explanation as to how an eight year old can sing this song, unaccompanied, with such expression of the emotions within the song. I mean, she's eight! It would be impressive if she simply remembered all the words but Angelina is breathtaking."[35] *Time* magazine online uses the same language in its headline: "This 7-Year Old's Incredible Voice Will Give You Chills as She Channels Billie Holiday."[36]

While these examples are quite different, the main impetus that drives interest in such vocal imitations is the friction between what is experienced phenomenologically as two disparate voices emitted by one person: the imitated and imitating voice. Fueling this friction are the many turns of disbelief about the degree of similarity between impersonated and impersonator, the effectiveness of the deception, and the moment when the gap between the impersonator's own voice and the voice he or she assumes is conceptually marked. These differences between the imitator's body and identity and the body and identity associated with the imitated voice can include aspects such as gender, age, and race. And there is disbelief about what *is* expressed (the expressive range of the impersonated voice) during the impersonation and whether or not it is commensurate with what the impersonator, as a singer, should be able to express emotionally. For example, after Angelina Jordan's first performance on *Norske Talenter* one of the judges responded:

> JUDGE: You are singing in a way one believes you have to be an adult to sing. Do you know what the song is about?
>
> ANGELINA: Yes. It is about a sad Sunday.
>
> JUDGE: [Quiet, nodding] . . . Yes, it is. It was fantastic to hear you sing.[37]

The surprise expressed here is not merely a response to the biological differences between bodies of two different ages. It is also prompted by the assumption that life experience leaves physical and emotional traces and thus offers artists access to emotional depth. Underlying the judge's reaction is a question: "What could a seven-year-old have possibly experienced that could give rise to such a deep delivery?" Angelina "sounds less like a 7-year-old and more like a jaded, middle-aged woman at a bar, blowing smoke in your face while telling you about all the rotten men in her life," the writer E. J. Dickinson muses about Angelina's performance. Attempting to make sense of it, she adds, "I'd be more inclined to call it a séance" before giving up on trying to account for Jordan's performance with a rational explanation.[38]

In addition to concrete biographical differences, Holiday and Jordan differ in terms of racial dynamics with regard to their respective audiences. Holiday sang as a black woman against the backdrop of the mid-twentieth-century United States, while Jordan sings as a European immigrant with a Middle Eastern background in the context of twenty-first-century Norway and a global audience.[39] The contrasting racial dynamic between Holiday and many of her impersonators is an obvious and interesting dimension. As scholars such as Eric Lott, Lisa Woolfork, and W. T. Lhamon have noted, impersonation across racial boundaries—in the form of blackface and misdirected and complex fantasy—has been discussed productively and importantly as a form of cultural misappropriation and vampirism.[40] Lott succinctly summarizes this phenomenon: while minstrelsy was "an established 19th-century theatrical practice, principally of the urban North, in which white men caricatured blacks for sport and profit" and its practitioners assumed racial superiority, imitation also implies some type of admiration.[41] Although scholarship along these lines is crucial, I address the naturalization of racial difference by explaining how general reductions of vocal timbre form the foundation upon which specific reductions, such as timbral racial differences, hinge.

Whether based on a perception of racial difference or on other aspects, as noted in my descriptions of impersonators, the impersonator's entertainment value lies in the perceived gap between the original performer and the imitator. Judgments about this gap hinge on the assumption that sound and vocal timbre are stable and knowable. The comparison takes place between the a priori idea of the original voice, the a priori idea of the imitator's real voice, and the imitated voice as it is heard by the listener. This comparison depends on stable categories.

What is the significance of that specific moment of *listener disbelief*—the pivot of imitation's entertainment value? The moment of disbelief simultaneously strengthens and erodes the cult of fidelity that depends on assumptions about stable and knowable sounds and voices. On one hand, the cult of fidelity is strengthened because it is comparison that constitutes the listening moment. In this comparison the listener holds an image of an original voice in his or her mind, comparing it with the evidence available as a more or less favorable reproduction with a greater or lesser degree of fidelity. The listener does not consider the vocal timbre at hand on its own merits; instead he or she engages with it in terms of an idea of another voice. On the other hand, the cult of fidelity is enfeebled. Simultaneously hearing both the voice of the singer at hand and that voice inflecting the idea of the imitated voice (with varying degrees of success) should, in principle, cause us to question the very foundation upon which the assumption of vocal essence rests.

Let's think about the situation in the form of the acousmatic question *Who is this?* Listeners who detect an impersonator or an impersonated voice conjure a multi-identified voice. This voice is simultaneously heard as unary (one person singing) and split, or layered (the separation between the "original" voice, the "original" voice of the imitator, and the sound of the first voice in the second). Such perceptual work requires a high degree of abstraction combined with compartmentalization—and depends on assumptions about stable, knowable voice.

Imitation Is in the Ear of the Beholder

"It takes two to tango," as the song goes. To imitate takes three. The most fitting description of the listener's role in this equation is not as a judge of relative fidelity but as the key protagonist. This is because listeners pull out their mental tape measures in order to precisely determine the gap between imitated and imitating voices, with this gap constituting the focal point of the imitative act. Listeners also form the third and determining party in the triangulation between "original" and "copy." There is a kind of pyrotechnic thrill in the joining of the two. (On the other hand, as Steven Connor notes, one cannot imitate oneself. It is only within this gap between two entities where the vocalizer has the choice to *not* imitate that the choice of imitation can exist.)

It is not enough that the so-called original and copy are present. Recognition is the key component: the third party recognizes the original, the current source, and the gap between the two. Given the issues discussed earlier, this seems self-evident. However, I mean to address another layer of the listener's role as protagonist. To return to a previous question in a different form, if a person sounds exactly like Billie Holiday, but nobody hears his or her voice, can that vocal act constitute an imitation?[42]

There is no essential or unified voice. Instead repeatable patterns where divergences are ignored create the sense of one. From a voice and sonority perspective, what is repeated in what may be perceived as vocal imitation is a degree of vocal pattern that is sufficient for recognition to take place. In the same way that we ignore anomalies in order to form ideas about unique voices, we ignore them when we identify vocal imitation. In other words, we first create an image of a unified voice. Next, we keep this idea in mind in order to recognize it elsewhere. Then we must recognize the unique voice of the imitator so that we can hear that the imitation diverges from the unique voice.

In summary, the ingredients necessary for recognition of a vocal imitation to take place are:

1 Knowledge of the original voice
2 A memory of the original voice
3 The ability to hear the imitator's original voice
4 Recognition of the imitation voice as superimposed on the imitator's original voice

While these four criteria are necessary for imitation to take place, we can also begin to get a sense that imitation is not grounded in an a priori voice in sonorous terms alone. Instead imitation is fully dependent on the scaffolding that props up the necessary reference to the a priori. Within a situation where a voice sounds very similar to another voice—where an auditory pattern seems identical to another auditory pattern—a number of conditions in addition to these four points must be in place for imitation to be perceived. In other words, if the four core components are present but the listener does not judge the overall vocal act to be an imitation, no imitation has taken place.

In short, a given vocal moment may be identical to another, but this sameness does not ensure that the listener judges the vocal moment to be an imitation. If the sound is identical, but all or some of our four points are not fulfilled, the vocal moment is not assumed to be an imitation. The level of imitation does not hinge on sonorous similarity; extrasonorous factors determine whether or not a given vocal act is considered an imitation.

How is it, then, that we recognize a vocal act as imitation? Paradoxically, unlike what appears on the sound-centered list of criteria, imitation is not bound to sonic similarity. Rather it is called forth through a nexus of nonsonorous comparisons and criteria, and it is believable because of the underlying naturalization of identification—an act of naming that is based solely on *interpretation*. At the base of the assessment of whether the vocal act is an imitation lies the question of the vocalizer's intention. If the vocalizer's intention is not to imitate, the equation then shifts: if the singer who is believed to be an imitator sounds like the original without consciously intending to do so, no imitation takes place—even if person B sounds so similar to person A that he or she may be mistaken for person A. If somebody accidentally sounds similar to another person, the genesis of that vocal sound was not grounded in the a priori. At the core of the mechanism that allows us to recognize a vocal act as imitation lies the cult of fidelity, the assumption that produces listening that hinges on comparison with a priori and knowable sounds.

When the acousmatic question is answered with *identification* of a voice in the negative—or as an imitation of an original—the response is politically energized. The fact that the singer is the actual producer of the sound we hear is evident. Regardless of the listener's reaction, in producing sound that is heard as imitation, the singer possesses the technical ability to create a particular pattern of sounds in a practiced way. This is the same idea that we generally use to credit a singer with creating an "authentic" work of art and to begin to assign an identity to the singer. But when the listener judges this creation an imitation, the person singing is erased; the singer is understood to act merely as an empty conduit for the "original" voice. The listener erases the vocalizer through the perception of imitation. In place of the singer as artist, the listener positions an imaginary proxy of his or her own creation and attributes to that proxy a number of characteristics (e.g., age, emotion, culture, race). Treating the singer as a proxy transfers these characteristics to him or her, effectively creating an identity that is a shadow of the listener's own mind. This process, which replaces a unique interpersonal experience with a proxy that carries our own prejudices, offers a micro-example of the work that racism, sexism, and other derogatory judgments perform. The process constitutes an overriding or erasing of an authentic experience with an imagined idea, a proxy for what we believe the authentic to be.

However, there is an additional, and deeper, layer to the process. When the acousmatic question is answered with identification of a voice in the positive— or as the original—this response is equally politically energized. The listener erases the vocalizer through a projected perception of him or her as iconic—in the case of Billie Holiday, as reduced to selected elements of her biography, viewed through the lens of the stereotypical tragic, sexualized, and wasted black female figure who lacks agency.

These two responses to the acousmatic question—Angelina sounds like Billie Holiday; Billie Holiday's voice oozes with her tragic biography—are equally reductive. Both are produced by a listening pedagogy formed within the cult of fidelity. Within the discursive-analytical space of the cult of fidelity, where voice is reduced to iconic identification, there is no voice for Holiday. Janell Hobson claims that, while Holiday's marginality is celebrated and made "hyperaudib[le]," "black women's voicelessness in cultural discourses on American music heritage and, ironically, in political narratives" is reinforced. She continues, "Black women—including [Marian] Anderson and Holiday—are often presented singing in the service of someone else rather than for themselves."[43] Farah Jasmine Griffin also astutely observes that black women's voices are called upon to carry out the labor of "heal[ing] a crisis in national unity as well as provok[ing] one."[44] Hence, because the listening pedagogy formed within the cult of fidelity is politically charged by reducing voices to iconic identifications, this type of listening extends its reductive effects to people and relationships.

But what can be done to address this problem? Are there alternative ways to frame these voices besides naming and identification? Such a reframing would allow us to practice a different kind of politics of listening: a return to hearing an artist, even in imitation.

The voice artist Eliza Jane Schneider details the process by which she learns voices from a sonorous and kinesthetic imitative perspective.[45] She has traveled across the United States, Canada, England, Ireland, Scotland, South Africa, New Zealand, and Australia, as well as to seven Caribbean islands, the Philippines, South Korea, and Hong Kong, recording examples of dialects, meeting individuals, and observing speech patterns and geographical idiosyncrasies.[46] With a sound database of seven thousand interviews with native speakers of variant forms of English, Schneider approaches each voice as a technical puzzle waiting to be solved. For example, as she prepared to audition for eight characters on Comedy Central's animated show *South Park*, she loaded sound bites from VHS and online resources onto her Roland SP808 groove sampler.[47] Each of its sixteen pads with sixty-four sound banks was filled with the characters' audio files, and Schneider listened and deconstructed the voices incessantly. Her listening and practice helped her to win the roles.[48] Schneider, who also serves as a dialect and accent coach for actors, has broken vocal performance into the following parameters: pitch, tempo (speed), tone, timbre, resonance/vocal placement, rhythm, meter, volume, lilt, emotion, dynamics, timing, breaths, laughs, pauses.[49]

Schneider's practice-based approach aligns with my own performative-analytical framework, outlined in the introductory chapter, which focuses on sound, style, and technique. If we strip away our projections about a vocal sound's *meaning* and the vocalizer's *intention*, we no longer hear a voice or a vocalizer as "channeling" another voice. Without these projections what remains is consideration of an artist who has control over his or her vocal technique and communication style.[50] Whether this artist is Holiday, a Holiday imitator, or all people who use their voices to express themselves and communicate with others, a careful listener can deconstruct the vocal act into stylistic choices and technical prowess. This listening practice debunks vocal timbre as autobiography, gender, race, and expression of the deepest essence, allowing listeners to understand vocal timbre as skill, artistry, and communicative intention. Ears turned away from a detailed and practical knowledge of vocal production perpetuate the micropolitics of timbre. Building self-knowledge and educating others about vocal style and technique offers a path to denaturalizing voice.

Considering Holiday from a Performative-Analytical Approach: The Stylist and Technician

Applying this alternative framework to Holiday's work highlights her technical and creative abilities (as, indeed, it does for Angelina Jordan).[51] By highlighting Holiday's technical and creative abilities, we no longer approach her within the limitations of the three dominant imitation patterns mapped earlier. My approach dovetails with Daphne A. Brooks's reading of Zora Neale Hurston's long overlooked vocal recordings as "archival and ethnographic endeavors" and is a refreshing antidote to both the overdetermined literary and feminist icons of the past few decades and the "perpetually romanticized figure of the melisma-driven, black female singing diva."[52] As Emily Lordi notes, while acknowledging that some individuals have "artistic talents," "it is imperative to analyze the practices that years of training allow singers to effect."[53] For example, in terms of style, Kate Daubney compares Holiday's singing to instrumental vocalization technique and finds that Holiday's timbre is comparable to that of the saxophone family. The context of Daubney's comparison is a discussion of Holiday's "lack of professional voice training"; the comparison may not ring true for listeners, but it does operate on a nonautobiographical level. While Holiday may have lacked formal education, the musicians she learned from were of the top echelon. For example, Daubney notes that "the imitative reference" of Holiday's timbral style "is found most prominently in her stylistic dialogues with tenor saxophonist Lester Young, with whom Holiday had a close personal and musical relationship. On the recordings where they performed together, there is a mutual imitation in the shaping of phrases, the use of timbre and the quality of tone which not only shows Holiday to have drawn from Young's style, but also that Young could evoke Holiday's voice."[54]

Discussions of style can also take place in terms of music to which Holiday had access. Examining the challenges for women to enter the spaces where musicians exchanged knowledge, Katherine Baber notes, "The exceptions were black singers like Ivie Anderson, Ella Fitzgerald, Billie Holiday, and Helen Humes, who were widely considered to be the peers of male musicians as they did have access to the blues and jazz culturally."[55] Daubney's descriptions of

BIFURCATED LISTENING • 169

Holiday's contrasting improvising strategies also describe her voice: Holiday "sought an extremely effective contrast with the piano, her voice standing out against the percussive, bright sound. . . . [Teddy] Wilson would improvise melodically with great rhythmic fluidity and across an enormous pitch compass, and his use of chords surpassed anything her voice could do; Holiday rose to the challenge by apparently singing within herself, yet it is the simplicity and smoothness of her delivery which creates the most effective contrast."[56]

Vibrato is a vocal stylistic trait that is closely associated with genre and the individual singer; many singers have a signature vibration that runs through every vocal line. In contrast, Daubney finds that Holiday is very economical and intentional with her vibrato: "In every line of the lyrics of this song however, she uses the oscillation of tone, or a small modulation of pitch to accentuate the sound of her voice and the use of this effect in conjunction with the rhyming lyrics is particularly striking: 'storm' and 'warm,' 'remember' and 'December,' 'gloves' and 'love,' 'fire' and 'higher.'"[57] In these analyses Holiday's interpretive powers are highlighted and her communicative genius accounted for; in "the subtleties of her phrasing and her flawless sense of swing, she offers us a glimpse into the human emotion of despair," Sara Ramshaw suggests.[58] Other stylistic traits offered include "a preponderance of sliding or 'kinetic' pitches; a drop of pitch on the voiced consonants L, M, N and Y; and soft or 'blurred' diction." Mostly focusing on the mechanics of speech and song, Hao Huang and Rachel Huang note that there are "melodic and rhythmic consequences of these mannerisms; we will then recontextualize them in terms of linguistic analysis of spoken English." Huang and Huang assert, "The range and placement of slides, abetted by soft, equivocal diction, are some of the important carriers of emotional meaning in Billie's performances."[59]

Considering Holiday from the point of view of vocal technical details can help map the range of her expression, detailed in over forty books written about her.[60] Drawing on the traditional chronological charting of composers' careers into three stylistic periods, in his 2015 biography John Szwed divides Holiday's oeuvre into early, middle, and late career.[61] Szwed identifies these periods as jazz musician, sophisticated international singer, and "a saucy miss and a broken drunk, a perp in a mug shot and a smiling matron posing with a pet," respectively. He identifies variety in these interpretations of Holiday and offers a long list of names she went by. In the same swoop, he critiques previous authors and justifies yet another biography by explaining that "much of what we think we know about Holiday . . . is questionable, and over time accounts of her life have been bent to serve some other purpose than telling her story." Szwed, on the contrary, shares that he intended to write a book about her music and to offer "a meditation on her art and its relation to her life."[62]

"Racism, drugs and alcohol abuse, and the brutality of some of the men in her life were sufficient to justify her mournful repertoire and a style that reinforced it," Szwed says, echoing earlier Holiday biographers. "But suffering and pain are neither necessary nor sufficient to produce a great artist." Such a perspective, peering above essentialized and naturalized notions of voice, is possible when considering singers in terms of style and technique. Whether acquired at a very early age or late in life, Szwed concludes, it was style and technique that allowed Holiday "to bring dignity, depth, and grandeur to her performances that went far beyond simply displaying the bruises she suffered."[63]

In response to the acousmatic question, we can choose what to listen for and decide how to respond. So if I hear Holiday's voice as a musician's instrument rather than as the materialization of an autobiography, what is the difference? Doesn't such listening also rely on a priori categories by, for example, comparing her voice to instrumental sounds? It does. But it does not assume that her timbre and performance style are essential. These comparisons are not self-referential, and Holiday's skill and commitment as a musician are acknowledged. Here she performs a presence with which the listener can interact, rather than standing in as a conduit, an echo of predetermined ideas. *The singer is elevated to the status of agent over his or her own voice.*

Picking up on the threads that run through the criticism and popular press on Holiday during her life and thereafter, and at the same time acknowledging her as an artist and jazz singer, Cassandra Wilson contextualizes her own impetus for the anniversary album *Coming Forth by Day.* In a radio interview Wilson reflects, "There is this great sensationalism around the icon Billie Holiday." She explains the impetus behind her drastic rearrangements and interpretations of the Holiday songbook: "I want to set this record straight in terms of giving her recognition in terms of her [musical] contribution more than focusing on the negative aspect." Wilson explicitly does not imitate Holiday. As she explains, this would be "rude," almost "insulting."[64]

According to Wilson, "imitating" Holiday would not acknowledge Holiday's contribution as a musician with a lasting legacy. Straightforward imitation, in this view, constitutes neither honest nor deep engagement. However, from our performative-analytical approach, we can appreciate imitators' technical skill. We can approach their performances with appreciation for their analyses of Holiday's technique and style in order to produce them as she did. Within such a perspective, we can appreciate imitative performers for their technical virtuosity, as stylists and technicians in their own right. And if, instead of admiring these singers for "channeling" Holiday, we appreciate them for studying her and showing us the results of their studies, we acknowledge rather than erase them.[65]

Summary

When presented with the acousmatic question, wherein we assume that voice is the distillation or essence of immediate emotions, life experience, ancestral destiny, or biological determinism, a listener will hear a given voice within the context of the cult of fidelity, with every vocal utterance framed as either original or copy. As a result, when a listener encounters an imitative voice and hears it as unaligned with the immediate emotions, life experience, ancestral destiny, or biological determinism expressed by the sound of the voice, the listener may experience tension. At this point the listener has two options for responses to the acousmatic question. Rejecting the idea of essential voice, the listener may continue to consider the "imitated voice" as evidence that voice is style and technique rather than essence. If we develop this path, we may realize that there is no imitation. Both inconsistencies in the singer's performed identity and similarities to other voices can be explained in terms of style and technique. On the other hand, and this is the phenomenon discussed in this chapter, when we refuse to give up the idea that voice is essence, we perceive the imitative performance as false, making sense of that reality by assigning an identity to the voice (say, "Billie Holiday") and separating that vocal identity from the identity of the actual singer. Thus the activity of assigning the identity "Angelina Jordan" to a 2014 singer of "Gloomy Sunday," and of hearing Jordan's voice as a Holiday imitation, can take place. Jordan as Holiday imitator is an essential Jordan and a secondary (false or copied) Holiday.[66]

If we apply listening practice within the cult of fidelity to a nexus around Holiday, we may see that there are at least three layers of imitation taking place. In the first and most obvious layer, Jordan and the other singers discussed here are heard as Holiday. In the second layer, Holiday is reduced to a few points in her biography and heard as the figure of the archetypal tragic black woman. In the third layer, Holiday is heard as a stand-in for the tragic black woman and, by extension, for a monolithic group of African Americans and racialized voices. None of these vocal events is heard in its unrepeatable and unpredictable co-unfoldings between vocalizer and listeners. Instead listeners perform a micropolitics of timbre wherein vocal events are heard with a constant comparison to preestablished categories focused on the relative relation to the a priori.

The broader point I seek to communicate within this chapter is, of course, that the case of Holiday is not unique; it exemplifies a broad, pervasive pattern. The kinds of reductions and naturalizations I have enumerated take place in any naming of a voice, and its social and cultural legitimacy is supplied from multiple sources. For every singer who is heard as an imitation of Holiday, his or her voice and persona are reduced to essence. For every time that Holiday is heard as and reduced to the archetypal tragic black woman, people are turned away from jobs or housing opportunities based on reductions of their voices to assumed nonwhite identities.[67] For every time a person is heard as gendered and racialized, a vocal timbre is believed to have revealed his or her essence.

The nexus of reductions around Holiday is not limited to the singers who try to imitate her, and audiences have the capacity to consider another voice as an imitation. Moreover the nexus of reductions around gender and race are also not limited to people who hold sexist or racist views and values. If, as john powell puts it, "we realize that race is neither objectively real nor purely imagined, we must define it in a manner that accounts for its socially constructed, mutable nature."[68] We may consider powell together with Michael Omi and Howard Winant, who posit that race signifies and symbolizes "social conflicts and interests by referring to different types of human bodies."[69] Such thinking has set the stage for my thinking about the human body's transmutability and, directly connected, the transmutability of the voice produced from within that body. Equally, "social conflicts and interests" are tied to and codify vocal performances.

While skin color functions as a permanent and indisputable racial signifier, voice is cast as an even stronger marker of race. Strict codification and enforcement of visual readings of the body arise directly from its encultured meaning. Listening practices around vocal timbre—a parameter equally malleable and unstable as skin color or, arguably, more so—have not even, at least to date, been subjected to thorough critical inquiry.

Voice is not innate; it is culture. It might seem as though the imitations I have discussed prove that we can know voice. Otherwise, the argument might go, how can we recognize an imitation? And how can we differentiate the imitation from the original, recognize the original, and distinguish the differences? This argument arises because the "social conflicts and interests" that Omi and Winant discuss are signified and symbolized through references to the human body, and also include vocal timbre's use in explaining the human body as difference. In this way, voice is not innate because we hear it according to the differences assigned by a given culture. Whatever markers we may recognize, we also recognize the codification. Indeed, vocal timbre has been and continues to be crucial to the process of "racial formation," which Omi and Winant define as "the sociohistorical process by which racial categories are created, inhabited, transformed and destroyed."[70] And, thanks to the efforts of critics and activists, work that has been carried out around the benefits and rights that are denied and extended based on race, today, perhaps even more so than in earlier times, and the processes of racial construction and maintenance thereof are subconscious.[71]

Listeners' assigning identity to singers in order to preserve the idea of essential voice is one of the ways in which the micropolitics of timbre play out. Based on this book's definition of voice as encultured and collective, this dynamic describes racial attitudes played out, not internally on an individual level, but rather through broader, group-based social and cultural factors. My shift of focus from the behavior of individual racists to collective forces does not mean I vacate listeners from responsibility. Instead it means that with deeper insight into the process of racialization, we can better address it: if the micropolitics of race is carried out through listening informed by the collective, that is the very level on which we have to operate in order to bring about change.

Such a micropolitics of listening represents the desire to name and deal with the voice through preformed categories rather than accepting performance as bona fide, as style and technique. This type of collective political listening functions to uphold assumptions about voice as essence. The irony is that by deconstructing concepts and listening skills that seek out instances of imitation, the logic of an a priori original is also de-energized. Letting go of such assumptions regarding imitation would open a space for completely new interactions. Because we would no longer have the scaffolding of certainty that identification brings, this positioning would necessitate a point of vulnerability and uncertainty on our part, as well as create further vulnerability and uncertainty. This relationship to voice can come about only if we give up the right to be certain, to know, and to sit in judgment. This is an uncomfortable spot. Choosing to hear a voice as imitation rather than unknown territory maintains righteousness and certainty, and the affect is not limited to the pigeonholed, imitated person. That is, such a reduction thwarts both listeners' ability to relate to Holiday as well as their relation to the self and to their own position in the world.

Putting Jordan and Holiday together offers an overt demonstration of voice as style and technique and exposes the moments in which listeners oscillate between aligning the performer with style and technique and aligning him or her with essence. It is within that unsettled space that a singer's agency is highlighted. In that moment of disruption, listeners' assessments split. Listeners cast Jordan as an old soul, but also understand that her vocal apparatus is that of a young girl. The congruence between these two possible responses to the acousmatic question is stitched together by telling stories about Jordan that put her into the aficionado category, highlighting dedicated practice from a young age. By employing critical performance practice as an analytical framework, we can recognize Jordan's deliberate practice of the vocal sound. Jordan's study of Holiday's recordings can be understood as a kind of self-entrainment or self-imposed formal pedagogy. In that recognition there is space to put to rest the notion of essence—or even inevitable autobiographical entrainment—acknowledging Jordan's style and technique. "Analysing singers' creative choices," Lordi writes, "allows us to see that these artists are sources, not objects, of knowledge."[72] Thus we can witness how various forms of entrainment are funneled into artistry and agency through style and technique.

Because listening is so deeply naturalized, I have built my case arguing for Holiday's artistic agency in a rather roundabout way. We need singers who theorize voice through practice, through critical performance practice, to expose what I conceive as *limit cases*, or what J. Martin Daughtry has termed "productively defamiliariz[ing] the voice," in order to cast naturalized listening into doubt and, from a space of unfamiliarity, build self-reflexive listening.[73]

To me, and to some of the listeners I witnessed, Jordan is just such a limit case. Her performance offers a disruptive moment for the routine acousmatic question. By listening to Jordan, the idea that her voice cannot be only essence or biographical entrainment is introduced. The recognition that Jordan's sound is not pure essence opens the possibility for considering that other singers making such sounds are also not pure essence. Thus, by defamiliarizing Holiday via Jordan, we may apply our critical performance practice lens to understand Holiday's voice as both funneled through various forms of entrainment and exerting her artistic agency by intentionally shaping her voice and performance.

6

WIDENING RINGS OF BEING

The Singer as Stylist and Technician

MEAD: You say . . . there are no "Negroes" outside of America. I know exactly
what you mean. . . .

   We'll deny your hair, we'll deny your skin, we'll deny your eyes. We deny you.
We deny you when we accept you; we deny the ways in which you are not exactly
us, by ignoring them.

BALDWIN: Yes.

MEAD: And what black power is saying is: I want to accept myself first, and my
parents, and I want to enjoy the way my mother and father look and from there—

BALDWIN: Then we'll see.

—Margaret Mead and James Baldwin, *A Rap on Race*

It is the context of the listening or the hearing that embodies the voice with meaning.

—Farah Jasmine Griffin, "When Malindy Sings"

The Listener Is an Active Agent

I have built a case to show that voice is neither essential nor singular, and thus
voice is neither knowable nor formulated a priori. Rather a given voice comes
into being and is defined by and founded on myriad circumstances, none of
which—alone or in combination—defines the voice. *The Race of Sound* parallels my more general study of sound, *Sensing Sound*, in which I argue that in
experiencing and naming the thick event of the falling tree *as sound*, a decision,

a cut has been made, and made by someone. In heeding the silent acousmatic question, and in naming the event, the listener is not a passive observer who is in or out of "the know"—who recognizes an F-sharp, say, or can tell whether a recorded voice is that of Billie Holiday or one of her imitators. The listener generates and produces the reduction to sound of, for instance, the awesome event of a falling tree—and this reduction stands in for an experience. I have myself been encultured through most of the concepts and language about sound, music, voice, and race that I critique in this book. Because that language serves to fix and naturalize rich phenomena into race and other categories, I will consider the book's overall concepts and conclusion in a prismatic form. I do so in an effort to counteract the reality as actualized through language and to counteract language as I know it, the potency of which I cannot pretend operates independently from the power structure this project seeks to call out.[1]

I return to the three correctives regarding voice that I identified in the introductory chapter.

- Voice is not innate; it is cultural.
- Voice is not singular; is it collective.
- Voice's source is not the singer; it is the listener.

In considering the ways in which vocal training is not immune to deep-seated assumptions about a given singer's essential nature, we can determine that a voice's character is not based on innate or essential biological or material qualities but that a particular vocal timbre is the result of a body's enculturation through training.

Thus, in chapter 1, we observed that while singers are trained carefully within a centuries-old musical tradition full of strict heuristic practices, the actual execution of this training is not isolated from the general ways in which we regard and form assumptions about people. In short, what is understood as the most essential aspect of voice—timbre—is the result of a practice of enculturation. While only some situations are identified as voice lessons, each and every moment of listening, and every moment of vocalization, is a voice lesson wherein we do, or do not, adhere to the established conventions. The micropolitics of timbre is carried out when the naming of the results of these lessons is naturalized.

In chapter 2 we saw that, due to the prejudice they faced, Marian Anderson and other early African American opera singers were perceptually framed within markers of blackface and ethnosympathy. Despite external recognition and hirings by major opera companies, their acclaim was only half-won. In other words, despite the level of skill and mastery exhibited by African American singers, they are heard through difference. By uncovering this perceptual filter, I show that voices operate socially. The reception of these African American opera singers' voices is not founded on the singers' perceptions of themselves, nor on their demonstrable skills and artistic accomplishments; rather it is based on an encultured understanding of race. In other words, a given audience member's perception of these singers is limited by his or her cultural frame of reference. An audience enacts the micropolitics of timbre when its perception of a vocalizer is limited to hearing only its own collective listening mind.

In the audience perceptions of Jimmy Scott in chapter 3, we saw the same disconnect between Scott's sense of himself and his audience's vision of him. There are multiple means of projecting identity onto a singer, from embedding a given identification in a vocal student's voice through voice lessons, to hearing race as overriding every other aspect of the voice, to the packaging of a singer for publicity purposes. Scott's record company did not honor his self-identification in publicity materials; instead they presented him under a number of alternative identifications. It is worthwhile to note that, in the case of both Anderson and Scott, we see strong indications that their own sense of self was in opposition to their public framing. I don't sense a lot of external or demonstrative resistance on their parts, but I do sense a firm ability to self-identify in ways that differed from public pronouncements regarding them. Scott in particular represents a graphic case of the third corrective: the listener produces meaning and thus, in a sense, defines the singer.

The case of Vocaloid, addressed in chapter 4, is an extreme example of how listeners project their own limited worlds in their interactions with voices—and even with technology that resembles or represents vocal sounds. While the initial concept pitched the voice synthesis software as more than a machine— indeed as a real singer—audiences, in the form of users, freely transformed the voice synthesis into any fantasy that could be materialized. While the options for vocal production might be limitless with voice synthesis software, the identities associated with the voices it can produce are still connected to the categories we identified in the previous chapters, namely gender, race, and age. Vocaloid's listeners-as-users directly reveal what they hear by creating it, which may seem like a peculiar fringe case, but my position is that, rather than an anomaly, this example illustrates the process that takes place during listening in general.

The answer to the acousmatic question is, most commonly, only vaguely articulated, and only to oneself. It is, however, acted on, although most of the time we are unaware of the assessment we have made. The Vocaloid example instrumentalizes the process of asking and answering the acousmatic: we can see and hear users' concrete assessments in the songs and characters they create.

But whether our response to the acousmatic question involves creating a vocal track or silently framing a voice within our own minds, our conceptual world guides and limits each response.

In chapter 5, in studying the mythification of Billie Holiday's voice—the projection of an essence onto her vocal timbre and its so-called imitations—it is easy to conclude that it is the listener who creates difference. But in asserting that the listener manifests difference, we also create an other, and, in turn, we project our own worlds back onto this entity, "the listener," that we manifest. However, if we continue to tease out the details of Holiday's case, we may find that it is also possible to listen to how we listen without manifesting an entity. If we listen to how we listen, or to how others listen, we can gradually shift our focus from the (imagined) entity-that-listens. And that is what we must do now; we have been concerned with who is doing the listening and whether they are getting it right or wrong, but we must pay more attention to the process that facilitates a given assessment.

By shifting our attention to the process of listening, we can turn away from identification. It is the listener, then, who activates and carries out the collective and who also enculturates every vocal utterance through his or her acceptance or denial of naturalized meaning. In short, the answer to the acousmatic question does not lead us to knowledge about the vocalizer. Instead it invariably points to the listener—who is always an active agent.

It is important to note explicitly that the same relationship to listening is repeated on the part of the singer. In other words, the meaning named by the singer-as-listener does not arise from the projected vocal sound itself. Instead, in the same way as the listener discussed earlier, the singer-as-listener ascribes a complex of meaning to the vocal sound. This meaning complex is assembled from a combination of the singer's own assessment of the sound, what he or she gathers by eavesdropping on what others hear, and what he or she believes they hear.

By shifting our assumption of the singer from pure producer to producer and listener, we can recognize that he or she is listening to and also assigning meaning to or withholding it from a given labeling of his or her vocal timbre. When we approach vocal timbre and meaning in this way, the usual disciplining dynamic of correct versus incorrect changes. It is at the point of naming that the singer-as-listener endorses or rejects a given projection. This means that any projection of meaning onto a voice is not only an external judgment but can also be participated in or rejected by the singer. This is the entry point for the question regarding agency, and also for the singer-as-listener for whom participation or rejection can take countless forms.

Listeners are not in a bind; they have a choice. There are two options. The first is to remain within the cult of fidelity by essentializing the voice, or even by framing voices as zero-sum results of entrainment, trapped in material-cultural circumstances—to continue to name the voices we hear and to believe that this is the way the world works. Let's call this the choice of listening stance A, in the form of listener A. We have seen listener A's choices throughout the cases we have discussed. Voice teachers named and heard ethnic voices when they used their own personal measuring sticks to divide people into groups, applied the results to voices, and compared those voices to a priori ideas of the marked and unmarked. When audiences and critics listening to African American classical singers heard these voices as other and as racialized rather than as classically trained, these listeners selectively organized the visual and aural information of a thick event to reflect their own inner worlds, within which people are divided according to selected aspects of their visual appearance. While all American singers come to the European operatic tradition as outsiders, this type of listener explains African American singers' outsider qualities as different from those of American singers who appear to have a European heritage.

While each instance of naming-through-listening—including the examples I have given above—is a manifestation of concepts not grounded in the singers to which they are applied, the phenomenon is more overt in the cases of Jimmy Scott and Vocaloid. Listeners, in the form of audiences and publicity agents, manifested Scott through descriptions (as child, woman, death, etc.) and imagery (via his album covers). In the case of Vocaloid, listeners—software users and fans—manifested voices through their compositions, descriptive language, and visual depictions of the constructed singers. In the case of Holiday, listeners produced a voice by limiting their interactions with her to archetypal tropes. Each case ignores the skill and decision making involved in vocal events.

The path taken by listener A does not lead to open-ended engagement with the world; it is purely self-referential. In mindlessly naming, and in believing that the names accurately capture the external world, listener A can hear the world only in the terms he or she has already set out. Recall that this book's initial strategy was to refuse to take any description of a voice for granted. Instead of taking a response to the acousmatic question at face value, we pull back and ask, Who is the listener stating "This is the voice of a black man . . . of an African American opera singer . . . of a seven-year-old girl who imitates Billie Holiday"? What distinguishes listening stance A from listening stance B?

The key offered by *The Race of Sound* is that there is a choice in listening, and that it is possible to move from listening stance A to listening stance B. How one approaches that choice divides listeners into the two stances. When we listen, we do not simply automatically measure and compare to an a priori. We are not *phonometrographers* "weighing and measuring sound."[2] Every measurement is preceded by countless decisions. When we answer that the falling tree is simply a loud sound, this answer is preceded by multiple sets of decisions that have pared down the thick event into a single sensory mode. In the same way, when we answer that Billie Holiday's voice "is sadness and longing,"[3] we make multiple sets of decisions in order to reduce the heterogeneity of a vocal moment, and the vocalizer's style and technique, into one name.

The practice of the pause is an antidote to glossing over the choices that precede each moment of naming. Listener B accepts this option. What I referred to in the introduction as *critical performance practice methodology* finds one manifestation in *the pause*.[4] Evoking the word's French etymological root, *pausée*, I gesture toward the aspect of *interruption* that is nontemporal. I use "the pause" to indicate anything from a sense of expansion of the mental, intellectual, and emotional space to nonautomatic reflections about meaning. In short, the pause is not about listening for a greater degree of accuracy but about attending from a state that can help interrupt the way we usually listen.

Pausing has the potential to move us from unexamined essentialization to a consideration of our participation in the process of reduction. I proposed earlier that voice, sound, singing, and listening together constitute a continuously unfolding vibrational practice wherein we focus in on particular nodes of this encounter; I now propose that the pause that acknowledges the style and technique that contribute to the vocal moment provide a simple technology that allows us to turn away from believing in, exercising, and perpetuating unexamined definitions of difference. It is precisely when we practice the pause, taking a moment to acknowledge that the name is only one of many in a chain of potentialities, that we avoid preserving a strain of naturalization carried out through timbre.

The listener is an active agent, perpetually poised between two paths. In taking listening stance A, the path of the cult of fidelity in response to the acousmatic question, listeners operate under its assumptions, understanding voice as the sound of an essential being. From this perspective the voice's sound simply evidences, and thus communicates, the essence of that person. The sound is understood as faithful to an a priori idea, and those sounds that are understood as incomplete, or as failing to fulfill the a priori, are measured and understood in relation to an ideal that is believed to be stable and knowable.

The path of style and technique presents an alternative for engagement. Assuming listening stance B, we approach voice as a snapshot of a much larger collection of styles and techniques. First, we understand this snapshot as a limited and circumstance-dependent window and as exhibiting only one of an infinite number of additional styles and techniques. In other words, we understand that any given timbre is ascribed to vocal practice rather than being an essential trait. We also understand that voices may be entrained into any vocal timbre—whether appropriate to a musical genre such as classical, soul, rock, or singer-songwriter—or any style associated with identities, such as woman, man, African American, or working class. Second, even when naming, we understand that this activity does not carry meaning within it, or within a given collection of styles and techniques. Instead we understand the name through human-made associations. That is, we understand a given voice as a pattern created from styles chosen and techniques executed.

As soon as we attempt to name and explicate the thick event or the vocal encounter, investigation into voice takes us to singers themselves. Because as with basic musical parameters, the question of what voice and music are, and what voice and music can contribute, is not answered theoretically, with reference to existing categories; rather it is answered practically. My investigation into voice as style and technique, then, expands my basic concern with the study of music as intermaterial vibration. Approaching and relating to voice as style and technique is a domain-specific example of my own call for an organology of intermaterial vibration.[5]

When we examine sound and music from an intermaterial vibrational perspective, we notice that what is understood as "mechanical radiation in all material media" under the framework of the science of acoustics will have different names across scholarly disciplines. Each identifying name, including "sonic and ultrasonic," "shock and vibration," "noise," "musical scales," "instruments," "bioacoustics," and "seismic waves," to name a few, means something distinct to a select group of people and holds little or no meaning or import to another group.[6] In the same way, if we break down each vocal encounter, we can easily understand it as a collection of styles and techniques that have different names, or shorthands—including soulful, tragic, and feminine—for different people. No single naming holds an advantage over the others, since any given collection of styles and techniques is no more essential than another snapshot that features a slightly different collection.

The practice of the pause involves noticing these many competing answers—a multitude of possible namings. Each of them crosses the others out; when there are two strong competing ideas, one does not override the other. No one phenomenon can be neatly measured and indisputably verified so that it points back to a *single* a priori. Instead each points to something larger. It is always this name, and this name, and this name, and this name . . . this, and this, and this, and this, and . . . Each name only points to something more complex than any one name can contain. Each name we assert is limited to the person who asserted it; each name points back to its issuer(s) rather than to the rich and unnamable phenomenon that he or she sought to capture by it. T. S. Eliot describes this in his play *The Cocktail Party*:

> What we know of other people
> Is only our memory of the moments
> During which we knew them. And they have
> Changed since then.[7]

Another way to further consider how infinite possibilities erase the efficacy of measurement is to compare the relationship between form and function. As signs in the form of words hold no meaning in themselves, timbres in themselves also carry no meaning. Moreover it is only in our ability to recognize timbres' distinctness from one another that we can distinguish the character of a single timbre. In other words, there is no meaning held within the form itself, and any and all meaning is generated outside the form.

In applying the practice of the pause, we clear a space in which we may notice that vocal patterns are not imbued with essential meanings. The practice of the pause can also help us to understand vocal patterns that may be ascribed to entrainment and, in that capacity, may be connected to a sense of inevitability. If the singer avoids believing that a vocal sound is inevitable, that singer has moved from the certainty of entrainment into style. In other words, instead of reproducing culture that exists accidentally in the world of entrainment, the singer intentionally reproduces what he or she has been entrained for: the singer *chooses* which world to make. Whether or not other people hear the voice as essential or entrained is incidental.

For example, when a listener hears the sound that we refer to as Billie Holiday's voice, that listener believes that an indisputable, essential person, Billie Holiday, exists, entrained as the qualities enumerated in her oft-repeated biography. Granting Holiday the capacity of choice can change our perception and critical assessment of her voice, and we may consider the style and technique that she employed as perhaps pulled from the reservoir of her life experience. However, thinking about voice through style and technique frames any vocal material as holding the potential to emit infinite amounts and ranges of sound, many of which we could not even have imagined.

"Look: An African Child!"

In order to move through some of the necessary arguments, this book has at times operated through an artificial division between singer and listener. My theoretical and practical points about listeners is not that their position is separate from that of the vocalizer. Any assessment or decision making regarding vocal practice is made from the position of the listener, including assessments and decisions made by the vocalizer. This book has basically said that singers put song into the world, offering up vocal sounds and themselves, both of which the listener subsequently objectifies. However, at this point we can examine this phenomenon in closer detail. I will do so by way of two anecdotes.

As the 1970s drew to a close, I was a little girl queuing up with my family on one of the hundreds of ferry docks that line the coast of Norway. As it can take hours between ferries and the weather was nice, I was playing in the sunshine. The ferry dock area is akin to a marriage between a harbor and a parking lot. Across this vast space, a little boy called to his mother, "Look, an African child!" His outstretched arm, with an outstretched finger, was pointing at me.

As an individual born in South Korea and transported by my adoptive parents to homogeneous Norway, I was most likely the first person this child had seen who did not resemble the others he knew. I was, frankly, as ignorant about the larger world as he, and my knowledge of other groups of people was also limited to images in newspapers or on the single state television channel available to all Norwegians until 1988. I did not feel offended; I did not know enough about the label to identify with or reject it. For me, the label was not filled with meaning, either positive or negative. The child who was reaching for ways to describe me reflected his own inner world, not mine. He must have thought that all people with black hair came from Africa—a misunderstanding that I heard articulated in more detail in other contexts.

The story joined our family's repertoire; we enjoyed telling it because the label applied was so mismatched it provided entertainment in its very absurdity. It could feel absurd because there was no identification with the label, which felt so distant that it did not even conjure a negative identification: the name-calling felt so unrelated to me that the reaction "I am not African" did not arise.

Three decades later I was running a children's song group for Norwegian expatriates in San Pedro, California. A child in the group was curious about me, asking me why my Norwegian Colombian son and I spoke Norwegian when we didn't look Norwegian. This time I was stung; I felt offended that I had not been seen for who I was.

2<

What had changed? I had lived away from Norway for one and a half decades and, as an expatriate, had developed a much stronger sense of my Norwegian-speaking identity. I had also learned to identify with labels: I was a Norwegian person living in Los Angeles. I felt defensive and vulnerable after so many years of being questioned within an American context regarding my cultural, national, linguistic, and timbral identity. We can examine this twist in my relationship to the various labels applied to me by returning to the issue of listeners and singers and my question regarding their separation.

Singers and listeners are not separate categories or roles; we are all singers and listeners simultaneously. It is not only the so-called listener, presented with a voice, who heeds the silent question *Who is this?* The so-called singer is also constantly faced with the same silent question: *Who is singing?* On the surface, the answers can range from "It is I, singing with my silly, playful voice" or "It is I, imitating my mother's voice" to "It is I singing, nailing my Metropolitan Opera audition" and "It is I, the woman Nina." We can already anticipate that, with closer examination, we will find that descriptors or identifiers such as "silly, playful voice," "imitation," "successful opera singer," and "recognized gendered voice" lie on the surface. This first category of vocal identification may be captured by the actor Jaroslaw Fret's "two opposing sentences: 'I *have* a voice' and 'I *am* a voice.'"[8] The description "my silly, playful voice" and others exemplify *having* a voice. That is, I have the capacity to sound silly and playful, and I am exercising that capacity now. We may easily grasp how "my silly, playful voice" is style and technique, harnessed and exercised. We may also deconstruct the style and technique—what Fret thinks of as a "stage of voice"—that went into a particular performance.[9]

The assumption that one layer of the voice is staged is based on a further assumption that there is a sincere, natural voice, emitted from an essence. In this assumption, the natural voice executes the style and technique that presents as the staged voice (the "I" in the statement "It is *I* singing, with my silly voice"). However, when we peel back these layers and continue to ask what makes up the seeming *I* of the voice, we find that it is a further series of styles and techniques. As I mentioned, any given material voice can make any vocal sound. Thus whichever pattern is settled on is the result of no more than circumstances that have led to deep vocal patterns. Therefore these deep vocal patterns may be seen as style and vocal technique rather than as an essential voice that points toward an essential self.

I would like to both exemplify the concept of "this and" (which may also be thought of as "this with" and "and this also") and discuss the issue of the singer and the listener as one and the same by returning to the two anecdotes related earlier. When, as a child, I heard external listeners identifying me with labels based on their incomplete readings of patterns across the sensorium, I did not feel touched by those labels. Based on the discussion thus far, I propose that this was because I myself, as an observer, had not yet applied labels. Because I did not have fixed labels with which others' labels either did or did not correspond, I did not perceive fidelity or dissonance in relation to the meanings applied to me. Hence, on my part, there was no attachment to or investment in the identification. I could consider my applied styles and techniques and imagine how external observers might process them in order to arrive at the identities they attached to me. However, again, this process did not feel personal. I operated as if there was no particular importance to a given label—as if it were one of many assessments of patterns of style and technique. At this moment, when I was unaffected by external labels, I operated outside the cult of fidelity.

However, thirty years later, when I, as a listener, was offended and thus affected by labels, I had switched to operation within the cult of fidelity. Prior to the encounter with the child who asked why I spoke Norwegian, I had already calibrated a clear set of identifications and labels in relation to my vocal patterns and overall presentation. The young boy's assessment did not correspond with those. While we can infer that I was hurt at not being considered a true Norwegian, on a deeper level the issue lay in my listening to myself and deriving what I believed to be a true version of me, and then responding to what I perceived as a mismatched identification.

In this way we are all listeners at all times. And not only do we assess each vocalization and name it, as discussed in chapter 1, but this act forms the basis of the vocal process. Voice is inherently social and collective, created through a feedback loop composed of communal vocal and listening practices. Every utterance, and every instance of listening to oneself and others, is a voice lesson. Everyone is both a singer and a listener, and this iterative process is the foundation of the vocal and listening culture that produces voice.

In *Sensing Sound*, I established that there is no a priori knowable and identifiable sound and that there is only "particular material-vibrational transmission." Therefore "the specific ways we have conceptualized music's building blocks—as species of sound with particular parameters—limit our knowledge of music's ontology, epistemology, and ramifications."[10] Moreover, traditional vocabulary, concepts, and theories do not possess the capacity to capture the nature of music and voice.

The Race of Sound traces a similar trajectory. It points out that simply naming the voice does not begin to capture the thick event. Through naming, we do not achieve knowledge about the vocalizer; we know only how the listener has named the voice that he or she perceived. A listener who believes that the world is what it appears to be in his or her imagination engages in solipsistic listening. In this type of listening, listeners cast their acoustic shadow over everyone they name. And when the vocalizers themselves function as listeners, they can cast the same acoustic shadow over themselves, limiting their world to preformed ideas. For example, the point about the recent encounter where my Norwegianness was questioned is not so much that the little boy was mistaken or that I identify myself in a particular way. The point is that I was clinging to a stable and seemingly knowable category about myself, and I experienced dissonance between that identification and the identification imposed upon me. It was the dissonance between my naming of myself and the boy's questioning of that naming, rather than the specific nature of the questioning, that caused me pain.

In rejecting the identification projected upon me, I did not scale back my understanding of the moment in order to consider style and technique. Rather I saw my own categories as correct and the child's as wrong. Again, whether his assessment was actually correct or incorrect did not matter. What mattered is that whatever identification might have been suggested to me—whether or not it aligned with my own—I would have compared it to my own and only my own, and any identifications aligning with mine would have fit into my world. In other words, within that situation my perception was solipsistic. And, while the child may have clung to an essential category of race (say, every person with black hair hails from Africa), I equally essentialized myself by not loosening enough to recognize that his was one assessment and mine was another and that each could sit side by side, filling out the interpretation of a particular style and technique (the expression of which was "black hair").

In other words, every vocal pattern can be understood as essential, entrained, or simply as style and technique. Assessing a voice or person as essential implies that the person is a priori defined, through and through, by that meaning. Assessing a voice or person as limited to entrainment implies that a person is inescapably the sum of his or her environment and life circumstances and can control only those circumstances to the degree that he or she can affect them. Assessing a voice or person as the product of style and technique implies an assumption that whatever I hear is a product of the singer's vocal abilities. Therefore whatever I choose to name those vocal sounds or abilities points only to me, the namer. When voice is heard as essence or as entrainment, it is assumed that a given name captures the singer. When voice is heard as style and technique, the assumption is that a given name describes only the style and technique of a vocal sound—but this name, this sound, does not define the singer.

Becoming aware of existence within fixed, solipsistic identification is brilliantly captured by the seventeenth-century poet Tukaram:

> I was meditating with my cat the other day
> and all of a sudden she shouted,
> "What happened"
> I knew exactly what she meant, but encouraged
> her to say more—feeling that if she got it all out on the table
> she would sleep better that night.
> So I responded, "Tell me more, dear,"
> and she soulfully meowed,
> "Well, I was mingled with the sky and now look—
> I am landlocked in fur."
> To this I said, "I know exactly what
> you mean."
> What to say about conversation
> between
> mystics?[11]

This poem expresses the feelings of shock and limitation that arise during identification, feelings I experienced as an adult when my Norwegianness was questioned. When we are landlocked within a limited identification, we are profoundly disconnected from the world, while, at the same time, we can recall the feeling of connection. For example, shortly after I became a mother, I was shocked to notice that I did not recognize my own child's voice. I prided myself on being an attentive and detailed listener to voices, and, more generally, I had always heard that mothers had an instinctive connection to their child's particular voice. While this is the case for some animals where social and spatial circumstances necessitate such identification, I did not experience it. Instead of selectively recognizing only my son's voice, I heard all children's voices as my child's. I would feel a sense of alarm on hearing any baby crying and would often leap to my feet, only to discover that the crying was not my son's.

I paused to think about this when testimonies surrounding the killing of Trayvon Martin made headlines. On the night of Martin's death, a neighbor called 911 to report the altercation. A person is heard screaming in the background of the recorded 911 call. When the recording was introduced in court, differing news headlines appeared—from "Screams on 911 Recording Were

Trayvon Martin's, Mother Testifies" to "Zimmerman Mom: That's My Son Screaming on Tape."[12] In other words, "Mothers of both Martin, Zimmerman testify they heard their own son calling for help on 911 tape," as *Fox News* summarized.[13]

The implication, leading to allegations, was that one of the mothers lied.[14] When listening to the desperate cries for help on the 911 recording, each of the mothers responded to the question *Who is crying?* with a sentiment that could be summarized as "This is my son crying for help. I am his mother. I would recognize his voice always and everywhere." Each mother maintained that it was *her* son's cry for help, and thus it was assumed that one of them lied. In other words, the drama hinged on the presumption that one of the mothers did not recognize her son in that voice and knowingly lied when she said she could identify him.[15] While this may have been the case, if the mothers—and everyone who heard the screams—met the world within a perceptual framework based on listening for style and technique, I would suggest that both mothers, and all parents as well as most listeners, would hear *a person* cry and that, without limitations, each would choose not to shield himself or herself from the pain of a child of humanity. And I would suggest that these mothers, like all compassionate human beings who care about other people, would react with despair at not being able to help.

However, within the listening framework of the cult of fidelity—and especially within a legal context that takes it for granted—a listener would simply ask whether the cry for help came from his or her son. In the same way, we respond to voices that support and fulfill our expectations of naturalized categories. Our expectations are fulfilled when we encounter a black man who "sounds like a black man," an African American classical singer who can sing spirituals with the correct idiomatic style, and so on. Each cry for help that is categorized as "my son" or "not my son" is veiled by the acoustic shadow that causes the meaning and signification of the cry to point only to the listener himself or herself: Is this a person who I already love, and who is in my personal frame of reference? Does this person fit within my world, as I comprehend it?

When listening beyond identification and limited compassion, we may hear every cry as though the vocalizer were our own child. If this type of listening were to be encouraged within the figure of sound framework, it would be a matter of expanding the listening into an even more detailed and accurate account of the world. Outside the figure of sound, it is instead about dissolving the reference points, so that the pain of social injustice is also my pain. And so that the pain of mothers and fathers who have lost a child to gun violence is all parents' collective pain and mandate to address.[16] When listening beyond identification and limited compassion, I propose, we would hear a person unencumbered by our own reference points and unmarked by the solipsistic shadow of our own mind—and that the possibility of hearing the cry as composed of styles and techniques could allow us to hear both "my son" and "a son"—to allow "my son" to be "a son" and "a son" to be "my son," neither the ocean nor the sand. This son is more expansive than the limitations of my own solipsistic identification.

Building on the two types of listeners, listener A and listener B, I further identify three evolutionary steps away from essentialization. That is, the micropolitics of listening is a tool that can be used not only to naturalize but also to denaturalize. I have formulated these steps in relation to the ways the acousmatic question is approached and answered (located to the left of the equals sign in table 6.1) and the ways the answer was assembled (at the right of the equals sign).

To flesh out the explanations of these formulas, let me return to Billie Holiday. According to formula A (listening stance A), my listening is contained within the limits of my own symbolic world. I can hear Holiday only through the images I have already formed about women, African Americans, Holiday as an icon, and so on. In other words, listeners are tasked with comparing what they hear with a preformulated set of a prioris. Within this dynamic a given voice is either the essence of an a priori (Billie Holiday as the iconic Billie Holiday; "a black voice") or an imitation of this essence (Billie Holiday not singing as we expect her to do; Angelina Jordan's imitation of Holiday; someone who "doesn't sound black"). This type of listening does not grant the singer agency. The singer simply fulfills or does not fulfill the listener's a prioris, which have been collected as a result of a specific set of circumstances.

According to formula B (listening stance B), the listener's listening is expanded to release his or her symbolic referential frame and acknowledge that voices are the result of style, technique, and conditions. Within this approach Holiday sounding like the iconic Holiday, Holiday on an "off day" with a bad cold, and Jordan's imitation are understood as performances based on style and technique. The listener's ability to experience the singer as separate from himself or herself, as a person with agency who executes technique and style, releases the singer from the listener. The singer is granted an independent existence and agency. That is, Holiday as an iconic singer exists because style and technique are exquisitely executed; Holiday with a bad cold exists because her sore throat and lack of sleep have modified this technique; and Jordan's imitation exists because she was able to decipher and execute vocal patterns. Here there is a clear

TABLE 6.1. Response to the Acousmatic Question Formula

Progression	*Response to the acousmatic question*	*Process of arriving at a response*
Formula A	S	1+0
Formula B	O	0+1
Formula C	∞	1+1+ ... n

0 = 0 (zero) defined in a binary with 1 (one).

1 = 1 (one) defined in a binary with 0 (zero).

S = Self (self, with no relationality to the Other). One. Subject, the solipsistic self.

O = Other (the self cannot see himself or herself in the Other; the Other is defined by its very difference from the self). An imaginary, limited "you" or Other who is defined by the listener's a prioris.

∞ = the infinity of 1s, which are in reality (1+0) or (0+1).

S = 1 + 0: Formula A describes solipsistic listening, wherein listeners are limited to naming themselves as phenomena in their world. While we might assume that the object named refers to someone other than oneself, in this response to the acousmatic question, the *answer* always points to the listener. The 0 is Object, an imaginary, limited Other, purely defined by listeners' available a prioris. This Other is also defined by its perceived difference from the subject.

O = 0 + 1: Formula B describes a situation in which singer and listener are catapulted into a third position, realizing that neither is subject and neither is object. When able to sense a voice as style and technique, the listener must take in the voice of the other as subject. At the same time, the listener recognizes that this "taking in" is also a subject position. The existence of two subjects creates a third position, the infinity of all positions, which leads us to the erasure of self and to the recognition of you and of all possibilities and multiplicities. This leads us to the third formula.

∞ = 1 + 1 ... n: From the perspective of Formula C, we consider no one position more important than any other. Indeed, we understand any particular position as the result of a choice based on many possibilities. In the thick event, and in the potentiality of styles and techniques, framing and naming point only to these sets of particularities. And in doing so, they point equally to all others.

separation between "I" and "you," and both combine to create a third position. This voice is not 50 percent "I" and 50 percent "you"; instead it exists within an unrepeatable constellation of circumstances.

Considering the same example from the opposite point of view, we cannot access the totality of the figure "Billie Holiday" through any particular reading, but a partial understanding may be accessed through attention to momentary techniques. When listening from this position, we do not hear Holiday (the complete being) but rather the specific sound of a person who is bending notes while forcing sound across a sore throat. Jordan's imitation is unique in the same way. She is recognized as Holiday not because she is "channeling" Holiday but because she applies vocal techniques and stylings that lead to vocal sounds similar to those created by the person Billie Holiday. Rather than lauding her for passive imitation, listeners' recognition of Jordan's execution is based in her ability to perform vocal choice. This recognition redeems her presence—Jordan performing a particular style and technique—and returns it to the foreground of our attention.

The third formula, formula C, expresses the idea that, if a voice may be understood as holding two positions involving style and technique, it can also hold an infinite number of different positions. When a collection of styles and techniques is distinguishable through one name, it may also be distinguishable through another name, and another, and another, and yet another. Given this infinity of possibilities, any assumptions about one distinction's correctness are already erased. According to this formula, we can recognize that Billie Holiday's vocal style and technique can be heard as patterns that we know by names such as "battered woman," "hypersexual," "victim," "the conscience of a nation," and, and, and, and . . .

Moreover, within the third formula the concept of "me" as a separate identity and the recognition that there is something that is not-me coexist. The effect is something that is not me or you, yet it includes both of us—and each of us is only one formulation of infinite possibilities. At this point, then, there is no way to separate me from you without severing the relationship. Because each voice has infinite potentiality, any given materialization holds no more power than the infinite number of other possibilities. In other words, Holiday's instrumentalization of certain sets of styles and techniques does not define her, any more than any of the other existing infinite number of styles and techniques. It points only to infinity.

Why Did the Chicken Cross the Road?

To rearticulate this discussion in the materialist language used earlier, it is the conceptualization of intermaterial vibration as given figures of sound that obstructs for infinity, as captured by formula C, wherein the particularities of styles and techniques, framing and naming also point to infinite potentiality. Some may read formula C and my argument about intermaterial vibration as simply a continuous chain of possibilities where the limit and range are simply the number of modes of listening, and some may feel that I "overstate the case against the figure of sound," as one friend observed in relation to this material. The observation was offered in the form of a joke: *Why did the chicken cross the road? Because everything is vibration.* "What is funny about this punch-line . . . is how incongruous an answer it is to the question posed," the humor-ous colleague offered, going on to observe, "The punchline doesn't answer the *relevant* question, which is to provide motivation for the chicken's action. . . . The vibrational account fails to motivate why individuals employ the 'figure of sound' in the first place."[17] However, in this book I've sought to address pre-cisely this issue. On the one hand, I posit that listening practices developed and naturalized within a given audible culture do give rise to conventions of figures of sound—for example, pitches that are in and out of tune and voices that are aligned or not aligned with a given identity. On the other hand, as my colleague rightly pointed out, the story is more complex than such an explana-tion can capture.

In my earlier work I posited that because sound does not exist in a vacuum and is always realized through a specific material entity, we can know it only within its unfolding intermaterial dynamic. The argument was built on a one-to-one relationship describing vibration in relation to its transmitting and transducing material. I made the argument in that form in order to address the basic naturalized parameters of sound. In *The Race of Sound* I deal with more complex categories of naturalization, and in that context I have the opportunity to develop that argument. Specifically, herein I have dealt with namings and categorizations of *people*, including those namings related to race and gender. Sound and voice are realized through matter, and therefore their particular re-lational unfolding is interdependent with the nature of the transmitting mate-rial. In the case of voice, the material adapts according to daily practice. In *The Race of Sound*, I move the argument one step further by addressing the chang-ing nature of the transmitting material—that is, singing and listening bodies.

The analogy that for me is the most intuitive comes not from sound but from the visual world. If a ray of light passes through a room full of dust, we can see that the angle of the light is 45 degrees. If the ray of light were to pass through a glass of water, we could see the light beam change its angle due to the change in materiality, approximately 28 degrees due to the glass and 32 degrees due to the differences between the substances glass and water. Each of these materialities realized certain aspects of its potentiality due to circumstances—say, the dusty air, glassness, and waterness. Therefore it is not because of a nonnegotiable a priori reason that each of them presents as dusty air, glass, and water, hence of-fering the beam of light the ability only to present within those specific inter-material ranges. Instead these intermaterial realizations come about because of the specific performances of dusty air, glass, and water.

In the same way that light fractures differently, sound travels at different speeds through dissimilar material.[18] Considered in relation to the acoustic condition, this difference affects our sense of the sound's clarity. For example, if the sound moves quickly, it can sound very "muddy," as previous sounds may still linger while new sounds are iterated. Hence much as light fractures in distinct ways with particular angles, when the so-called same sound or vibrational energy is transmitted through different materialities, it can be expressed differently through each materiality.

The body, made up of different types of organic material, is in constant formation. As anybody who has engaged in a particular type of exercise or other physical activity knows, the body physically acquires knowledge and skills. The body can move more gracefully than previously imagined, can possess more explosive or enduring energy, and can carry out more precise handiwork after this adaptation process. As I have addressed extensively throughout my work, daily vocal activity transforms the body's organic material in the same way. Therefore, while people's ability and expression can be utterly transformed by exercise, people going through an extensive sprint training program perceive that altered body as still their body.

Let's tie the visual analogy back to sound, voices, and bodies. What was described in our visual analogy as performing and emphasizing the potentiality, ability, and character of glassness is, in the body-voice-sound situation, the same as a person sounding one way prior to sustained training and another after training. Just as a singular light source is refracted in one angle through glass and another angle through water, a voice can sound one way prior to enculturation into a given sociocultural category and another when encultured. Moreover the same person can simultaneously be encultured into more than one sociocultural category or musical genre and move between them with ease, as a light can easily move from glass to water.

We could discuss the beam of light moving through these materials—and, by way of analogy, the racialized voice—in two ways. We could say, imprecisely, that as light passes through different materials, it changes into airy light (as made visible through dust), glassy light, or watery light with the angles of refraction of 45, 28, and 32 degrees, respectively, thus suggesting that there are three different kinds of light and that each is essentially itself and itself alone. Such an assumption narrates a story of essential types of things, defined in turn by their characteristics. This narrative seems to explain the way the light appears to us in each of its states, but at the same time it invokes the misleading implication that fundamental differences are expressed through what we experience as dusty light or watery light. They are not.

A second way to consider the apparently changing characteristics of refracted light is to see that light per se always possesses all of the qualities that can be observed in each individual state—through dust, glass, or water—but that the presence of a particular material focuses our attention on one set of qualities—say, dusty light. When we talk about light in this way, we can see that, although the light appears to express different angles and looks different from one state to another, the light itself is not changed; it contains all of the same characteristics in each state. It is the material through which the light passes that causes particular features to be highlighted. The racialized voice works the same way. There is no a priori set of vocal timbres that define or express blackness or whiteness. In terms of our light analogy, the empirical elements of timbre remain an identical set of mechanical potentialities in all individuals until the kinetic sound is "passed through" some refracting material. The refracting-material analogy can be used when considering both the ways in which the listener brings his or her own interpretation to the scene, and the ways in which vocalizing bodies are entrained through daily vocal practice. At this point, in the listener's view, the voice appears to be the very material through which it is realized (i.e., it *is* glassness or *is* a black voice), but what is really happening is that we now see or hear two things: the light or the timbre and the material it has passed through. Here, within the figure of sound framework, the listener stops thinking about vocal-timbral limitlessness, concluding that the material through which the voice only passes is the essential and sole expression of that voice.

In this analogy, to perform glassness is the same as to vocalize under a particular sociocultural condition that stabilizes the body and voice so that they sound a given timbre. Performing glassness is the same as performing the daily inner choreography that shapes the material vocal apparatus into easily performable sounds. Producing these timbres feels like second nature, and a given listening community can recognize them as, for instance, a black voice. That is, race is not expressed timbrally because vibration is realized in some material relationship, the a priori range of which is, say, whiteness or blackness. Instead, in reaction to a particular sociocultural circumstance, a vocalist's materiality performs one of its potentialities. This realized potentiality, in turn, has been indexed as whiteness or blackness according to sociocultural norms regarding timbral style and technique, and—in combination with a vibrational entity in the form of the singer and the listening body—is thus heard as whiteness or blackness.

However, naturalization of a given timbral realization is a false choice. For example, as a vocalizer and as a listener, due to my participation in the thick event and my unlimited ability to understand the various ways available to frame portions of it as this style and that technique, I possess infinite potential, with each particularity zeroing out all others and none left standing as the most significant. Therefore any specific naming or identification of this action, or of that style and technique—for instance, "specific mother to specific son"—is only added to "infinite mother." My recognition of a specific son is only added to my recognition of all sons. Because I am composed of an infinity of styles and techniques, and because I happen to materialize this one now, I am both This and . . . Norwegian and . . . The "This" doesn't change the " . . . ," which is infinity. And "and" doesn't change infinity, and therefore represents a nonissue. Luigi Russolo identified this phenomenon, saying, "To enrich means to add, not to substitute or to abolish."[19] Josh Kun formulates it as a call to think about music as a space of difference, within which listeners recognize that there are no a priori indices but that "we are all strangers among sounds made by others."[20]

As I have put it previously, "singing and listening are aspects of a thick event and are distinguished from it only through naming."[21] In the same way, race and ethnicity are aspects of a continuous field of style and technique and are distinguished from its limitless potentiality only through naming. If there is no essential human form besides an a priori idea that holds that form together, there can be no essential race, ethnicity, or other identity marker besides the a priori idea that holds such a marker together. We are materially specific, continuously unfolding events. Or, in the language of *The Race of Sound*, we are continuously unfolding style and technique.

Just as there is no zone between the end of the ocean and the beginning of the land, there is the infinity of possible styles and techniques and the infinity of ways of naming a given pattern drawn from these styles and techniques. There is no one pattern that expresses the present moment. With infinite potentiality, all measurements zero out the importance of any one in particular.[22]

The paradox is that there is only the moment of listening and of responding to the call of the acousmatic question. The ocean and the beach. How do we avoid identifying with either? And what happens when we identify with one of them? In the awareness of the infinite we can exercise nonidentification with ocean-beach or past-future. As mentioned, the antidote to indexing timbre is the pause. Within the pause we may recognize our clinging to the process and the results of identification, and we may become aware of each moment's infinite potentialities.

Tukaram's cat has a moment of nonidentification before she is hurled back to being landlocked in fur. The important point is that, at that moment, the cat has knowledge of infinity, and her landlocked state is understood within that broader perspective. Moreover the cat has the incentive to step out of her

fur-bound state. No one identification is a limitation. I am Korean-born and . . .
I am trained in a European classical vocal tradition and . . . I speak the regional
dialect of the place called Molde and . . . I speak English and . . . My hormonal
composition is this and . . . I have experienced hardship and also much luck,
and . . . I am almond-eyed, Norwegian-raised, and . . . and . . . and . . . and . . . ∞

Returning to listening, in response to the acousmatic question, I can say:
This is a white man's voice. I can then pause to imagine the infinite potentialities of style and technique; I can recognize my own way of organizing the world
and see that I have applied it to organize selected patterns into what I now identify as this particular voice. These styles and techniques could be organized into
any pattern. In this way, any identification is one of many. In other words, it is
1+1+1+1 . . . ∞ where no one ties us permanently to a particular identification,
and even when there is a temporary identification, we know, as does the cat,
that there is another.[23] Outside the cult of fidelity, the answer to the acousmatic
question is *It is this and . . . ∞*. The answer is descriptive and not essential, and
the descriptive dimension is tied to the *describer* (listener) rather than to the
described (the vocalizer).

The point is not simply to enable us to grasp people's complexity and add
more and more identities to those we already perceive. Let's return to the pause
introduced at the beginning of this chapter and note that it actually occurs in
the formula in table 6.1, but only as a detail. When two objects act simultaneously as interrelated, neither is the subject or object within that relationship.
Here neither is identified as the namer of the other.

We considered the listener vis-à-vis the singer and the singer vis-à-vis the
listener. To assign a definition of listener or singer, we needed to use one of the
two elements as subject and as the head of the frame of reference, thus reducing the second element to object. I don't mean anything in these designations
other than that one element has some hierarchical relationship to the other,
and the definition of the two elements then becomes the manifestation of that
hierarchy.[24] In short, the cult of fidelity lends itself to relationships that *are* only
relationships because of the defined hierarchy between x and y.

When we remove the hierarchy—the idea that one element is more important or relevant than another (in Kun's words, when we become "strangers
among sounds")—but retain the interconnectedness, we create a logical conjunction (Λ). The logical conjunction (Λ) is the statement A Λ B is true if A and
B are both true; else it is false and produces a nonreferential relationship *among*
rather than between. That is, two things share a relationship without one of
them determining that relationship.

But by rethinking the joke about the chicken, we can move one step fur-

TABLE 6.2. Response to the Acousmatic Question Formula,
Including Logical Conjunction

Progression	Response to the acousmatic question	Process of arriving at a response
Formula A	S	1+0
Formula B	O	0+1
	Λ	$(1+0) + (0+1)$
Formula C	∞	$1+1+\ldots n$

ther. My response to the joke is not to say that "everything is vibration," nor that we can conceptualize any vibrational pattern into any given identity. Instead I would simply say that the chicken crossed the road because it is not the chicken that didn't cross the road, or the chicken that half-crossed the road, or the chicken that crossed the road and then returned. The chicken didn't cross the road because it is unique, or because everything is vibration. All of these chickens are in connection, are related, but this relationship and each expression of it isn't a linear one of cause and effect, time and space, before and after; it is a relationship that is manifest through *realization of the fact of the relationship*. In this formulation, we would expand our formula to show the pause created by the conjunction of Formula A and Formula B (see table 6.2).

In the conjunction we see that Formulas A and B are not in opposition to each other. Instead the conjunction spells out that each 1 is (1+0) and each 0 is (0+1) and includes any possible combination of 1s and 0s. Each point contains the binary. Through the conjunction, we can move to Formula C, where no single point overrides another. Because we are translating from a linear, subject/object–based discourse, the process of arriving at the response is expressed as 1+1+ . . . n. However, this does not mean that we are only talking about the infinite collection of a variety of namings and identities (mother, daughter, scholar, runner, singer . . . n), but that scholarly discourse, always partial in its perspective, fumbles in this inadequate way toward grasping the inexpressible whole. While we might be reliant on such methods and partial perspectives, my work strains to make this problem visible and audible. In the language of sound, it aims to attend to the micropolitics of listening by offering a methodological question that denaturalizes listening.

Unless I am aware of my beliefs, I am imprisoned by them. Thus, while the acousmatic question is crucial and can help us to gain insight into both the non-fixity of any one position and our active participation in any articulation, one question cuts deeper—indeed deepest. That question is this: Who would I have to be, and what would I have to feel, if I did not cling to any given identification, and instead practiced inquiry through the pause?[25] As the thirteenth-century poet Rumi asks:

Why do you stay in prison
when the door is so wide open?
Move outside the tangle of fear-thinking.
Live in silence.
Flow down and down
in always widening rings of being.[26]

Appendix

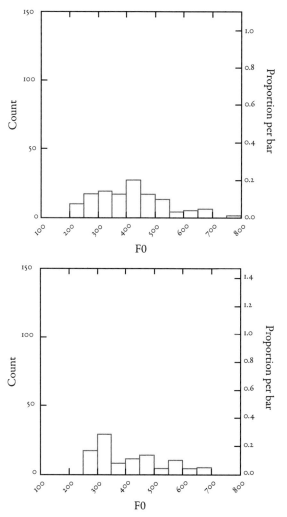

FIGURE A.1 Smokey Robinson, "Ooo Baby, Baby." Prepared by Jody Kreiman.

FIGURE A.2 Frankie Valli, "Big Girls Don't Cry." Prepared by Jody Kreiman.

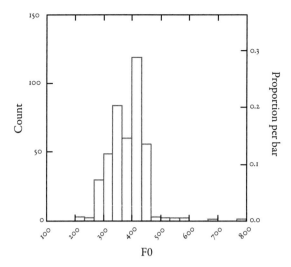

FIGURE A.3 Marvin Gaye, "Trouble Man." Prepared by Jody Kreiman.

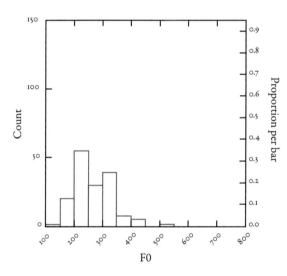

FIGURE A.4 Jimmy Scott, "On Broadway." Prepared by Jody Kreiman.

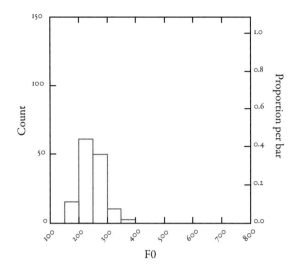

FIGURE A.5 Jimmy Scott, "I Wish I Knew." Prepared by Jody Kreiman.

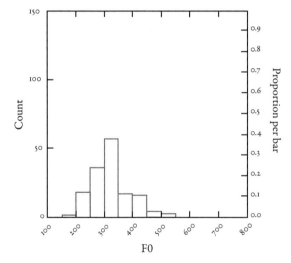

FIGURE A.6 Jimmy Scott, "This Love of Mine." Prepared by Jody Kreiman.

Notes

1. Schaeffer, *Traité des Objets Musicaux*, 91. For a discussion of Schaeffer and the acousmatic discussion, see Kane, "*L'Objet Sonore Maintenant*," 3.

2. Francis Barraud, *His Master's Voice*, 1900, oil on canvas, EMI Music's Gloucester Place, London.

3. Kane, *Sound Unseen*, 5–6.

4. Mladen Dolar and Slavoj Žižek consider the acousmatic condition specifically in regard to the acousmatic voice. As Brian Kane summarizes, Dolar and Žižek investigate "acousmatic voice as a form of social interpellation" and they "explicitly describe the Lacanian 'object voice' as acousmatic" (*Sound Unseen*, 6, 11). In fact Kane argues "that Dolar reifies the acousmaticity of the voice, making it into a permanent condition, and that his treatment of the acousmatic voice is phantasmagoric, masking the technique at play in the psychoanalytic session" (11). In contrast, as I exemplify throughout this book, the acousmatic *question* presents an opportunity to undo reification.

5. For recent summaries and overviews of the assumed primacy of the voice as interiority within Western thought, see Konstantinos Thomaidos, "The Re-vocalization of Logos? Thinking, Doing and Disseminating Voice," in Thomaidos and Macpherson, *Voice Studies*, 10–22; Weidman, "Anthropology and Voice" and "Voice."

6. Joanna Demers, email correspondence with the author, August 10, 2015.

7. Cavarero, *For More Than One Voice*, 5.

8. Cavarero, *For More Than One Voice*, 7.

9. Butler, *The Ancient Phonograph*, 18.

10. Butler, *The Ancient Phonograph*, 18. See especially the introductory chapter and chapter 5.

11. For an overview of this issue, see Smalls, "Linguistic Profiling and the Law."

12. Early on, I took a seminar with George Lipsitz on race and popular culture, and I worked with George Lewis on issues of race in music generally, and in improvisation specifically. I also worked with Jann Pasler and Anne Seshadri on postcolonial theory and with Deborah Wong on the performativity of race in the United States. This eclectic training oriented my approach to scholarship.

13. These gaps in understanding of vocal production, product, and perception, often expressed as ambiguities, are found not only within a critical humanistic framework. Kreiman et al. noted as late as 2014 that "two important questions about voice remain unanswered: When voice quality changes, what physiological alteration caused this change, and if a change to the voice production system occurs, what change in perceived quality can be expected?" ("Toward a Unified Theory of Voice Production and Perception," 1).

14. See, for example, Kreiman et al., "Toward a Unified Theory of Voice Production and Perception."

15. "Color" was also a medieval Latin term used between the mid-thirteenth and mid-fifteenth centuries that pointed to repetitions as embellishments.

16. American National Standards Institute, *Acoustical Terminology*, 45, and Helmholtz, *On the Sensations of Tone*, both cited in Kreiman and Sidtis, *Foundations of Voice Studies*, 7.

17. Similarly, working within linguistic anthropology, Nicholas Harkness has dealt with the tension of the "ongoing intersection between the phonic production and organization of sound on the one hand, and the sonic uptake and categorization of sound in the world on the other." He writes, "Treating the voice as a phonosonic nexus has allowed me to explore how vocalization is situated at the intersection of multiple frameworks of meaningfulness and distinction as a form of culturally regimented semiotic engagement with and inhabitance of social worlds" ("Anthropology at the Phonosonic Nexus," 5).

18. Kreiman et al., "Toward a Unified Theory of Voice Production and Perception," 2. They go on to explain, "A significant body of behavioral and neuropsychological data . . . shows that listeners perceive voice quality as an integral pattern, rather than as the sum of a number of separate features" (2).

19. Kreiman and Sidtis, *Foundations of Voice Studies*, 113.

20. For example, countertenor Patrick Dailey speaks in a normative masculine voice but sings in falsetto in a manner that does not signal the female register, as many drag performers' voices do. For more on this, see chapter 3.

21. Lipsitz, *The Possessive Investment in Whiteness*, has served as a major text for me while addressing homeownership, education politics, inheritance patterns, and federal policy.

22. Obadike, "Low Fidelity," 135–37.

23. Meyer and Land, "Threshold Concepts and Troublesome Knowledge," 3.

24. Adler-Kassner and Wardle, *Naming What We Know*.

25. Meyer and Land, "Threshold Concepts and Troublesome Knowledge," 3.

26. Relatedly, in an article addressing the perception of female voices in leadership positions, Jordan Kisner writes that Michelle Obama has shared that, as a young woman, she was taunted for "talking like a white girl," only to be criticized later for sounding "too loud, or too angry, or too emasculating" during Barack Obama's presidential campaign. Audie Cornish, an NPR host, is "frequently accused of 'code-switching' to sound more white for public-radio audiences," Kisner reports. Cornish observes that she speaks with the same voice whether she is on or off the air. Jordan Kisner, "Can a Wom-

an's Voice Ever Be Right?," *The Cut*, accessed August 1, 2016, https://www.thecut
.com/2016/07/female-voice-anxiety-c-v-r.html#.

27. Although, in reality, pitch also contributes to the timbral makeup, this is a frequent definition. What this definition *does capture* is that if two instruments or sound sources play the same pitch and duration, what distinguishes them from one another is timbre.

28. While it is impossible to entirely separate timbre from a statement's pitch, duration, and verbal content, one way we know that timbre influences our perceptions independently of these categories of communication is that, if a verbal statement conveys one message but its tone communicates another, adult listeners will tend to believe the tone of voice rather than the words. Thus timbre can contribute to listeners' consideration of identity, emotional state, truthfulness, age, and vocal genre, among other aspects of vocal expression. For the complexity and the enormous amount of literature addressing the recognition of identity, personality, emotion, age, and physical characteristics based on vocalizing, see Kreiman and Sidtis, *Foundations of Voice Studies*, 110–89, 302–98. For recognition of vocal (music) genres based on timbre, see Huron, *Sweet Anticipation*.

29. Such an argument has been made possible by the work of scholars such as Stuart Hall. "Cultural identity," he explains, is not "a fixed essence . . . but a *positioning*," and race is a matter of "'becoming'" ("Cultural Identity and Diaspora," 226, 225). Thank you to Shana Redmond, who reminded me about this foundational text.

30. It is noteworthy that voice as a signifier of uniqueness is set within an intensely Western metaphysics.

31. Farah Jasmine Griffin also explains recognizable vocal performances, such as "the black woman's voice," in terms of cultural style: "I do not mean the voice that comes out every time any black woman anywhere opens her mouth to sing. Nor do I want to imply that there is something in the structure of the black diaphragm, neck, throat, and tongue, teeth, or mouth that contributes to a certain vocalization. No, I don't mean a black voice as markedly different as skin color or texture of hair. *Instead I am talking of a cultural style*. A particularly New World style with roots in West Africa. . . . In the United States it is a style transformed, nurtured, and developed in the tradition of the spirituals, field hollers, and work songs and sustained in black church and/or blues and jazz venues" ("When Malindy Sings," 105–6, italics mine). While not using the terminology "style and technique," Jason King also addresses performance as authorship in his discussion of Roberta Flack. King writes, "If we consider the role of energy as a defining factor in the production and reception of music, Flack emerges as an auteur precisely because of her ability to use her voice and complementary musical skills to traffic in 'vibe'" ("The Sound of Velvet Melting," 172–73).

32. Baldwin, *The Devil Finds Work*, 6.

33. To date, no work has been carried out regarding a given voice's plasticity and possible vocal range and the actual amount that is used. One ongoing research project studies vocal patterns within everyday use. See Kreiman et al., "The Relationship between Acoustic and Perceived Interspeaker Variability in Voice Quality."

34. Denes and Pinson, *The Speech Chain*, 5.

35. See Kreiman et al., "Toward a Unified Theory of Voice Production and Perception," 3.

36. This position resonates with Alva Noë's argument that "sound is not a physical phenomenon but a perceptual entity, arising within the mind." If this were not the case, "then variation between listeners' experiences . . . could not be satisfactorily explained" (*Action in Perception*, 112).

37. Marcel Mauss, "Body Techniques," in *Sociology and Psychology*, 104, 121.

38. Woodson, *The Mis-Education of the Negro*; Foucault, *Discipline and Punish*.

39. There are recognizable affinities between this position and that of actor network theory's material-symbolic dynamic recognition. I address some of the relations between the two in chapter 2, on the discursive networks formed around Marian Anderson.

40. This phrasing, which I found very useful, comes from one of the anonymous reader reports, conveyed in an email from Ken Wissoker, September 19, 2017.

41. See the collaborative project I direct, Keys to Voice Studies, http://keystovoice .cdh.ucla.edu/, as an example of putting different scholarly areas in conversation.

42. For an overview on work and views on the voice surviving from Occidental ancient times, see Shane Butler, "What Was the Voice?," in Eidsheim and Meizel, *The Oxford Handbook of Voice Studies*; Butler, *The Ancient Phonograph*.

43. Thank you to Monica Chieffo for the stimulating conversation (June 11, 2015) that got me thinking along these lines.

44. Beahrs, "Post-Soviet Tuvan Throat-Singing (*Xöömei*) and the Circulation of Nomadic Sensibility"; Butler, *The Ancient Phonograph*; Daughtry, "Afterword"; Fales, "The Paradox of Timbre"; Kessler, "Anachronism Effects," 26–60; Kinney, "The Resonance of Brando's Voice"; Kreiman and Sidtis, *Foundations of Voice Studies*; Levin and Süzükei, *Where Rivers and Mountains Sing*; Marshall, "Crippled Speech"; Norton, *Singing and Wellbeing*; Ochoa Gautier, *Aurality*; Rahaim, *Musicking Bodies*; Schlichter, "Do Voices Matter?"; Weidman, *Singing the Classical, Voicing the Modern*.

45. *The Family Group of the Katarrhinen* (*Die Familiegruppe der Katarrhinene*), artist unknown, in Haeckel, *Die Natürliche Schöpfungsgeschichte*; Nott and Gliddon, *Types of Mankind*, 458.

46. For a detailed discussion of the relationship between anatomy, vocal pedagogy, and musical abilities, see Nina Sun Eidsheim, "Race and the Aesthetics of Vocal Timbre," in Bloechl et al., *Rethinking Difference in Music Scholarship*, 338–65.

47. Du Bois, *The Souls of Black Folk*, 2.

48. I am here echoing Du Bois's influential title, *The Souls of Black Folk*.

49. Aristotle, *On the Soul* 2.8.420b, in *The Complete Works*.

50. Cruz, *Culture on the Margins*, 43.

51. In "The Secret Animation of Black Music," Radano provides the following quote: "Despite their kinship with hogs in nature and habit, the Negro has music in his soul" (anonymous Georgia physician, 1860). I include the quote here to illustrate the connection between a concern with the body in its material, concrete form and a focus on the sound of the voice and its assessment.

52. "The social life of things" is Arjun Appadurai's well-known phrase, and Radano

evokes it when describing the ways in which "the abstract labor behind the record's production in world markets gives way to the life of exchange and re-imagined uses" ("The Secret Animation").

53. Considering Charles Sanders Peirce's model of the sign, the signified, and the active role of the interpretant—the listener—we can synthesize the takeaways from this book's case studies into the following patterns. Aspects of the voice that were framed or understood as material and "objective" were used to argue for a particular meaning. These symbolic dimensions directed daily practice, and hence shaped the material. In other words, a composite meaning directly affected the range of possibilities for the vocal body, its daily habituation, and the resulting material vocal body. This circularity acted as a self-fulfilling prophecy around various (often unarticulated) focal points. The very focal point or meaning that was reinforced triggered the practice. In other words, if sonic fidelity with overall presentation (visual, identity expressed, etc.) is not experienced by the listener and interpretant, we see that the interpretant actively arranges various aspects of the thick vocal event to create coherence according to a given cultural and societal frame.

54. Davis, *Blues Legacies and Black Feminism*, 163, 165, 163.

55. Quoted in Gillespie, *Film Blackness*, 6; Stuart Hall, "New Ethnicities," in *Stuart Hall*, 443.

56. Gillespie, *Film Blackness*, 158, 155, 6. This argument resonates with those of other scholars. See, for example, Johnson, "Black"; Wright, *Physics of Blackness*. Thank you to Shana Redmond for pointing me to these works.

57. Iyer, "5 Expansive Wadada Leo Smith Recordings." The word *ankhrasmation* combines the Egyptian word for "vital life force" (*ankh*), the Amharic word for "head" or "father" (*ras*), and a word for "mother" (*ma*).

58. All the quotes in this paragraph can be found in West, "What I Am Interested in Is Sound."

59. Lordi writes this about O'Meally and Griffin, and I consider her work to offer a contribution toward the same end (*Black Resonance*, 9).

60. The sixty-year timeframe spans Marian Anderson's 1955 Metropolitan Opera debut to 2015.

61. Others have addressed the political aspect of listening, including Bickford, *The Dissonance of Democracy*; Bretherton, *Christianity and Contemporary Politics*; Cusick, "'You Are in a Place That Is Out of the World'"; Dobson, *Listening for Democracy*; Goodman, *Sonic Warfare*; Lacey, *Listening Publics*; McDermott, and Bird, *Beyond the Silence*; Muers, *Keeping God's Silence*; Schmidt, *Hearing Things*.

62. I return to a more in-depth discussion of Peirce in chapter 1.

63. Sterne, *The Audible Past*, 137–78; Du Bois, *The Souls of Black Folk*, 2.

64. Butler, *Gender Trouble* and *Bodies That Matter*; Mauss, "Body Techniques," 104, 121; Foucault, *Discipline and Punish*; Bruner, "Narrative Construction of Reality"; Haraway, "Situated Knowledge"; Schechner, *Performance Studies*.

65. Carpenter, *Coloring Whiteness*, 195.

66. Moten, *In the Break*.

67. Brooks, "'All That You Can't Leave Behind'"; Brooks, "Bring the Pain"; Brooks,

"Nina Simone's Triple Play"; Stoever, *The Sonic Color Line*; Wald, *It's Been Beautiful*. Echoing Moten (*In the Break*), while we share the approach of listening "in the break," my work diverges from theirs (including Moten's) in that I do not believe I can convey a more fine-grained story beyond tracing sounds and actions to their intermaterial vibrational node or performance and the perception and reception of that node, and observing that meaning is drawn. I also note that this meaning is recirculated into intermaterial vibrational practices but do my best to resist the urge to add another version to the mix.

68. Kun, *Audiotopia*, 25.

69. Du Bois, *The Souls of Black Folk*, 2.

70. As I do not parse the historically situated meaning of F-sharp, I also do not carry out historiographic readings of terms and concepts such as "black voice" and "white voice." This book addresses the contextual dependency of meaning: as given pitches do not hold the same meaning across historical times and contexts, coding held within descriptions of voices are not static. While some readers will certainly think a book on voice and race should provide a detailed breakdown of the historic specificity of a vocal category's coding, and I agree this is very necessary, I see as my main task in this particular book to establish the broader concept that people listen to vocal timbre according to racial categories.

71. This resembles Peter Szendy's chapter "Listening (to Listening): The Making of the Modern Ear," in *Listen*, 99–128.

72. Vocal fry goes under a number of other terms, including pulse register, laryngealization, pulse phonation, creak, popcorning, glottal fry, glottal rattle, glottal scrape, strohbass, irregular phonation, and evaluations such as an "epidemiological prevalence of vocal fry in young speakers" and vocal fry's "potential hazards" to vocal health (Wolk et al., "Habitual Use of Vocal Fry in Young Adult Female Speakers," e115). See also, for example, Blomgren et al., "Acoustic, Aerodynamic, Physiologic, and Perceptual Properties of Modal and Vocal Fry Registers"; Hollien et al., "On the Nature of Vocal Fry."

73. In the symbolic position, vocal fry would be considered in terms of its meaning and signaling, including its gendered and generational dimensions.

74. Within the disciplinary tradition of theater, Konstantinos Thomaidos probes "the role of voice in contemporary practice as research (PaR) in the performing arts" ("The Re-vocalization of Logos?," 10).

75. I echo Alexandra T. Vazquez's phrase from the title of her insightful book *Listening in Detail*.

76. Lott, *Love and Theft*.

77. Brooks, "'This Voice Which Is Not One,'" 38.

78. Radano, "The Sound of Racial Feeling," 126.

79. Radano, "The Sound of Racial Feeling," 129.

80. Spivak and Rooney, "In a Word"; Muñoz, *Disidentifications*.

81. I echo Shana Redmond here. Her opening line in *Anthem* is "Music is a method."

82. Cavarero, *For More Than One Voice*.

83. See Alisha Lola Jones, "Singing High: Countertenors, Treble Timbre, and Transcendence," in Eidsheim and Meizel, *Oxford Handbook of Voice Studies*.

1. *Clifford v. Commonwealth of Kentucky,* 7 S.W.3d (Ky. 1999), 371.

2. Foucault, *Discipline and Punish,* 136.

3. Marcel Mauss, "Body Techniques," in *Sociology and Psychology,* 104, 121.

4. Sterne, *The Audible Past,* 13.

5. Hutcheon and Hutcheon, *Bodily Charm,* 123. For a detailed discussion of recognition, see the introduction to Bloechl et al., *Rethinking Difference in Music Scholarship,* 1–52.

6. As a classical singer, I trained in music conservatories in Norway and Denmark and took voice lessons in New York for five years. I then moved to Los Angeles and subsequently to San Diego, and in both places I participated in higher education vocal training communities. While I am still a member of these communities, I discontinued taking and giving lessons in 2007, so my account of sixteen years ends at that point.

7. Most of the interviews took place in teachers' private studios. In one case the interview was conducted in a coffee shop, and on one occasion the interview took place by telephone. I conducted the interviews during the 2005–6 academic year, enabled in part by the UCSD Center for Study of Race and Ethnicity's Chicano/Latino Studies and Ethnic Studies Summer Fellowship.

8. My participation in and knowledge of classical vocal communities is specific to the places and times I've noted. My observations have also been affected by what I, and my life circumstances, brought to the scene. My knowledge about vocality in the classical vocal world is broadly informed by the attitudes I have observed in response to others' and my own visual presentation, accent within the context of the English-speaking United States, and vocal school—Korean, Norwegian, and Scandinavian, respectively. In this chapter I limit my inquiry to the specific observations made by the voice teachers I interviewed. As such, I do not purport to make broad statements about voice teachers per se. While some readers may find my interviewees' observations extreme or at least out of the ordinary, based on my many years as a participant observer, they did not strike me as outliers—neither as statements by voice teachers nor as statements that might be made by the general public. Therefore, while these specific case studies come from the world of classical vocal practice, my observations here are much broader in both application and ramification.

9. I use pseudonyms throughout to refer to voice teachers and students who participated in this research. Words used by voice teacher identified as Allison in this chapter, interview with the author, Sept. 1, 2005.

10. Allison, interview.

11. I use the word "diagnosis" in a loose way here, but with a wink toward the porous boundaries between a voice teacher's aesthetic and medical listening. Because the body is the singer's instrument, it is more common for voice teachers and students to discuss overall health issues, offer health advice, and refer students to be examined by specific medical doctors, than in teacher-student relationships I have observed around other instrument learning in music conservatory environments. I make this observation based on personal and anecdotal experience. Additionally, otolaryngologists, who mainly

serve people who are not professionally dependent on their voices, stress general body care (hydration, healthy work environment, avoiding drugs, treating gastroesophageal reflux, etc.) in their work on vocal health, which also goes by the term "vocal hygiene."

12. Voice teacher identified as Dorothy in this chapter, interview with author, June 20, 2005.

13. What may produce an Armenian or Korean versus an American sound? The question is asked here within the context of the United States. While a distinct timbre might be attributed to the singer's mother tongue, this timbre is also believed to be retained when singers sing in other languages. More important, I have not heard this observation regarding vocal health made about singers who appear to be European American. The parallel between Armenian Americans (who may or may not share Armenian as their first language) and European Americans is that both sing in foreign languages—say, Italian—but the connection between vocal health and ethnicity is made only in regard to those appearing as Armenian American.

14. Marius Schneider, "Primitive Music," in Wellesz, *The New Oxford History of Music*, 42.

15. Merriam and Merriam, *The Anthropology of Music*, 255.

16. Schneider, "Primitive Music," 27.

17. Their rhetoric also evidences similar assumptions about nationality and ethnicity, but the scope of this chapter only allows for a discussion of race.

18. The early twentieth-century teacher-student relationship between the Chinese American Vaudevillian Lee Tung Foo and his voice teacher Margaret Blake Alverson captures this dynamic. Theirs was a relationship that "broke racial barriers but never transcended their limits" (Moon, "Lee Tung Foo and the Making of a Chinese American Vaudevillian," 23). See also Alverson's own account of the story in Margaret Blake Alverson, "Lee Tung Foo," in *Sixty Years of California Song*, 161–66.

19. Potter, *Vocal Authority*, 54.

20. While past pedagogical texts connected race and vocal timbre, some current respected pedagogical texts do not. For my in-depth discussion of racial formation in classical vocal training, see Eidsheim, "Voice as Action." For the latter, see Potter, *Vocal Authority*, 47.

21. Miller, *Solutions for Singers*; Leslie Rubenstein, "Oriental Musicians Come of Age," *New York Times*, November 23, 1989; Miller, *National Schools of Singing*, 220.

22. For a thorough discussion of this concept, see Eidsheim, *Sensing Sound*.

23. The assessments here, in terms of gender, are infinitely complex. Why is it left unexamined whether the voice in question could even be the sound of a male imitating a female voice? Or, indeed, a female impersonating a man's voice, a child's, an animal's, and so on?

24. "Nader: Obama Trying to 'Talk White' and 'Appeal to White Guilt,'" *Huffington Post*, July 7, 2008, http://www.huffingtonpost.com/2008/06/25/nader-obama-trying -to-tal_n_109085.html/.

25. Merton, "The Self-Fulfilling Prophecy."

26. This phrase is close to Steven Goodman's phrase "the micropolitics of frequency" (*Sonic Warfare*, 187). While Goodman's terminology is useful, I do have some strong

reservations about it, as I understand the term and concept of "frequency" to imply stability—akin to the figure of sound. I discuss this further in *Sensing Sound*.

27. What is now referred to as the international style of singing is based in the Italian bel canto school, but is also flexible enough to be well received in several other regions of the world. Indeed, the "international school of singing" generally refers to the style practiced by singers who travel among the most prominent world opera stages.

28. Richard Miller notes that, although there are recognizable national tonal preferences and techniques, no nation exhibits monolithic conformity. He estimates that over half of the teachers within a given national school adhere to the national tonal preference, while the remaining singers and teachers are devoted to international practices (*National Schools*, xix). Tone preference is also influenced by teacher migration and relocation. For example, many German teachers associate themselves with the historic international Italianate School as a result of the legacy of the master vocal pedagogue G. B. Lamperti, an Italian expatriate who taught in Munich. For more on voice teacher genealogy, see Sampson, "Operatic Artifacts."

29. In addition one's preference for a particular repertoire can affect the sound of one's voice, as the repertoire's method of "setting the voice" and demanding certain techniques from it will shape the voice.

30. A vocal onset is the way a singer performs the beginning of a musical phrase. This may be accomplished with an attack or by "easing" more softly into the note. To those unfamiliar with vocal technique this might not seem like such a radical difference, but for vocal pedagogues and singers it is very important. Listeners who are not voice professionals might not consciously register these different onset practices, but attentive listeners can develop an awareness of an overall difference in the sound.

31. In contrast, there is the Nordic "soft" onset, wherein airflow precedes sound; the German *weicher Einsatz* (whisper onset), a reaction against the earlier *Sprenginsatz* (hard onset), and so on (Miller, *National Schools*, xix–xx).

32. For a discussion of the concept of vocal work see Schlichter, "Un/Voicing the Self."

33. Goodman, *Sonic Warfare*, 189–94.

34. When we move beyond monosensory ideas of music, we easily sense the "cracks" in these beliefs (Eidsheim, *Sensing Sound*).

35. See Stoever-Ackerman, "Splicing the Sonic-Color-Line" and "Reproducing U.S. Citizenship in *Blackboard Jungle*," for fuller definitions of the term *listening ear*.

36. Aronowitz and Giroux, *Education under Siege*.

37. We can address this from an intensely material point of view. See Eidsheim, *Sensing Sound*; Moten, *In the Break*; Stras, "The Organ of the Soul."

38. The "work" carried out through the FoS becomes clear when we consider it in contrast to multisensorial listening.

39. *Clifford v. Commonwealth of Kentucky*, 371.

40. *Clifford v. Commonwealth of Kentucky*, 375–76.

41. Of course much of the hermeneutic work that is carried out deconstructs the process of interpretation through interpretation itself. While much of that work is invaluable to understanding the process of racial construction, the challenge remains in

areas that cannot easily undergo hermeneutic analysis, including certain aspects of vocal timbre and categories that, due to their naturalization, are impenetrable to any kind of critical analysis.

42. Doyle, *Hold It Against Me*, 94–95.

2. PHANTOM GENEALOGY

1. Quoted in Burroughs, "Indian Summer," 61.

2. Olin Downes, "A Door Opens: Marian Anderson's Engagement by 'Met' Should Help Other Negro Singers," *New York Times*, October 17, 1954.

3. There are, of course, operas written in the United States in which the libretto is in American English; however, the core of the repertoire and certainly its historical roots are European.

4. Singers often acknowledge their teacher's genealogy as others point to their family tree or academic mentor. For a network analysis of voice teachers and their students, see Sampson, "Operatic Artifacts."

5. Moten, *In the Break*.

6. Kimberlé Crenshaw, "Why Intersectionality Can't Wait," *Washington Post*, September 24, 2015, https://www.washingtonpost.com/news/in-theory/wp/2015/09/24/why-intersectionality-cant-wait/?utm_term=.f36a372254ab. Crenshaw's formulation in this opinion piece was especially clear, and I use it here. The full sentence: "Intersectionality, then, was my attempt to make feminism, anti-racist activism, and anti-discrimination law do what I thought they should—highlight the multiple avenues through which racial and gender oppression were experienced so that the problems would be easier to discuss and understand." To read the detailed discussion in which she introduces her analytical framework of intersectionality, see Crenshaw, "Mapping the Margins."

7. Piekut, "Actor-Networks in Music History," 192. Piekut notes that, within such an analytical framework, it is helpful to consider music in regard to "the extent to which it requires collaborators in order to touch the world, each irreducible to the next—molecules that transfer energy and vibrate in concert; enzymes that produce feelings of anticipation, release, and pleasure; technologies of writing, print, phonography, amplification, and digitality to extend the 'here and now' to the 'there and then'; instruments that are themselves tangles of labour, craft, and materials; human or machine performers that render text or code into event; archives and repertoires that extend cultural meaning historically; corporeal protocols that discipline the performing body; and finally the regimes of material-semiotic meaning that condition each sounding and make it significant" (191).

8. Piekut, "Actor-Networks in Music History," 191.

9. Piekut, "Actor-Networks in Music History," 191.

10. Bernheimer, "Yes, but Are We Really Colour Deaf?," 759; Stoever, "The Contours of the Sonic Color-Line"; Smith, *Vocal Tracks*, 136.

11. This relates loosely to Joanna Demers's explanation of thought fiction in music—a notion that is untrue but nonetheless produces real effects. Demers, "Musical

Fictions: Hegelian Conditions for the Possibility of Musical Thought," unpublished manuscript.

12. Barg, "Black Voice/White Sounds."

13. Oby, *Equity in Operatic Casting*. See also Shirley, "The Black Performer."

14. George Shirley, "Il Rodolfo Nero, or The Masque of Blackness," in André et al., *Blackness in Opera*, 260–74.

15. Naomi André, "From Otello to Porgy: Blackness, Masculinity, and Morality in Opera," in André et al., *Blackness in Opera*, 11–31.

16. The concept of voice as essence has been critiqued thoroughly, including by Bergeron, *Voice Lessons*; Cusick, "On Musical Performances of Gender and Sex"; Eidsheim, *Sensing Sound*; Ochoa Gautier, *Aurality*; Kreiman and Sidtis, *Foundations of Voice Studies*; Meizel, "A Powerful Voice"; Schlichter, "Un/Voicing the Self"; Weidman, *Singing the Classical*.

Richard Powers's radiant novel *In the Time of Our Singing* powerfully portrays the personal triumphs and tragedies of an American mixed-race family, as they intersect with those of the nation from 1955 to 1992. Whereas music and singing bind the entire family together through the upbringing of three children, the oldest son is an exceptionally gifted singer who trains at Juilliard and goes on to an international career with his brother as accompanist. The book sensitively portrays the hardships that might have been experienced by any interracial family in mid-twentieth-century America, and it also vividly conveys the particular complexities experienced by the oldest son, who is perceived as black (although he is also half German Jewish), while undertaking training and pursuing a career as a classical singer.

While eldest son Jonah's brilliant New York debut is described by the book's narrator, his younger brother and accompanist, Joseph, as transcendent—beyond time and race—the fictional *New York Times* reviewer could not but cap an otherwise congratulatory review by concluding that Jonah was "one of the finest Negro recitalists this country has ever produced." When Jonah finally receives an offer from the Metropolitan Opera, it is in the role of a nameless "Negro" in a contemporary production. Discouraged, he leaves for Europe, where he enjoys a successful career as a tenor. But it is when Jonah enters the world of early music, a movement then in its infancy, that he is able to experience a (musical) era predating the racial discord experienced by his Jewish father before he fled Europe and endured by his African American mother and their interracial family.

Voice lessons, vocal anatomy, and musical form are described in the minutest and most accurate detail. (As a person trained in the classical vocal tradition I recognized every intrigue and technical point.)

17. While identification of race in relation to popular music genres is entangled in racial stereotypes, it is not completely arbitrary. (The music industry has worked to create links between race and genre for marketing purposes.) For a discussion of genre and race in contemporary musical life, see Brackett, "Questions of Genre in Black Popular Music."

18. Jonathan Greenberg provides an interesting discussion of three phonemes with strong racial (black) and geographic connotations, and Ethel Waters's manipulation of these phonemes and related racial expectations ("Singing Up Close," 200–247).

19. Language acquisition is an integral part of voice training. In addition, singers learn the International Phonetic Alphabet in order to read, transcribe, and reproduce the phonetic realization of any language.

20. In brief, timbre refers both to the overall sound that enables us to distinguish one instrument from another, and to the different sounds within a single instrument. This composite sound is made up of different partials, or frequencies. In classical vocal production a concentration of partials around 3,000 Hz—known as the singer's formant—is favored. This creates the characteristic "ring" in the voice (the intense "core") and enables it to cut through and be heard over the massive sound of a symphony orchestra. Many vocal pedagogical texts feature in-depth discussions of the physics and vocal training that go into its production. Two classic texts are Sundberg, *The Science of the Singing Voice*, and Vennard, *Singing*.

21. Quoted in Brooks and Spottswood, *Lost Sounds*, 30.

22. Quoted in Smith, *Vocal Tracks*, 135.

23. Not only is it difficult to distinguish race physically or anatomically, but it is just as difficult to distinguish a male from a female voice based on a given vocal apparatus. This suggests that much of the difference between male and female voices is acquired. See Cusick, "On Musical Performances of Gender and Sex"; Eidsheim, "Voice as a Technology of Selfhood," 1–27, 20–66.

24. One of the most exciting additions to the American opera scene is the National Grand Finals winner of the 2011 Metropolitan Opera National Council Audition, Ryan Speedo Green. Green later appeared at the Metropolitan Opera and New York City Opera and in Europe. To his memoirist, Green recounts the many painful moments he experienced as an African American opera singer. Central among them were the times he was asked to sing "Ol' Man River." Not only did performing that song force him to perform an inferior position, but the request arose within a structural situation in which people of privilege asked a less-privileged person to perform a certain position within the U.S. racial hierarchy. See Bergner, *Sing for Your Life*, 196–201.

25. Later in life, during her time in England, she was invited to study with Sir George Smart, the queen's organist and music director. LeBrew, *The Black Swan*, 18.

26. In his discussion of recording media's influence on the voice, Jacob Smith cites both class and technology as reasons why minstrel, folk, and traditional material were sung and recorded by operatic voices. For the former, Smith draws on Robert Toll's *Blacking Up*, writing, "Minstrel troupes such as the Ethiopian Serenaders 'sought the respectability of "high" culture'" (*Vocal Tracks*, 141), and William Howland Kinney's *Recorded Music in American Life*, which argued that folk material was sung with an operatic approach because of the prominence of European classical music on the phonograph market. Black voices—because of their "sharpness or harshness that the white man's has not" (quoted in Smith, *Vocal Tracks*, 136)—were thought to be better suited for recording. This could not, however, have been believed in earnest, as most minstrel recording artists were white. According to Smith, only George Washington Johnson and Bert Williams were substantially recorded and widely distributed during this era.

27. Naomi André, Karen M. Bryan, and Eric Saylor, "Introduction: Representing Blackness on the Operatic Stage," in André et al., *Blackness in Opera*, 3.

28. Story, *And So I Sing*, 21.

29. Review, *New York Herald*, April 1, 1854, quoted in Lawrence and Strong, *Strong on Music*, 413.

30. Greenfield also received letters from supporters with detailed advice "respecting [her] dress." One recommendation was to dress with "great modesty and with much simplicity" and goes into details: "Wear nothing in your hair, unless it be a cluster of white flowers in the back; never wear *coloured* flowers, nor flowing ribbons. Let your dress be a plain black silk, high at the back of the neck, and open in the front about half way to the waist: under this, wear a square of lace, tarltan [*sic*], or muslin, doubled and laid in folds to cross over the breast." The letter continues another two long paragraphs and is signed "Your friend, E.S.M." Quoted in Young, *The Black Swan at Home and Abroad*, 11.

31. Quotations from Story, *And So I Sing*, 23, 25.

32. Chybowski, "The 'Black Swan' in England." On the topic of British audiences, Chybowski writes, "Audiences went to Greenfield's performances looking and listening for what they expected based on Greenfield's former slave identity—an untrained musicality that accentuated the bodily aspects of the voices as the natural human instrument. Reviews of Greenfield's performance characterize her voice as 'wholly natural,' and as 'lacking the training and exquisite cultivation that belongs to the skillful Italian singer'" (15).

33. Both quotations from Chybowski, "The 'Black Swan' in England," 4.

34. The linguist D. L. Rubin forcefully demonstrates that nonsonic information plays a crucial role in how we perceive voices and determine racial identities in general. Asked to rate the comprehensibility and intelligence of a lecture recorded by a native speaker of American English, paired with a photo of either an Asian-looking or a Caucasian-looking lecturer, listeners gave lower ratings to the recording paired with the Asian-looking lecturer. Since the same recording accompanied both photos, researchers concluded that the listeners expected the Asian-looking lecturer to speak in accented, simplified English and therefore heard her speech that way. See Rubin, "Nonlanguage Factors Affecting Undergraduates' Judgments of Nonnative English-Speaking Teaching Assistants."

35. Quoted in Trotter, *Music and Some Highly Musical People*, 78.

36. Quoted in Graziano, "The Early Life and Career of the 'Black Patti,'" 571. For a number of those reviews, see 543–96; Trotter, *Music and Some Highly Musical People*, 66–87.

37. Graziano, "The Early Life and Career of the 'Black Patti,'" 565. For a list of Jones's repertoire, see 589–91.

38. Smith, *Vocal Tracks*, 154, 140–41.

39. Graziano, "The Early Life and Career of the 'Black Patti,'" 568.

40. Graziano, "The Early Life and Career of the 'Black Patti,'" 587.

41. In 1889 Jones performed with the Georgia Minstrels at Dockstader's Theater in New York. Graziano provides an astute analysis of the reasons Jones returned to minstrelsy ("The Early Life and Career of the 'Black Patti,'" 585–89).

42. *New York Dramatic Mirror*, January 11, 1896.

43. Lott, *Love and Theft*, 235.

44. Cruz, *Culture on the Margins*, 3.

45. Cruz, *Culture on the Margins*, 1, 119.

46. Cruz, *Culture on the Margins*, 4, 7.

47. "Amusements," *New York Times*, January 31, 1875, quoted in Stoever, "Contours of the Sonic Color-Line," 1.

48. Review, February 2, 1875, quoted in Stoever, "Contours of the Sonic Color-Line," 8.

49. Chybowski, "The 'Black Swan' in England," 14.

50. Review, *Chicago Tribune*, January 8, 1893.

51. "Negroes as Singers," *Washington Post*, April 25, 1903, quoted in Smith, *Vocal Tracks*, 136.

52. Barg, "Black Voice/White Sounds," 123.

53. Vechten, "A Few Notes about *Four Saints in Three Acts*," 7.

54. "Stein Opera Sung by All-Negro Cast," *New York Times*, February 9, 1934.

55. Thomson, *Virgil Thomson*, 217.

56. Stein, *Everybody's Autobiography*, 278.

57. Barthes, "The Grain of the Voice."

58. Barg, "Black Voice/White Sounds," 151.

59. Review, *New York Times*, February 9, 1934.

60. John Mason Brown, review, *New York Evening Post*, February 21, 1934.

61. W. J. Henderson, "American Opera Keeps Struggling," *American Mercury* (May 1934): 104–5.

62. F.P.A., *Herald Tribune*, February 22, 1934, quoted in Watson, *Prepare for Saints*, 344.

63. Thomson, *Four Saints in Three Acts*, 47.

64. Interview in *Aida's Brothers and Sisters*, directed by Jan Schmidt-Garre and Marieke Schroeder (West Long Branch, NJ: Kultur Video, 2000), VHS.

65. Oby, *Equity in Operatic Casting*.

66. Story, *And So I Sing*, 183–84.

67. Interview in *Aida's Brothers and Sisters*. However, Bobby McFerrin, the singer, composer, conductor, and son of Robert McFerrin, the first African American to sing at the Metropolitan Opera, believes that Gershwin should be applauded for his *attempt* at creating an African American story. Interview in *Aida's Brothers and Sisters*.

68. Anderson, *My Lord, What a Morning*; Keiler, *Marian Anderson*; Jones, *Marian Anderson*.

69. Quoted in Keiler, *Marian Anderson*, 30.

70. Keiler, *Marian Anderson*, 47–48.

71. London seemed friendlier for blacks. Anderson's longtime friend and informal mentor Roland Hayes had experienced great success there a few years earlier, including performing for the king and queen. Keiler, *Marian Anderson*, 68.

72. Reviews, *London Times*, June 16, 1928, quoted in Keiler, *Marian Anderson*, 79, 80.

73. See Keiler, *Marian Anderson*, 78; Cook, "The Negro Spiritual Goes to France," 48.

74. Sheean, *Between the Thunder and the Sun*, 25.

75. For a list of Anderson's repertoire, see Keiler, *Marian Anderson*, 337–52.

76. Keiler, *Marian Anderson*, 166.

77. Anderson's longtime accompanist Kosti Vehanen recorded Toscanini's remark (Vehanen and Barnett, *Marian Anderson*, 130). Donald Bogle is quoted in Turner, "Marian Anderson," 18. Bogle and Keiler regretted that Anderson's artistic achievements were dwarfed by her image as a "tattered social symbol" (Bogle, quoted in Turner, "Marian Anderson," 18; Keiler, *Marian Anderson*, 7).

78. Quoted in Bernheimer, "Yes, but Are We Really Colour Deaf?," 759–60. For a discussion about the visual descriptive language of voices of singers, see Eidsheim, "Voice as a Technology of Selfhood."

79. Quoted in Bernheimer, "Yes, but Are We Really Colour Deaf?," 760.

80. Adam Bernstein, "Robert McFerrin Sr. Was First Black Man to Sing with the Met," *Washington Post*, November 29, 2006, http://www.washingtonpost.com/wp -dyn/content/article/2006/11/28/AR2006112801534.html. McFerrin went on to do some work in Hollywood, including vocals for Sidney Poitier in the 1959 movie version of *Porgy and Bess*.

81. Story, *And So I Sing*, 184.

82. Haggin, *Music and Ballet*, 105–6. In 2004 the Royal Opera House famously fired the American soprano Deborah Voigt from the role of Ariadne. Having lost a substantial amount of weight, she has been singing with critical acclaim for several major opera houses in the United States and was rehired by the Royal Opera House. However, some critics wondered whether her weight loss had led to her "vocal decline." Peter Davis, "Deborah Voigt's New Problem," *New York*, May 1, 2006, http://nymag.com/art /classicaldance/classical/reviews/16855/.

83. Fay, *The Ring*, 61. Estes later sang Wotan in Berlin to favorable criticism.

84. As was the case with Hope Briggs, mentioned below.

85. Story, *And So I Sing*, 189.

86. Over the past several years—arguably due to practices such as the Metropolitan Opera's *Live in HD* video simulcast, which features close-up shots of singers—some of this seems to have changed. The case of Deborah Voigt's highly publicized firing from the Royal Opera House also suggests that there have been some changes in this regard. While the Royal Opera's spokesman, Christopher Millard, declined during a *New York Times* interview "to say whether weight was the main reason for the decision to replace Ms. Voigt," Voigt explained that the company had "sacked her for being too fat to fit into the little black dress" worn by Ariadne in Richard Strauss's opera *Ariadne auf Naxos*. In her autobiography, she notes that Luciano Pavarotti was often lauded for his "huggable, teddy-bear roundness." See Robin Pogrebin, "Soprano Says Her Weight Cost Her Role in London," *New York Times*, March 9, 2004, http://www.nytimes .com/2004/03/09/arts/music/09VOIG.html.

87. Story, *And So I Sing*, 189.

88. The expatriate Jessye Norman seems to be an exception, with much more of her idiosyncratic repertoire independently selected, compared to any other opera star of her caliber.

89. For more on Hope Briggs's 2007 dismissal from the San Francisco opera, see Eidsheim, "Marian Anderson and 'Sonic Blackness' in American Opera."

90. Interview in *Aida's Brothers and Sisters*.

91. In this period, vocal expectations in popular media such as radio were similar, William Barlow observes:

> Candidates for black roles in comedy or variety series had to demonstrate that they could speak "Negro dialect" as defined, and in some cases even taught to them, by white entertainers and scriptwriters. As a result, African Americans were routinely rejected for black radio roles because, as one frustrated actress stated, "I have been told repeatedly that I don't sound like a Negro." The few black entertainers actually hired for roles endured a ridiculous ordeal of instruction. Lillian Randolf, for instance, spent three months working on her racial accent under the tutelage of James Jewel, the white originator of *The Lone Ranger* radio show, before she was finally hired for a role in his *Lulu and Leander* series on WXZ in Detroit, Michigan. Johnny Lee, a black comic on *The Slick and Slim Show* on WHN in New York City, complained: "I had to learn to talk as white people believed Negroes talked in order to get the job." This situation persisted well into the 1940s. Actor Frederick O'Neal, who portrayed a character in the *Beulah* radio series during the war years, recalled: "After I appeared on the *Beulah* program several times, the producer insisted that I use more dialect in my speech." And as late as 1947, Wonderful Smith, a popular African American comedian with *The Red Skelton Show*, was fired by the series producers because, in Smith's words, "I had difficulty sounding as Negroid as they expected.'" (Barlow, *Voice Over*, 30–31)

92. In "The Paradox of Timbre," Cornelia Fales has elucidated the question of timbre and listener projection of what is sounded. In her discussion of the "whispered inanga" musicians of Burundi, she concludes that listeners project the hearing of a melodic line that in fact is not sounded.

93. For a thorough discussion of vocal timbre, race, physiology, and training, see Eidsheim, "Voice as a Technology of Selfhood," 1–27, 30–66.

94. Piekut, "Actor-Networks in Music History," 193.

95. This resonates with Eric Drott's ideas about genre in "The End(s) of Genre."

96. Cruz, *Culture on the Margins*, 1.

97. Turner, "Marian Anderson," 17; Downes, "A Door Opens."

98. Henderson, "Minstrelsy, American."

3. FAMILIARITY AS STRANGENESS

1. We also use voice categories such as boy soprano and female tenor. But in this very common formal presentation of voices, males occupy the bottom pitch range and females the upper.

2. From infancy to puberty, boys' and girls' voices are similar due to similar thyroid cartilage angle and vocal fold length. If we compare prepubescent boys and girls, there are no statistically significant physiological differences in terms of laryngeal size or the

overall vocal tract length (Kreiman and Sidtis, *Foundations of Voice Studies*, 110–16). (There are of course individual variations between voices.) Babies' larynxes are placed high in the neck, fibers are underdeveloped, "tissue layers are not differentiated, and there is no vocal ligament" (112). Everything from the size of the tongue relative to the vocal cavities, a lack of teeth, an immature respiratory system, and so on contributes to what we identify as an infant vocal sound. Between birth and puberty all of these areas gradually mature at a similar rate for boys and girls. However, when considering the acoustic signal, scientists (and the average listener) often observe differences. Specifically "by age seven or eight, boys have consistently lower formant frequency than girls" (113). Summarizing Vorperian, Jody Kreiman and Diana Sidtis observe that "existing physiological data do not completely explain this difference in formant frequencies, because sex-dependent differences in overall vocal tract length do not exist for these young children" (113; Vorperian et al., "Development of Vocal Tract Length during Early Childhood"). This difference, then, must at this point be attributed to the performance of gender.

For both men and women, voices undergo growth and maturation and generally do not reach a fully mature state until about twenty-one years of age. Aging also contributes to vocal change. For example, from birth to older age, the larynx gradually moves from the third or fourth vertebrae position to the fifth at adulthood but continues to lower throughout one's lifetime. In fact physical divergence between male and female voices is set in motion between the ages of eleven and fourteen, with pubescent boys' vocal growth. The cracking we hear during that "voice change" is the challenge of navigating a vocal instrument that changes overnight and within which different parts, for a period of time, are not optimally coordinated. The female voice also grows considerably, and vocal folds can grow up to 34 percent in length, reaching an adult size of 12 to 21 mm and a vocal tract average of 144 mm in length. The male vocal folds can grow up to 60 percent in length, reaching an adult length of 17 to 29 mm and a vocal tract average of 156 mm in length (Kreiman and Sidtis, *Foundations of Voice Studies*, 113–14). Discussions and perceptions of female and male voices focus inordinately on differences, to the detriment of understanding similarities—in the realm of both the physical and the performative.

3. Guillory, "Black Bodies Swingin'."

4. Richard Williams, "Jimmy Scott Obituary," *Guardian*, June 15, 2014, http:// www.theguardian.com/music/2014/jun/15/jimmy-scott; Matt Schudel, "Jimmy Scott, Hard-Luck Singer with a Haunting Voice, Dies at 88," *Washington Post*, June 13, 2014, https://www.washingtonpost.com/entertainment/music/jimmy-scott-hard-luck-singer -with-a-haunting-voice-dies-at-88/2014/06/13/270725b6-48c3-11e3-a196-3544a03c2351 _story.html?utm_term=.4a251becb00a; Peter Kepnews, "Jimmy Scott, Singer Whose Star Rose Late, Dies at 88," *New York Times*, June 13, 2014, http://www.nytimes.com /2014/06/14/arts/music/jimmy-scott-singer-whose-star-rose-late-dies-at-88.html.

5. David Ritz, "The Triumph of Jimmy Scott (1925–2014)," *Rolling Stone*, June 16, 2014, https://www.rollingstone.com/music/news/the-triumph-of-jimmy-scott-1925 -2014-20140616.

6. For further biographical information, see *Jimmy Scott: If You Only Knew*, directed

by Matthew Buzzell (Los Angeles: Rhino Home Video, 2000), DVD; Ritz, *Faith in Time*; *Little Jimmy Scott: Why Was I Born?*, directed by Melodic McDaniel (Bravo Profiles, Jazz Masters, 1998), DVD; Joseph Hooper, "The Ballad of Little Jimmy Scott," *New York Times*, August 27, 2000, http://www.nytimes.com/2000/08/27/magazine/the-ballad-of-little-jimmy-scott.html.

7. Affecting 1 in 10,000 to 86,000 people and occurring more frequently in males than in females, Kallmann syndrome is characterized by delayed or absent puberty and an impaired sense of smell. A form of hypogonadotropic hypogonadism, the condition affects the production of hormones that control sexual development. The results in males include being born with an unusually small penis (micropenis) and undescended testes (cryptorchidism). Later symptoms include failure to develop secondary sex characteristics, including facial hair growth and deepening of the voice in males, or no menstruation and little or no breast development in females. For others affected by Kallmann syndrome, puberty is incomplete or delayed. Additional features vary, including within the same family. For further information, see Neil Smith and Richard Quinton, "A Patient's Journey: Kallmann Syndrome," *British Medical Journal* 2012;345:e6971; U.S. National Library of Medicine, "Kallmann Syndrome," accessed March 13, 2015, http://ghr.nlm.nih.gov/condition/kallmann-syndrome; and the Kallmann Syndrome Organization homepage, accessed March 13, 2015, http://www.kallmanns.org.

8. Scott stopped growing at the height of four feet eleven. At the age of thirty-four, due to what his physician referred to as "delayed hormonal development," Scott grew over a few months to five feet six. His voice did not seem to have been affected (Ritz, *Faith in Time*, 119).

9. Ritz, *Faith in Time*, 16.

10. Ritz, *Faith in Time*, 29, 31.

11. Ritz, *Faith in Time*, 32.

12. See Ritz, *Faith in Time*, 92–98, for a discussion of the Savoy case.

13. The Jimmy Scott page on the website Artists Only, accessed August 1, 2007, www.artistsonly.com/scothm.htm.

14. Although both Scott's challenges and successes may be attributed in part to his hormonally affected voice—arguably the closest modern equivalent to the sound of the castrato—the depth of his musical artistry is evident in his distinctive timbre, vibrato, phrasing, and pronunciation.

15. The quote in the subheading of this section, "That Boy's Alto Voice," is from Hooper, "The Ballad of Little Jimmy Scott."

16. Ritz, *Faith in Time*, 59.

17. *Everybody's Somebody's Fool*, orchestra dir. Lionel Hampton, Decca Records 9–30412, 1957, 45 rpm.

18. Ritz, *Faith in Time*, 64–65.

19. Ritz, *Faith in Time*, 63–64.

20. Jimmy Scott, *The Source*, with Billy Butler (guitar), Bruno Carr (drums), Ron Carter (bass), et al., recorded March 3–5, 1969, Atlantic 8122–73526–2, 2001, CD; *Falling in Love Is Wonderful*, Tangerine Records, 1962, reissue by Rhino Records, 2002, CD.

It was Joe Adams, Ray Charles's manager and coproducer of the record, who came up with the cover idea.

21. Ritz, *Faith in Time*, 157–59, 133.

22. Ritz, *Faith in Time*, 158.

23. In "Black Faces, White Voices," Jeff Smith suggests that the dubbing of Dorothy Dandridge's and Harry Belafonte's voices was prompted by particular racial politics.

24. Ritz, *Faith in Time*, 132.

25. Gordon, *Monteverdi's Unruly Women*, 62–63.

26. For further discussion regarding these issues surrounding the castrato voice, see, for example, Feldman, *The Castrato*; Freitas, *Portrait of a Castrato*.

27. *Philadelphia*, directed by Jonathan Demme (Culver City, CA: Columbia TriStar Home Video, 1993), VHS.

28. If I were to analyze the music in this movie, I would carefully note the foreshadowing of the Callas aria to which Beckett listens in a much later scene, a scene that also serves to move the emotional plotline forward. In the scene, Beckett is much weaker, seated in a wheelchair, and loses himself in Callas's voice. While the musical genre is quite different, Callas was scrutinized for her use of the so-called chest voice in the lower register; hence both her voice and Scott's were timbrally othered.

29. *Twin Peaks*, "Beyond Life and Death," episode 29, directed by David Lynch, aired June 10, 1991.

30. Grey, "Black Masculinity and Visual Culture," 401.

31. Grey, "Black Masculinity and Visual Culture," 402. There are, however, new modes of black masculinity emerging today, such as the performance work of Andre 3000.

32. Hooper, "The Ballad of Little Jimmy Scott."

33. Halberstam, *In a Queer Time and Place*, 55, and "Queer Voices and Musical Genders," 190. Halberstam is careful to offer a broad definition of "transgender," explaining, "The term transgender can be used as a marker for all kinds of people who challenge, deliberately or accidentally, gender normativity" (*In a Queer Time and Place*, 55).

34. The vocal range indicates the range a given voice group should be able to sing comfortably within. In most cases singers within each voice group are able to sing either higher or lower. For a historical discussion of vocal range, see Jackson, *Performance Practice*, 456. For references given to vocal ranges, see guides for singers, choir instructors, and composers and reference works in music theory, music, and library cataloguing: Frisell, *The Baritone Voice*, 14; Mabry, *Exploring Twentieth-Century Vocal Music*, 82; Joyce et al., *Scoring for Voice*, 5; Reneau, "Determining Basic Voice Classification of High School Choir Students," 10; Miller, *The Complete Idiot's Guide to Music Theory*, 226; *The New Harvard Dictionary of Music*, s.v. "voice"; Koth, *Uniform Titles for Music*, 87.

35. Sam Cooke, vocal performance of "A Change Is Gonna Come," by Sam Cooke, rereleased 1986, on *The Man and His Music*, RCA Victor PCD1-7127, CD; Marvin Gaye, vocal performance of "Trouble Man," by Marvin Gaye, rereleased in 1994, on *Trouble Man*, Motown 31453-0097-2, CD; Roy Orbison, vocal performance of "Blue Angel," by Roy Orbison and Joe Melson, rereleased in 1988, on *For the Lonely: 18 Greatest Hits*,

Rhino R2 71493, CD; Roy Orbison, vocal performance of "Blue Bayou," by Roy Orbison and Joe Melson, rereleased in 1988, on *For the Lonely: 18 Greatest Hits*, Rhino R2 71493, CD; Smokey Robinson and the Miracles, vocal performance of "I Second That Emotion," by Smokey Robinson and Al Cleveland, rereleased February 22, 1994, on *Smokey Robinson and the Miracles: The 35th Anniversary Collection*, Motown 374-636-334-2, CD; Smokey Robinson and the Miracles, vocal performance of "Ooo Baby Baby," by Smokey Robinson and Pete Moore, rereleased February 22, 1994, on *Smokey Robinson and the Miracles: The 35th Anniversary Collection*, Motown 374-636-334-2, CD; Otis Rush, vocal performance of "I Can't Stop Baby," rereleased in 2012, on *Double Trouble*, Complete Blues SBLUECD084, CD; Swan Silvertones, vocal performance of "Brighter Day Ahead," released in 2001, on *Savior Pass Me Not*, Vee Jay COL-CD-7227, CD; The Temptations, vocal performance of "Get Ready," by Smokey Robinson, digitally remastered by This Way Productions, May 23, 1995, on *Best of the Temptations*, Motown 53 0524-2, CD; Frankie Valli and the Four Seasons, vocal performance of "Big Girls Don't Cry," by Bob Crewe and Bob Gaudio, rereleased 1988, on *Frankie Vallie and the Four Seasons: Anthology*, Rhino R2 71490, CD; Stevie Wonder, vocal performance of "Uptight," by Sylvia Moy and Henry Cosby, rereleased in 2002, on *The Definitive Collection*, Motown 440 066 164-2, CD; Stevic Wonder, vocal performance of "For Once in My Life," by Ron Miller and Orlando Murden, rereleased in 2002, on *The Definitive Collection*, Motown 440 066 164-2, CD; Scott, *The Source*.

36. This analysis is carried out in collaboration with Jody Kreiman.

37. See appendix 1 for additional detail.

38. For comparison, in *speech* the mean vocal ranges for men are around 82–164 Hz; women around 160–260 Hz; and children around 250–400 Hz. This means Scott's singing range in the three songs analyzed is comparable in the high woman or low child range, but the other examples fall comparably in the high speech range even for a child. In terms of the distributions, the performances of "Ooo Baby Baby" (Smokey Robinson) and "Big Girls Don't Cry" (Frankie Valli) have a lot of variability, with no one frequency range dominating the distribution; Scott's three songs have less variability and a clear mean; and "Trouble Man" (Marvin Gaye) is almost monotone. (See appendix 1 for additional detail.) While much of that is determined by the compositions, the different embellishments the singers use affect the distribution as well. For additional detail regarding the "contributions of fundamental frequency (F0) and formants in cuing the distinction between men's and women's voices," see Hillenbrand and Clark, "The Role of F0 and Formant Frequencies in Distinguishing the Voices of Men and Women."

39. Borsel et al., "Physical Appearance and Voice in Male-to-Female Transsexuals"; Bruin et al., "Speech Therapy in the Management of Male-to-Female Transsexuals."

40. Mount and Salmon, "Changing the Vocal Characteristics of a Post-Operative Transsexual Patient."

41. "Surgeons," Kreiman and Sidtis report, "have increased the tension in the vocal folds by surgically approximating the cricoid and thyroid cartilages; by removing part of the thyroid cartilage and the vocal folds (so that the folds are reduced in length and tension is increased); or by making a window in the thyroid cartilage and stretching the vocal folds forward, effectively moving the anterior commissure (but also accentuating the

thyroid prominence)." Moreover "attempts have also been made to alter the consistency of the fold by creating scar tissue, or to decrease the mass of the folds by stripping tissue. Finally, the front edges of the folds may be sutured together, decreasing their length and effective vibrating mass. Because FO is a primary cue to a speaker's sex, such surgical interventions may increase the perceived femininity of a voice. However, they are invasive and long-term rates are variable." They conclude that "simply increasing FO generally produces a voice that is more feminine, but not necessarily female"; indeed "voices with very high FOs may remain unambiguously male" as long as "other cues to the speaker's sex retain their male values" (*Foundations of Voice Studies*, 145).

42. Derived on the basis of an acoustical measurement, FO (the lowest periodic cycle component of the acoustic waveform) indicates the fundamental frequency of a sound; pitch is its perceived correlate. Because the two are perceptually understood very similarly, I have chosen to use the two intermittently in this book, using pitch as the default term but deferring to whichever specific form the literature I cite uses.

43. Kreiman and Sidtis, *Foundations of Voice Studies*, 133.

44. Kreiman and Sidtis, *Foundations of Voice Studies*, 145.

45. Breathy voice is a stereotype of female voice that is no longer as prevalent a vocal parameter in female singers' performances. However, invoking a stereotype can of course prove effective if intending to invoke markers of vocal femininity.

46. The length of the vocal tract during vocalization depends on the one hand on the actual length of the vocal tract, but on the other hand, on the vocal manipulations carried out by the singer—to an overwhelming degree. Hence hearing the timbral result of a short vocal tract does not necessarily mean that this vocalizer's default vocal tract is limited to that specific length.

47. "Perceptual tests showed that the utterances of the speakers who produced the greatest contrast in FO and loudness between male and female vocal production were correctly classified as male or female 99% of the time" (Kreiman and Sidtis, *Foundations of Voice Studies*, 145).

48. This summary of this literature is adapted from Kreiman and Sidtis, *Foundations of Voice Studies*, 145.

49. Kreiman and Sidtis, *Foundations of Voice Studies*, 145. They refer to Whiteside, "A Comment on Women's Speech and Its Synthesis." See also Hillenbrand and Clark, "The Role of FO and Formant Frequencies in Distinguishing the Voices of Men and Women."

50. Gelfer and Schofield also note that while it was expected that transgender individuals who were perceived to be female would be considered more feminine than transgender people who were perceived to be male, this did not seem to be the case. They hypothesize that "it is possible that the listeners had a predisposition to identify voices reading neutral, nonemotional sentences as male. That is, if a voice presented with some characteristics of a female voice and some characteristics of a male voice, listeners may have had a tendency to attend to the male characteristic and identify the voice as belonging to a male (although perhaps a feminine-sounding male)" ("Comparison of Acoustic and Perceptual Measures of Voice in Male-to-Female Transsexuals Perceived as Female versus Those Perceived as Male," 32).

51. In addition to falsetto, a particular portion of the voice could be timbrally bracketed off in a variety of ways, including by straining or breathiness. See Cusick, "On Musical Performances of Gender and Sex," for a discussion of screaming and straining as a way of performing masculinity.

52. There is a long history of male singing in a higher than expected register, falsetto being one of the vocal techniques enabling this. A broader cultural reading of falsetto is beyond this chapter, which limits its scope to establish that Scott's contemporaries sang in comparable higher pitch range yet were read as masculine. For insights on falsetto in relation to masculinity, see Mark Anthony Neal's excellent discussion in *Songs in the Key of Black Life* (47). Neal starts out by observing, "In reality the falsetto voice is the product of hypermasculine performance, be it derived from the regular Regent Mack-Daddy infomercial circuit—inspired no doubt by the original 'playa-revs' like Ike, Father Devine, and 'sweet' Daddy Grace—or the brothers flexing for real in HBO's *Pimps Up, Hoes Down*." Neal quotes Russell Simmons saying, "'High pitched falsetto, crying singers were the most ghetto. . . . For all the talk of love there was something very pimp-like, manipulative and fly about that sound.'" And, reading Robin Kelley, Neal also reminds us that "falsetto voice was part of an elaborate black oral form known as toasting." For a discussion of falsetto in relation to disco, a genre with generous use of falsetto, see Anne-Lise François, "Fakin' It/Makin' It." She describes falsetto as "the voice of exception, crisis, and interruption, if not intervention. But it is also a rhetorical deployment of difference, a staging of an otherness imposed from without by oppressive economic, racial, or gender-based structures" (445).

53. Vennard, *Singing*, 67. See also Deguchi, "Mechanism of and Threshold Biomechanical Conditions for Falsetto Voice Onset."

54. I do believe this particular way of timbrally bracketing off the higher portions of the vocal register is different from what Ollie Wilson has called "the heterogeneous sound ideal tendency" in black musical aesthetics ("Black Music as an Art Form," 3).

55. To read more about "Camille," see Hawkins and Niblock, *Prince*, 127; Morton, *Prince*, 135; and Paul Casey, "Prince's Dirty Mind," *Pop Shifter*, last modified January 30, 2012, http://popshifter.com/2012-01-30/princes-dirty-mind/2/.

56. Edgerton has also identified timbre as the parameter that makes Scott's voice "closely resemble female voices" (*The 21st-Century Voice*, 41).

57. Alisha Lola Jones, "Singing High: Countertenors, Treble Timbre, and Transcendence," in Eidsheim and Meizel, *Oxford Handbook of Voice Studies*, n.p.

58. Commentary on falsetto in gospel include Cooper, "Wade in the Water"; Williams-Jones, "Afro-American Gospel Music."

59. Jones, "Singing High." Jones reports, "Protocol competency is signified with a salutation such as one that starts with 'First, giving honor to God' or 'Praise the Lord, everybody'" (n.p.).

60. Jones, "Singing High." Narrow ideas about vocality in regard to gender generally, and in regard to masculine vocality, are of course not limited to issues around black masculinity. See, for example, Allison McCracken's analysis of Rudy Vallée and Bing Crosby in *Real Men Don't Sing*. She demonstrates that the limits set to contain crooners also ended up dictating the limits for masculinity for male singers more generally.

61. Muñoz, *Disidentifications*, 5, 6.

62. Muñoz, *Disidentifications*, 93–118.

63. Muñoz cites Félix Guattari's discussion of the Mirabelles (*Disidentifications*, 85).

64. Goffman, *Presentations of Self in Everyday Life*.

65. I echo basic semiotic theory here. See, for example, Charles S. Peirce's work on the active and defining role of "interpreting" in the triangulation of sign, object, and interpretant (*The Essential Peirce*, 478).

66. Ritz, *Faith in Time*, xv.

67. Ritz, *Faith in* Time, 57, 70.

68. Hooper, "The Ballad of Little Jimmy Scott."

69. My reading is not derived from a psychoanalytic framework, but some readers may recognize a resemblance to Kaja Silverman's notion of the acoustic mirror.

4. RACE AS ZEROS AND ONES

1. However, there are very interesting dynamics in the realm of transnational transactions around this vocal synthesis technology and its packaging, user response, and audience perception. These transnational concerns are beyond the scope of this book, and I treat them in a separate article. Additionally, while I do address later developments of the software in relation to Hatsune Miku, for an in-depth discussion of this, see Francis, "Playing with the Voice."

2. Hatsune Miku's voice bank is based on samples recorded by the well-known voice actress Saki Fujita.

3. Michael Z. McIntee, "Dave Meets Vocaloid Star Hatsune Miku—Late Show," *CBS.com*, last modified October 8, 2014, http://www.cbs.com/shows/late_show /wahoo_gazette/1003272/. See also Teolee, "Miku on Letterman."

4. Eidsheim, "Synthesizing Race."

5. The first NAMM show was held on January 13 and 14, 2004. It has evolved to become one of the major international events introducing new music products. Vocaloid was first introduced through a demo at Musikmesse in Frankfurt in March 2003 and through Zero-G's website, launched on October 23, 2003.

6. Bill Werde, "Could I Get That Song in Elvis, Please," *New York Times*, November 23, 2003, http://www.nytimes.com/2003/11/23/arts/music/23WERD.html.

7. See "Vocaloid," Roblox, accessed June 1, 2015, http://www.roblox.com/groups /group.aspx?gid=344536. I use this definition of Vocaloid as a synthesis software throughout. However, at this point, the term is understood by some as an umbrella term for a holographic singer and its ecology of sounds, repertoire, persona, fictional characters, and stories.

8. Because of the translation that must take place between the written representation of a language and its sounded version, the applications are language-specific. At this time, the Vocaloid synthesis method is used only with English and Japanese; LOLA, LEON, and MIRIAM were voiced in English.

9. As explained in notes 7 and 10, Vocaloid is not true vocal synthesis.

10. For additional detail on the Vocaloid synthesis system, see Kenmochi, "Singing Synthesis as a New Musical Instrument."

11. An electronic voice synthesis apparatus was first patented in the United States by Homer Dudley of Bell Laboratories (Homer W. Dudley, Signal transmission, U.S. Patent 2,151,091, filed October 30, 1935, and issued March 21; see also Bell Laboratories, "Pedro the Voder"). In the late 1950s Bell Labs produced several speech synthesis systems that were capable of "singing." Although too computationally intensive for commercial use as a speech synthesizer, one of these systems, created by Lochbaum and Kelly, "Speech Synthesis," in 1962, was used in a collaboration with Max Mathews to generate early examples of singing synthesis. See also Risset, *An Introductory Catalogue of Computer Synthesized Sounds*, rereleased in 1995 on the compact disc *The Historical CD of Digital Sound Synthesis*, Computer Music Currents 13, Wergo 2033–2 (Mainz, Germany: Wergo Schallplatten). From this period of early speech signal processing, the channel vocoder (VOice CODER) and linear predictive coding (LPC) were created (Atal, "Speech Analysis and Synthesis by Linear Prediction of the Speech Wave"; Makhoul, "Linear Prediction"). LPC created a revolution in speech synthesis and compositional possibilities. Some of its success was due to the similarity between the source/filter composition produced by the mathematics of linear prediction and the source/filter model of the human vocal tract. In the 1980s frequency modulation synthesis and formant wave function synthesis (FOF, for *fonction d'onde formantique*) were used for singing synthesis. FOF was later dubbed CHANT. In general terms, vocal synthesis may be divided into two different models, spectral and physical. The spectral model is, roughly speaking, based on perceptual mechanisms and attempts to re-create the sound of the voice, while the physical model is based on production mechanisms and attempts to re-create the function of the voice (and, as a result, the sound). For more detailed information about different vocal synthesis models see Cook, "Singing Voice Synthesis."

12. Practically, what matters to amateur users who neither know nor care about these distinctions, and to a general public told that the voice it hears is a synthesized voice, is not the technical distinction between full and hybrid vocal synthesis. What matters is that they *believe* it is vocal synthesis.

13. For more information on language capabilities and challenges, see Bonada, "Voice Processing and Synthesis by Performance Sampling and Spectral Models"; Kenmochi, "VOCALOID and Hatsune Miku Phenomenon in Japan"; Bell, "The dB in the .db."

14. According to my latest (July 2015) count, current Vocaloid companies issue voice font software in the following languages: English (created by Zero-G and PowerFX, sometimes in collaboration with the fan-run project Vocatone); Spanish (Voctro Labs); Chinese (Vocaloid China Project, a division of bplats; VOCANESE); Japanese (Crypton Future Media, bplats/Yamaha, Ki/oon records by Sony, i-STYLE Project by Studio Deen, Internet Co. Ltd., AH Software, First Place). The Korean language issuer SBS Artech is defunct.

15. A Japanese company, Crypton Future Media, released Vocaloid Meiko, which uses the same synthesis method as the voices discussed in this paper, on October 5, 2004. Zero-G released Vocaloid PRIMA, "a brand-new plug-in VIRTUAL VOCALIST modeled

on the voice of a professional soprano opera singer, and powered by the all-new Yamaha VOCALOID 2 Singing Synthesis Technology," in January 2007.

16. As the VY tagline goes, "Power of imagination accelerates Creator's possibility." The female voice VYI was called MIZKI, a name the developers derived from Hanamizuki (Dogwood). But there is no character for the voice; instead both packages feature an image of a decorative sword, in pink and gold with blue accents, respectively ("VY1V3," Vocaloid, accessed June 1, 2015, http://www.vocaloid.com/en/lineup/vocaloid /vy1v3.html; "VY2V3," *Vocaloid*, accessed June 1, 2015, http://www.vocaloid.com/en /lineup/vocaloid3/vy2v3.html). Vocaloid's original announcement web pages are no longer available, but fans have preserved information and images on the two following sites: "VY1V3," Fandom, accessed April 5, 2018, http://vocaloid.wikia.com/wiki /VY1v3; and "VY2V3," Fandom, accessed April 5, 2018, http://vocaloid.wikia.com /wiki/VY2v3. VY1 and VY2 are referred to in gendered terms, female and male, respectively. Even though these voices were released without images of singers, the most frequent discussion among users and fans is on the topic of what these voices look like. While Cyber Diva—with the fan-given nickname Cuva—is another Vocaloid, like VY1/VY2 marketed without a name that could be understood as human, "Cyber Diva" does point to a general type of identity.

17. Discussions on Apple's Siri include Alchemist & Metaphysician, comment on "Human-Computer Interaction: Is There Research on the Psychology of Speaking to a Device, Like Siri?," *Quora*, November 2, 2011, http://www.quora.com/Human -Computer-Interaction/Is-there-research-on-the-psychology-of-speaking-to-a-device -like-Siri; Devine, "iOS 7.1 Makes British Siri More Human, and Female!"; Muniz, "Computer Programs and Humans in the movie *Her*"; Manohla Dargis, "Disembodied, but, Oh, What a Voice," *New York Times*, December 17, 2013, http://www.nytimes .com/2013/12/18/movies/her-directed-by-spike-jonze.html?_r=2; Peter H. Kahn Jr., "What We Shouldn't Learn from the Movie *Her*," *Psychology Today*, April 3, 2014, https://www.psychologytoday.com/blog/human-nature/201404/what-we-shouldn-t -learn-the-movie-her; *Her*, directed by Spike Jonze (Burbank, CA: Warner Bros. Pictures, 2013), DVD. Perhaps because the use of Vocaloid explicitly requires the user to input text (lyrics) and notes, and because users have been instrumental in helping to create the characters, discussions around artificial intelligence have not cropped up around this software.

18. Miriam Stockley is originally from South Africa but moved to the United Kingdom in her teens to pursue a music career. In 1995 she entered the spotlight with the album *Audiemus*, in which her voice is recorded layer upon layer, producing a mix that is supposed to sound like "African voices."

19. See "Vocaloid," *Vocaloid*, accessed June 1, 2015, http://www.vocaloid.com/en /index.html.

20. For a critique of the highly problematic images used, see Eidsheim, "Voice as a Technology of Selfhood," 109–17.

21. To see a discussion of the commercial use of this piece, see Taylor, "World Music in Television Ads."

22. Vocaloid's depictions of each of their synthetic voices feature very strong, offen-

sive racial references. For a critique of this aspect of the software, see Eidsheim, "Voice as a Technology of Selfhood," 110–17.

23. Robotarchie, forum post on Vocaloid-User.net, "When Will Vocaloid Meet Your Expectations?," April 12, 2004, http://vocaloid-user.net/forum/general-vocaloid -discussion/when-will-vocaloid-meet-your-expectations.

24. heatviper, "Mike Oldfield," forum post on Vocaloid-User.net, January 19, 2006, http://vocaloid-user.net/forum/general-vocaloid-discussion/mike-oldfield.

25. Jogomus et al., "2 Questions about Vocaloid," forum post on Vocaloid-User .net, August 5, 2005, http://vocaloid-user.net/forum/general-vocaloid-discussion /2-questions-about-vocaloid.

26. Werde, "Could I Get That Song in Elvis, Please."

27. Unless the identity of the source singer is part of the product's promotional material, information regarding the source voices is kept very secret; this information was given to me in conversation with developers who were unable to share their names. I have therefore not been able to verify it with the source singers themselves. However, I have no reason to doubt the general information that was shared with me. My general point stands, even if the details differ.

28. If Vocaloid's developers were comfortable recruiting a professional musician working outside the immediate cultural, social, and political context of a given musical genre, it could arguably have been equally reasonable to have hired nonblack British or Jamaican native speakers or, perhaps aesthetically closer, to have hired native speakers of American English, independent of their racial or ethnic identification. This is, of course, tricky territory. Historically the African diaspora has been connected in many ways and has nurtured affinities despite geographical dispersal. Therefore there is an argument to be made that black populations in the United States, the United Kingdom, and Jamaica share affinities and many commonalities in their connection to the African diaspora, but I am unconvinced that they are connected by syllable pronunciation.

29. By simply listening, I cannot tell if any default phonemes were edited to improve the pronunciation of the words.

30. Graceinliife, "[VOCALOID 1] Obsoletion→Retirement [MIRIAM, LOLA, & LEON]." "Obsoletion→Retirement" and "Disappearance of LEON" are fan covers of the cosMo songs "Division→Destruction" and "Disappearance of Hatsune Miku."

31. Pavel Vu, "(Lola) Light Comes My Way (Original)."

32. Muzehack, "Muzehack—Destruction ft. Vocaloid Leon."

33. Agatechlo, "The Disappearance of LEON."

34. Anarobik, "anaROBIK Home."

35. This piece of fan art is a well-known image among the Vocaloid community and is often re-created. I have not been able to locate the originator of these visual ideas and continue to pursue the question.

36. Soph, "(Leon) I'll Quit Singing (Vocaloid)." This is another example of fan-based art that creates a chain of reference. "(Leon) I'll Quit Singing (Vocaloid)" is based on "I'll Quit Singing" (*Yamete yaruyo utaite nanka*) (with English subtitles) by NamahageP. The original "I'll Quit Singing" song uses the character/voice font Kasane Teto, created in the UTAU software (Damesukekun, "Kasane Teto 'Yamete yaruyo utaite nanka' (I'll

Quit Singing) English Subtitles"). The lyrics were based on a cover created by Goth-icBlue07 using the voice font SONiKA (Afrostream. "[Sonika]—I'll Quit Singing (Sonika ver)."). A number of other covers exist.

37. "Zero-G Vocaloid Sale—October 2012," December 26, 2013, http://engloids.info /uploads/news_vocaloid-discontinuation-notice.pdf.

38. Agatechlo, "The Disappearance of LEON."

39. Werde, "Could I Get That Song in Elvis, Please."

40. Y. Okada, "Extraordinary Sales for Hatsune Miku as Nico Spreads the Music," *IT Media*, September 12, 2007, http://www.itmedia.co.jp/news/articles/0709/12 /news035.html.

41. The first name, Miku, translates as "future," and the surname, Hatsune, trans-lates as "first sound."

42. For more on the topic of idol, see Aoyagi, *Islands of Eight Million Smiles*.

43. The Crypton Future Media CEO and Hatsune Miku creator, Hiroyuki Ito, received the Blue Ribbon Medal of Honor—presented to "individuals who have made prosperous efforts in the areas of public welfare and education"—on November 2, 2013. See "Hatsune Miku Creator Hiroyuki Ito Receives Medal of Honor," *Japan Bullet*, November 17, 2013, https://www.japanbullet.com/life-style/hatsune-miku-creator -hiroyuki-ito-receives-medal-of-honor.

44. James Verini, "How Virtual Pop Star Hatsune Miku Blew Up in Japan," *Wired*, October 19, 2012, http://www.wired.com/2012/10/mf-japan-pop-star-hatsune-miku/.

45. In an interview Alex Leavitt says, "Crypton actively supports this re-appropria-tion process with its Creative Commons–like 'Piapro Character License.'" Patrick St. Michel, "In Japan, Anyone Can Be a Holographic Pop Star," *Atlantic*, October 22, 2012, http://www.theatlantic.com/entertainment/archive/2012/10/in-japan-anyone-can-be -a-holographic-pop-star/263927/. See also Alex Leavitt, "Miku: The Open-Source Girl Who Conquered the World," SXSW PanelPicker, accessed June 1, 2015, http://panel picker.sxsw.com/vote/3548. For more on this aspect of Hatsune Miku, see Bell, "The dB in the .db"; To, "The Voice of the Future."

46. For more on this cultural phenomenon, see Itō et al., *Fandom Unbound*.

47. GoogleChromeJapan, "Google Chrome: Hatsune Miku (初音ミク)."

48. Miku spinoff products are "everywhere," in "cacophonous electronics, comic, doll, fetish, porn, and costume stores," James Verini writes in "How Virtual Pop Star Hatsune Miku Blew Up in Japan." She has been written about in "touching devotional texts: a handsome edition entitled Miku-4 by a fan named Nagimiso, a volume of Miku-inspired poetry and Miku-poetry criticism by Eureka, and a collection of songs transcribed into sheet music called *Selections for Piano*, with a cover illustration of Miku seated at a baby grand." Also, "not surprisingly, this crowdsourced creativity has led to a sub-genre of sexualized Mikus, including brutal sadomasochistic motifs. There is, inevitably, a market for Miku porn." See also St. Michel, "In Japan, Anyone Can Be a Holographic Pop Star." For more on Miku from the point of view of "open source culture," see "Miku: The Open-Source Girl Who Conquered the World"; Lindsay Zoladz, "Hatsune Miku Is a Piece of Software. She May Also Be the Future of Music," *Slate*, November 20, 2014, http://www.slate.com/blogs/browbeat/2014/11

/20/hatsune_miku how_a_vocaloid_avatar_is_redefining_the_idea_of_a_pop_star
.html.

49. Verini, "How Virtual Pop Star Hatsune Miku Blew Up in Japan."

50. Fan-created art and projects based on Miku's character extend beyond the voice
font and music to include games such as MikuMikuDance, consideration of which is
beyond the scope of this chapter. Most of the 15,500,000 Google search results for
Hatsune Miku on July 15, 2015, led to fan-based projects, and not to Crypton Future
Media.

51. See, for example, "Aoki Lapis (VOCALOID3)," Fandom, accessed April 5, 2018,
http://vocaloid.wikia.com/wiki/Aoki_Lapis_(VOCALOID3).

52. John Walden, "PowerFX Vocaloid 2 Sweet Ann," sos, January 1, 2008, http://
www.soundonsound.com/sos/jan08/articles/sweetann.htm.

53. Engloids, "Interview: Bil Bryant (Production and CEO of PowerFX)," *Engloids's
Blog*, January 4, 2010, https://engloids.wordpress.com/2010/01/04/interview-bil-bryant
-production-and-ceo-of-powerfx/.

54. Engloids, "Interview: Bil Bryant."

55. "Vocaloid BIG AL New York, New York," March 8, 2010, https://www.youtube
.com/watch?v=4R6aiN3xerg, video no longer available; "Yamaha show Vocaloid
@ Musikmesse," KVR, last modified March 9, 2003, http://www.kvraudio.com/news/y.
Big Al's artwork was not chosen through a contest per se. It's unknown whether the
artist volunteered or was contacted by PFX to design him.

56. "BIG AL," Vocaloid Wiki, accessed June 1, 2015, http://vocaloid.wikia.com/wiki
/BIG_AL.

57. Details regarding these different phases fall outside the scope of this chapter; I
treat this in an article under preparation.

58. "Hello, Japan! MikuFes'09 Summer," *MikuFes*, last modified January 1, 2011,
http://www.mikufes.jp.

59. "Hatsune Miku-AFAX-I Love Anisong," Anime Festival Asia, last modified January 1, 2010, http://www.animefestival.asia/afax/i_love_miku.html; "Hatsune Miku
Virtual Idol to Hold 1st Solo Concert," Anime News Network, last modified
December 10, 2009, https://www.animenewsnetwork.com/news/2009-12-10/virtual
-idol-hatsune-miku-to-hold-1st-solo-concert.

60. "Hatsune Miku Live Party 2011," last modified March 1, 2011, http://5pb.jp
/mikupa/index_tokyo.html.

61. Notably this concert was streamed live on the Niconico Douga (also transliterated
to Nico Nico or Niko Niko) website (a video website á la YouTube) for international
viewers (Mikunopolis, 2011). Niconico Douga, last modified March 15, 2007, http://
www.nicovideo.jp/watch/sm33357.

62. Yoree Koh, "Toyota's New U.S. Saleswoman: Virtual Idol Hatsune Miku,"
Wall Street Journal, May 10, 2011, http://blogs.wsj.com/japanrealtime/2011/05/10
/toyotas-new-u-s-saleswoman-virtual-idol-hatsune-miku/.

63. Lady Gaga, Twitter, April 15, 2014, 4:10 p.m., https://twitter.com/ladygaga
/status/456207861832380416.

64. David Ng, "Pharrell Williams Teams with Takashi Murakami on Music Video,"

Los Angeles Times, May 13, 2014, http://www.latimes.com/entertainment/arts/culture/la-et-cm-pharrell-williams-takashi-murakami-music-video-20140513-story.html.

65. See note 45 on the open licensing of Miku-derived noncommercial products.

66. Kisekikui, "Hatsune Miku—Thoughtful Zombie (English Subbed)."

67. Cawotte, "Hibikase."

68. Voca Vamp, "(Hatsune Miku) Mikusabbath (UtsuP) (English and Romaji Subs)."

69. daniwellP, "(Official Music Video) Nyan Cat—daniwellP (Nyanyanyanyanyanyanya!)."

70. Greatmuta0402, "SUPER GT 2014 GSR 初音ミクZ4 Drag the Ground Feat Hatsune Miku."

71. Goodsmile Racing, "Goodsmile Racing Official Support Site," accessed June 1, 2015, http://www.goodsmileracing.com/en/.

72. Eidsheim, "Synthesizing Race."

73. For an image of the unveiling of the software art and the voice provider, see KagamoneyLen, Twitter, July 4, 2015, 12:18 p.m., https://twitter.com/KagamoneyLen/status/617412178581172224.

74. For an image of the original design, see fig. 4.22.

75. "Ruby VOCALOID4," posting to "Vocaloid Wiki: Sandbox/Ruby," no date, accessed July 8, 2015, http://vocaloid.wikia.com/wiki/Vocaloid_Wiki:Sandbox/Ruby#cite_note-21, page deleted.

76. Sasuke, "Ruby: New Female English VOCALOID," posting to VocaloidOtaku.net, July 9, 2015, http://www.vocaloidotaku.net/index.php?/topic/55772-ruby-new-female-english-vocaloid/page__st__1875__p__1276002&#entry1276002; "ruby (vocaloid)," Tumblr, accessed June 1, 2015, https://www.tumblr.com/search/ruby%20(vocaloid); "vocaloid ruby on Tumblr," Tumblr, accessed June 1, 2015, https://www.tumblr.com/tagged/vocaloid-ruby; "maeblythe asked," Tumblr, accessed July 14, 2015, http://mishas-dunkinronpas.tumblr.com/post/123431378324/hey-there-i-know-youre-behind-ruby-there-was-a.

77. mishakeet, Twitter account, accessed July 6–14, 2015, https://twitter.com/Mishakeet; mishakeet, Twitter, July 6, 2015, 12:12 p.m., https://twitter.com/Mishakeet/status/618135378957086721.

78. "maeblythe asked."

79. When scrolling through the Google image search results of "Vocaloid Ruby," only one image involving PowerFX shows up. This is a photo where PowerFX's image is unveiled next to Misha, the source voice, who is not alluded to in the image description.

80. noricakes, Twitter post, July 6, 2015, 9:43 a.m., https://twitter.com/noricakes/status/618097952796491776/photo/1.

81. robotarchie, "Is Vocaloid Any Good?," posting to Vocaloid-User.net, March 23, 2004, http://vocaloid-user.net/forum/leon-and-lola/is-vocaloid-any-good#p414.

82. quetzalcoatl, posting to Vocaloid-User.net, July 8, 2015, http://vocaloid-user.net/forum/leon-and-lola/is-vocaloid-any-good#p441.

83. roba, "Is Vocaloid Any Good?," posting to Vocaloid-User.net, March 28, 2004, http://vocaloid-user.net/forum/leon-and-lola/is-vocaloid-any-good#p538.

84. andromeda, "Is Vocaloid any Good?, posting to Vocaloid-User.net, March 28, 2004, http://vocaloid-user.net/forum/leon-and-lola/is-vocaloid-any-good#p541.

85. robotarchie, "Is Vocaloid Any Good?," posting to Vocaloid-User.net, March 28, 2004, http://vocaloid-user.net/forum/leon-and-lola/is-vocaloid-any-good#p543.

5. BIFURCATED LISTENING

1. MovieClips, "Amazing Seven Year Old Sings Gloomy Sunday/Billy Holiday (Angelina Jordan) Eng Sub." The clip is from a televised performance on the show *Norway's Got Talent*.

2. Addressing the complex racial politics arising from cross-racial impersonation, the motivations behind appropriation (such as "love and theft," which addresses this from a psychoanalytical point of view), and practices from overt minstrelsy to "sonic blue(s) face culture," to quote Eric Lott and Daphne Brooks, is beyond the scope of this chapter. See Lott, *Love and Theft*; Brooks, "'This Voice Which Is Not One.'" However, I plan to address these thorny issues in a separate piece, considering them through Ronald Radano's nuanced theory of slaves' singing voices as the property of property, thus an inalienable property. As he explains, today's ideas of "authentic" and "inauthentic" are due to slave era constructions in part, that cultural ownership of black music and its authenticity is connected to black visual presentation ("The Sound of Racial Feeling"), and later, in the late nineteenth century and the first half of the twentieth, when a dynamic within which "de-valuation and re-valuation of black music" "change[d] relationally, dialectically, following the self-valorizing expansiveness of capitalism" ("The Secret Animation of Black Music").

3. Carvalho, "Strange Fruit," 112. The quote in the subheading for this section, "Billie Holiday's Burned Voice," is from Rita Dove's "Canary" (1989), quoted in Griffin, *If You Can't Be Free, Be a Mystery*, 156. For perspective on the mythmaking generated by Billie Holiday's 1956 ghostwritten autobiography, *Lady Sings the Blues*, see critiques, including Griffin, *If You Can't Be Free*; Szwed, *Billie Holiday*. On performance, sensationalistic tabloid stories, and a posthumous biographical film akin to "a type of cultural 'identity theft,'" see Sutton, "Bitter Crop," 294.

4. Sutton, "Bitter Crop," 301.

5. "New Life," *Time*, April 12, 1948, 68, quoted in Sara Ramshaw, "'He's My Man!,'"95.

6. Cooke, *Jazz*, quoted in Daubney, "Songbird or Subversive?," 18.

7. Sutton, "Bitter Crop," 301.

8. Carvalho, "Strange Fruit," 112.

9. Hobson, "Everybody's Protest Song," 447.

10. Griffin, "When Malindy Sings," 107.

11. Quoted in Griffin, "When Malindy Sings," 107.

12. Carvalho, "Strange Fruit," 115.

13. Davis, *Blues Legacies and Black Feminism*, 177.

14. Sutton, "Bitter Crop," 304.

15. Margolick, *Strange Fruit*, 12.

16. Margolick, *Strange Fruit*, 9. Even the intense and public prosecution of Holiday for her possession and use of drugs was orchestrated. Johann Hari recently reported that the prosecution formed part of the Federal Bureau of Narcotics' strategy to gain public visibility and support, with the aim of receiving continued funding. See "The Hunting of Billie Holiday: How Lady Day Found Herself in the Middle of the Federal Bureau of Narcotics' Early Fight for Survival," *Politico*, January 17, 2015, http://www.politico.com /magazine/story/2015/01/drug-war-the-hunting-of-billie-holiday-114298_Page4.html#. VdvUz9NVikq.

17. Nicholson, *Billie Holiday*, 170.

18. Margolick, *Strange Fruit*, 9.

19. Nicholson, "Billie Holiday."

20. Blackburn, *With Billie*, 270.

21. Szwed, *Billie Holiday*, 3.

22. Griffin, "When Malindy Sings," 102–25.

23. Griffin, *If You Can't Be Free, Be a Mystery*, 31.

24. Griffin, "When Malindy Sings," 119.

25. For a rich discussion of vocal art and vocal recordings as "archival and ethnographic endeavors" (as opposed to the unmediated sound of "natural" voices), read Brooks, "Sister, Can You Line It Out?"

26. 5ninthavenueproject, "Joey Arias in His Debut Performance as Billie Holiday in 1986." Regarding the recording sessions for "They Can't Take That Away from Me" from March 1977: "This rehearsal performance contains an impromptu impersonation of Billie Holiday by Peggy Lee." Iván Santiago-Mercado, "The Peggy Lee Bio-Discography and Videography: Rehearsals and Home Sessions," May 6, 2014, http://www .peggyleediscography.com/p/LeeRehearsals.php; Richard Lane, "Véronica DiCaire Overflows with Talent and Voices at Bally's," *VegasChatter.com*, July 1, 2013, http:// www.vegaschatter.com/story/2013/7/1/18431/31021/vegas-travel/V%E9ronic+DiCaire +Overflows+With+Talent+and+Voices+At+Bally's, site discontinued; MegaConcert Love, "Nikki Yanofsky's Impression of Billie Holiday."

27. Stephen Holden, "Review: Joey Arias Incarnates Billie Holiday in the American Songbook," *New York Times*, February 26, 2015, http://www.nytimes.com/2015/02/27 /arts/music/review-joey-arias-incarnates-billie-holiday-in-the-american-songbook .html?_r=0.

28. Tony Bravo, "Joey Arias Channels Billie Holiday for Singer's Centenary," *SF Gate*, June 12, 2015, http://www.sfgate.com/art/article/Joey-Arias-channels-Billie -Holiday-for-singer-s-6323733.php.

29. Sedaris, "Music Lessons."

30. Karen, "Me Sing Pretty One Day: David Sedaris Sings the Blues," *Notes on the Road*, January 31, 2013, http://www.notesontheroad.com/David-Sedaris-Billie-Holiday -Video.html#.

31. Charles Isherwood, "Stepping into the Shoes of a Ravaged Singer: Audra McDonald in 'Lady Day at Emerson's Bar and Grill,'" *New York Times*, April 13, 2014, https:// www.nytimes.com/2014/04/14/theater/audra-mcdonald-in-lady-day-at-emersons-bar -and-grill.html?_r=0.

32. "Angelina Jordan Astar synger i finalen i Norske Talenter," *Videosidene*, May 23, 2014, http://www.tv2.no/v/816695/.

33. Gabrielle Bluestone, "Norwegian Seven-Year-Old Has the Voice and Soul of Billie Holiday," Gawker, March 9, 2014, http://gawker.com/norwegian-seven-year-old -has-the-voice-and-soul-of-bill-1540148926.

34. Burton, "Angelina Jordan, Age 7, Channels Billie Holiday's 'Gloomy Sunday' on 'Norway's Got Talent' Audition."

35. Fiona Harper, "Angelina Jordan Astar—Music Monday," *Lady, We Salute You!*, November 3, 2014, http://ladywesaluteyou.com/angelina-jordan-astar-music-monday/.

36. Melissa Locker, "This 7-Year Old's Incredible Voice Will Give You Chills as She Channels Billie Holiday," *Time*, March 10, 2014, http://time.com/18173/this-7-year -olds-incredible-voice-will-give-you-chills-as-she-channels-billie-holiday/?iid=time _readnext; MovieClips, "Amazing Seven Year Old Sings Gloomy Sunday/Billy Holiday (Angelina Jordan) Eng Sub."

37. MovieClips, "Amazing Seven Year Old Sings Gloomy Sunday/Billy Holiday (Angelina Jordan) Eng Sub," my translation.

38. EJ Dickson, "Norwegian 7-Year-Old Does an Amazing Impression of Billie Holiday," *Daily Dot*, Mar 8, 2014, http://www.dailydot.com/lifestyle/billie -holiday-norwegian-girl/.

39. Jordan's Middle Eastern background is not discussed in Norwegian or international media. She has been featured across Europe, the United States, and Australia. Pa1189j, "Angelina Jordan—Fly Me to the Moon—*The View* 2014"; MovieClips, "Amazing Seven Year Old Sings Fly Me to the Moon (Angelina Jordan) on Senkveld 'The Late Show'"; Franziska Krug, "'Das Herz Im Zentrum' Charity Gala in Hamburg, 2015," digital image, accessed August 16, 2015, http://herz-im-zentrum.de/index.php/15 -galerie/72-galerie-das-kleine-herz-im-zentrum-2015; Katarina Wendelin, "8-åriga Youtube-fenomenet fick kändissverige att gråta," *Svenska Hjältar*, December 12, 2014, http://www.aftonbladet.se/svenskahjaltar/article20010107.ab.

40. Lhamon, *Raising Cain*; Lott, *Love and Theft*; Woolfork, *Embodying American Slavery in Contemporary Culture*.

41. Lott, *Love and Theft*, 3.

42. The question is discussed in Eidsheim, *Sensing Sound*, 1.

43. Hobson, "Everybody's Protest Song," 44.

44. Griffin, "When Malindy Sings," 104.

45. For a thoughtful, ethnographic, and science-based study of vocal artists, I recommend Katherine Meizel and Ronald Scherer's insightful analysis of Véronique's fifty-voice Las Vegas show, which highlights the technique involved in carrying out imitations, a technique they dub "multivocality." Described from an acoustic perspective, summarizing Stevens and House, "Development of a Quantitative Description of Vowel Articulation," Meizel and Scherer note that singing impersonation "involves acoustic features that lead to the perception of timbre and are most likely related to formant frequencies and their relative intensities. The way listeners perceive vowels is most affected by the first two formants (F_1 and F_2), the frequencies and relative intensities of which are related to the location along the vocal tract of the primary constriction(s), the

size of the constriction, and dimensions of the lip opening and extent." See "Voice and Disjuncture in Celebrity Impersonation," in Eidsheim and Meizel, *The Oxford Handbook of Voice Studies*.

46. Schneider began traveling in 1993 and has collected nearly continuously since that time. Conversation with the author, April 20, 2015, and text message on August 24, 2015.

47. Schneider voiced the *South Park* characters Wendy, Shelly, Principal Victoria, Mrs. Marsh, Mrs. Cartman, Mrs. McCormick, Ms. Crabtree, and the Mayor for five years.

48. The playwright and actress Anna Deavere Smith is respected for her ability to imitate a wide variety of characters' voices—characters who often have very different biographies, ages, races, and genders than Smith herself. About her process Smith shares, "I get up and I start talking like another person, and start trying to occupy their words or be occupied by their words" ("Let Me Down Easy"). In a review of the play *Notes from the Field*, Edgardo Cervano-Soto summarizes Smith's creative process as "finding individuals closest to the narrative, interviewing and filming them, studying their mannerisms, memorizing their words, and ultimately, curating a showcase of those voices." "Anna Deavere Smith Takes on School-to-Prison Pipeline," *Richmond (CA) Pulse*, July 30, 2015, http://richmondpulse.org/2015/07/30/anna -devere-smith-takes-on-school-to-prison-pipeline/.

Smith describes her rationale this way: "Nobody talks alike. So I thought that one place to study identity would be in the actual speech of the voice. . . . I interview people, I take something that they said, and then I attempt to say exactly what they said, more than word for word, utterance for utterance, because I have come to see that it's in the way the utterances themselves are manipulated that identity comes forward. . . . What I really love to do is listen to people, and listen to stories." Big Think, "How Do You Get into Character?"

49. I am currently in the process of coauthoring a piece with Schneider on the technical breakdown of Holiday's voice.

50. This approach follows Emily J. Lordi's cue in *Black Resonance*. She discusses the "haunting" quality of Holiday's voice but argues against the cultural current that reads performances as "direct expressions of lived struggle" (110) and, instead, insists on considering Holiday's vocal work as a result of artistic choices (137–72).

51. As Holiday is the focus of this chapter, I will mention only in passing that Jordan's performance is yet another example wherein a singer's technical abilities exceed what would be viewed as her physical limitations, here related to age and vocal development. Yet Jordan's acute ear and technique surpass her physical difference from Holiday, as Jordan is clearly prepubescent at the time of her performance of "Gloomy Sunday."

52. Brooks, "Sister, Can You Line It Out?," 618.

53. Lordi, *Black Resonance*, 9–10.

54. Daubney, "Songbird or Subversive?," 21, 22.

55. Baber, "'Manhattan Women,'" 78.

56. Daubney, "Songbird or Subversive?," 17–28.

57. Daubney, "Songbird or Subversive?," 24.

58. Ramshaw, "'He's My Man!,'" 93. It doesn't take long, though, before Ramshaw launches into hyperbole: "No other voice has ever given such honest, intimate and profound expression" (93).

59. Huang and Huang, "She Sang as She Spoke," 288, 302. Overall these authors consider certain spoken consonants and the pitches of preceding vowels.

60. Szwed, *Billie Holiday*, 1.

61. For more on Holiday's three stylistic periods, see Szwed, *Billie Holiday*, 126–29.

62. Szwed, *Billie Holiday*, 2, 5.

63. Szwed, *Billie Holiday*, 3.

64. "Celebrating Billie Holiday's Centennial with Cassandra Wilson."

65. As Daphne Brooks notes, "bodies in dissent" are bodies that build on coexisting genres and expectations and bend them to their advantage. Bodies such as these understand the expectations placed on a black body that is understood as a slave body; in 1846 William and Ellen Craft took advantage of these expectations and escaped the South, William posing as the slave of his light-skinned wife, Ellen, who posed as the white master. Bodies in dissent do not accept any essential or naturalized traits overlaid upon them. They knew the expectations, played with them, and took advantage of their blind spots. See Brooks, *Bodies in Dissent*; Craft and Craft, *Running a Thousand Miles for Freedom*.

66. This tension is the focal point of today's talent competitions. The dramatic arc is built around the presentation of a person about whom members of the audience have certain ideas (an uncool teenager; an aging virgin; a young girl who sounds like an old soul), combined with the assumption that this identity should fail to yield an interesting or strong vocal performance. The "wow moment" of the program is created by the bursting of these expectations. The effect would not have been the same if the audience and judges had expected spectacular vocal performances from these individuals at the start. The twist is provided by the disruption of these expectations. For examples of talent show participants who defy judges' and audiences' expectations, see Imryanang, "Judges Lack Confidence in This Shy 14 Year Old until She Starts Singing!," August 18, 2013, https://www.youtube.com/watch?v=uxXcocqDyuw, source terminated; Smith, "Susan Boyle First Audition."

67. See, for example, Lippi-Green, *English with an Accent*; Massey and Lundy, "Use of Black English and Racial Discrimination in Urban Housing Markets"; Purnell et al., "Perceptual and Phonetic Experiments on American English Dialect Identification."

68. powell, *Racing to Justice*, 53.

69. Omi and Winant, *Racial Formation in the United States*, 55.

70. Omi and Winant, *Racial Formation in the United States*, 55.

71. Phillip Goff summarizes the context for his research on contextual explanation of racial inequality: "The latter part of the 20th Century saw an impressive decline in the overt expression of racial animosity towards non-Whites. This decline, however, was largely unaccompanied by a reduction in racial inequality. The seeming disconnect between racial attitudes and racial outcomes has troubled contemporary social scientists who had long assumed that individual-level racism accounted for racial disparities."

"Phillip Atiba Goff," Social Psychology Network, accessed April 1, 2015, http://goff
.socialpsychology.org/.

72. Lordi, *Black Resonance*, 10.

73. Daughtry, "Atmospheric Pressures."

6. WIDENING RINGS OF BEING

1. I have long pondered this dilemma. For example, when asked to offer a contribution to the panel "Musical Aesthetics of Race and Ethnicity," I did not believe I could responsibly use words as we know and understand them today, and instead offered a musical track featuring my nonverbal singing with an abstract video made by Sandro Del Rosario. National meeting of the American Musicological Society, Philadelphia, November 13, 2009.

2. Eric Satie rejects the label "musician." In a 1912 essay he describes himself as a "phonometrographer." For example, Satie confesses, "I enjoy measuring a sound much more than hearing it," and "On my phono-scales a common or garden F-sharp registered 93 kilos. It came out of a fat tenor whom I also weighed." See "What I Am," in *A Mammal's Notebook*, 101. See also Auner, "Weighing, Measuring, Embalming Tonality."

3. Simon Sweetman, "On Billie Holiday's Voice," *Blog on the Tracks*, February 28, 2013, http://www.stuff.co.nz/entertainment/blogs/blog-on-the-tracks/8361478/On -Billie-Holidays-voice.

4. As I mentioned in the introduction, what I derive from the critical performance practice methodology carried out in this book, which it seems most logical to call "style and technique" here, is what I have earlier called the "organology of voice." See Eidsheim, *Sensing Sound*, 163.

5. For an expanded discussion of this position, see Eidsheim, "Maria Callas's Waistline and the Organology of Voice."

6. Lindsay, "Lindsay's Wheel of Acoustics," 2242.

7. Eliot, *The Cocktail Party*, 33.

8. Ben Macpherson et al., "What Is Voice Studies?," in Thomaidis and Macpherson, *Voice Studies*, 214.

9. Macpherson et al., "What Is Voice Studies?," 214.

10. Eidsheim, *Sensing Sound*, 155.

11. Tukaram, "Landlocked in Fur," accessed April 1, 2015, http://cliffarnold.com /landlockedinfur.html.

12. Michael Muskal and Tina Susman, "Screams on 911 Recording Were Trayvon Martin's, Mother Testifies," *Los Angeles Times*, July 5, 2013, http://articles.latimes.com /2013/jul/05/nation/la-na-nn-trayvon-martin-mother-voice-20130705; "Zimmerman Mom: That's My Son Screaming on Tape," HLN, July 5, 2014, http://www.hlntv.com /video/2013/07/05/gladys-zimmerman-thats-my-son-screaming-tape.

13. Joshua Rhett Miller, Perry Chiaramonte, and Serafin Gomez, "Mothers of Both Martin, Zimmerman Testify They Heard Their Own Son Calling for Help on 911 Tape," *Fox News*, July 5, 2013, http://www.foxnews.com/us/2013/07/04/prosecutors -winding-down-case-in-george-zimmerman-trial/. In addition Zimmerman's father and

uncle testified that it was their son and nephew on the tape. Associated Press, "Zimmerman's Father Testifies It Was His Son Screaming on 911 Call," CBS *Tampa Bay*, July 10, 2013, http://tampa.cbslocal.com/2013/07/10/zimmermans-father-testifies-it-was-his-son-screaming-on-911-call/; Kim Lacapria, "George Zimmerman Cries as Uncle Offers Improbable 'Screams' Testimony," *Inquisitor*, July 6, 2013, http://www.inquisitr.com/833178/george-zimmerman-cries-as-uncle-offers-improbable-screams-testimony/.

14. Other Martin and Zimmerman relatives also weighed in on identifying the voice, both in court and in media reports. Lisa Lucas and Corky Siemaszko, "Trayvon Martin Shooting: Martin's Dad Says Screams on 911 Tape Were His Son's, Contradicting Police," *New York Daily News*, July 8, 2013, http://www.nydailynews.com/news/national/friend-ids-george-zimmerman-screams-911-tape-article-1.1392958; "Zimmerman's Father Testifies It Was His Son Screaming on 911 Call"; "George Zimmerman Cries as Uncle Offers Improbable 'Screams' Testimony."

15. One of the expert witnesses, Dr. J. P. (Peter) French, testified, "If you were simply presented with the screams in this case, with no background information, if it were simply edited out of the recording end-to-end and given to an analyst, I don't think you could even be sure that the person was speaking in English . . . [or] be sure that the person was male or female." That is, French affirms that the audio sample cannot even be identified to such broad markers as language and gender. Andrew Branca, "Zimmerman Case: Experts Call State's Scream Claims 'Absurd' 'Ridiculous' and 'Imaginary Stuff,'" *Legal Insurrection*, June 9, 2013, accessed April 1, 2015, http://legalinsurrection.com/2013/06/zimmerman-case-states-scream-claims-called-absurd-ridiculous-and-imaginary-stuff/.

16. For example, Sybrina Fulton and Tracy Martin started the Trayvon Martin Foundation (with the Circle of Mothers and Circle of Fathers concentrations), the overall commitment of which is to "end gun violence, strengthen families through holistic support, S.T.E.M. education for women and minorities and mentoring." *Trayvon Martin Foundation*, accessed July 5, 2017, http://trayvonmartinfoundation.org/. See also Ella Hillaire, "Five Years Later, Trayvon Martin's Parents Haven't Yet Started to Grieve," *Vanity Fair*, February 9, 2017 , http://www.vanityfair.com/news/2017/02/trayvon-martin-parents-interview.

17. These quotes are from an anonymous review of *Sensing Sound*.

18. For my discussion of sound in water, see Eidsheim, *Sensing Sound*, 27–57.

19. Quoted in Chessa, *Luigi Russolo, Futurist*, 1.

20. Kun, *Audiotopia*, 14.

21. Eidsheim, *Sensing Sound*, 183.

22. These ideas and positions are not unique. My main intellectual companion in writing this book has been powell, *Racing to Justice*. While approaching issues about race, dignity, community, and sense of self from a scholarly legal perspective, powell expresses similar sentiments regarding the need to "[move] beyond the isolated self" (xvii). He is weary, as I am, of the notion of "postracialism" as "targeted universalism" (3–28), and thus moves his inquiry of the racialized self into a discussion about the "multiple self" (163–96). In this discussion he touches on points of convergence with Buddhist philosophy. While I have never engaged in earnest with Buddhism, I know from powell's work, and from conversations with colleagues who do know the tradition, that

there are multiple points of convergence between Buddhist thought practices and where my investigation into listening has taken me.

23. On the flip side, this means that each positive power we wish to name is also not pinned down to a single expression. Shana Redmond beautifully exemplifies this in her reminder that "the underground sounds a little bit like this [plays excerpt of Nina Simone, 'See Line Woman'], and this [plays excerpt of Miriam Makeba, 'Ndodem-nyama Verwoerd'], and this [plays excerpt of Max Roach and Abbey Lincoln, 'Garvey's Ghost'], and [plays excerpt of Kendrick Lamar, 'Alright,' and the Pan African Space Station, and Kamasi Washington, and Cesaria Evora, and Margaret Bonds, and, and, and]." Each example is different at the level of what I think about as naming (e.g., genre), but all are examples of "the underground sound" and share in the "investment in a practice of fugitive blackness that refuses containment" ("Black Music and the Aesthetics of Protest"). I attended the talk; as of July 1, 2015, the panel discussion can be viewed here: http://hammer.ucla.edu/programs-events/2015/06/black-music-and-the-aesthetics-of-protest/.

24. For a poignant discussion of an example of this phenomenon, see these three by Radano: *Lying up a Nation*; "The Sound of Racial Feeling," 126; "Black Music Labor and the Animated Properties of Slave Sound."

25. Again, I am aware these positions are similar to those expressed within certain Buddhist worldviews. However, I do want to stress that the stances I take in this book are derived from following the logic of inquiry into the acousmatic question.

26. Rūmī Jalāl al-Dīn and Coleman Barks, "A Community of Spirit," in Rūmī and Barks, *Rumi*, 40.

Bibliography

Adler-Kassner, Linda, and Elizabeth Wardle, editors. *Naming What We Know: Threshold Concepts of Writing Studies*. Boulder: University Press of Colorado, 2015.

Afrostream. "[Sonika]—I'll Quit Singing (Sonika ver)." YouTube, April 26, 2010. https://www.youtube.com/watch?v=6ZPbwkvD7vc.

Agatechlo. "The Disappearance of LEON." YouTube, December 31, 2013. https://www.youtube.com/watch?v=4n73dI1a1vQ.

Alverson, Margaret Blake. *Sixty Years of California Song*. Project Gutenberg, 2006. http://www.gutenberg.org/files/19528/19528-h/19528-h.htm.

American National Standards Institute. *Acoustical Terminology*. ANSI Sl.1–1960. New York: ANSI, 1960.

Anarobik. "anaROBIK Home." YouTube. Accessed June 1, 2015. https://www.youtube.com/user/anaROBIK.

Anderson, Marian. *My Lord, What a Morning: An Autobiography*. New York: Viking Press, 1956.

André, Naomi, Karen M. Bryan, and Eric Saylor. *Blackness in Opera*. Urbana: University of Illinois Press, 2012.

Aoyagi, Hiroshi. *Islands of Eight Million Smiles: Idol Performance and Symbolic Production in Contemporary Japan*. Cambridge, MA: Harvard University Press, 2005.

Aristotle. *The Complete Works of Aristotle: The Revised Oxford Translation*. Edited by Jonathan Barnes. Translated by D'Arcy Wentworth Thompson. Princeton: Princeton University Press, 1984.

Aronowitz, Stanley, and Henry A. Giroux. *Education under Siege: The Conservative, Liberal and Radical Debate over Schooling*. South Hadley, MA: Bergin and Garvey, 1985.

Atal, Bishnu S. "Speech Analysis and Synthesis by Linear Prediction of the Speech Wave." *Journal of the Acoustical Society of America* 47, no. 1A (1970): 65.

Auner, Joseph. "Weighing, Measuring, Embalming Tonality: How We Became Phonometrographers." In *Tonality 1900–1950: Concept and Practice*, edited by Feliz Wörner, Ullrich Scheideler, and Philip Rupprecht, 24–46. Stuttgart: Franz Steiner Verlag, 2012.

Baber, Katherine. "'Manhattan Women': Jazz, Blues, and Gender in *On the Town* and *Wonderful Town*." *American Music* 31, no. 1 (2013): 73–105.

Baldwin, James. *The Devil Finds Work: An Essay*. New York: Vintage Books, 1976.

Barg, Lisa. "Black Voice/White Sounds: Race and Representation in Virgil Thomson's *Four Saints in Three Acts*." *American Music* 18, no. 2 (2000): 121–61.

Barlow, William. *Voice Over: The Making of Black Radio*. Philadelphia: Temple University Press, 1998.

Barthes, Roland. "The Grain of the Voice." In *Image, Music, Text*, 179–89. New York: Hill and Wang, 1977.

Beahrs, Robert Oliver. "Post-Soviet Tuvan Throat-Singing (*Xöömei*) and the Circulation of Nomadic Sensibility." PhD diss., University of California, Berkeley, 2014.

Bell, Sarah A. "The dB in the .db: Vocaloid Software as Posthuman Instrument." *Popular Music and Society* 39, no. 2 (2015): 222–40.

Bell Laboratories. "Pedro the Voder: A Machine That Talks." *Bell Laboratory Record* 17, no. 6 (1939): 170–71.

Bergeron, Katherine. *Voice Lessons: French Mélodie in the Belle Epoque*. Oxford: Oxford University Press, 2010.

Bergner, Daniel. *Sing for Your Life: A Story of Race, Music, and Family*. New York: Little, Brown, 2016.

Bernheimer, Martin. "Yes, but Are We Really Colour Deaf?" *Opera* 36 (1985): 755–60.

Bickford, Susan. *The Dissonance of Democracy: Listening, Conflict, and Citizenship*. Ithaca, NY: Cornell University Press, 1996.

Big Think. "How Do You Get into Character?" YouTube, April 23, 2012. https://www.youtube.com/watch?t=300&v=NkjADgWRq3Y.

Blackburn, Julia. *With Billie*. New York: Pantheon Books, 2005.

Bloechl, Olivia, Melanie Lowe, and Jeffrey Kallberg. *Rethinking Difference in Music Scholarship*. New York: Cambridge University Press, 2015.

Blomgren, Michael Yang Chen, Manwa L. Ng, and Harvey R. Gilbert. "Acoustic, Aerodynamic, Physiologic, and Perceptual Properties of Modal and Vocal Fry Registers." *Journal of the Acoustical Society of America* 103, no. 5 (1998): 2649–58.

Bonada, Jordi. "Voice Processing and Synthesis by Performance Sampling and Spectral Models." PhD diss., University of Pompeu Fabra, 2008.

Borsel, John Van, Elke Van Eynde, Griet De Cuypere, and Hilde Van den Berghe. "Physical Appearance and Voice in Male-to-Female Transsexuals." *Journal of Voice* 15 (2001): 570–75.

Brackett, David. "Questions of Genre in Black Popular Music." *Black Music Research Journal* 25, nos. 1–2 (2005): 73–92.

Bretherton, Luke. *Christianity and Contemporary Politics: The Conditions and Possibilities of Faithful Witness*. Chichester, UK: Wiley-Blackwell, 2010.

Brooks, Daphne A. "'All That You Can't Leave Behind': Black Female Soul Singing and the Politics of Surrogation in the Age of Catastrophe." *Meridians: Feminism, Race, Transnationalism* 8, no. 1 (2008): 180–204.

Brooks, Daphne A. *Bodies in Dissent: Spectacular Performances of Race and Freedom, 1850–1910*. Durham, NC: Duke University Press, 2006.

Brooks, Daphne A. "Bring the Pain: Post-Soul Memory, Neo-Soul Affect, and Lauryn Hill in the Black Public Sphere." In *Taking It to the Bridge: Music as Performance,* edited by Nicholas Cook and Richard Pettengill, 180–203. Ann Arbor: University of Michigan Press, 2013.

Brooks, Daphne A. "Nina Simone's Triple Play." *Callaloo: A Journal of African Diaspora Arts and Letters* 34, no.1 (2011): 176–97.

Brooks, Daphne A. "Sister, Can You Line It Out? Zora Neale Hurston and the Sound of Angular Black Womanhood." *Amerikastudien/American Studies* 55, no 4 (2010): 617–23.

Brooks, Daphne A. "'This Voice Which Is Not One': Amy Winehouse Sings the Ballad of Sonic Blue(s)face Culture." *Women and Performance: A Journal of Feminist Theory* 20, no. 1 (2010): 37–60.

Brooks, Tim, and Richard K. Spottswood. *Lost Sounds: Blacks and the Birth of the Recording Industry, 1890–1919*. Urbana: University of Illinois Press, 2004.

Bruin, M. D. de, M. J. Coerts, and A. J. Greven. "Speech Therapy in the Management of Male-to-Female Transsexuals." *Folia Phoniatrica et Logopaedica* 52 (2000): 220–27.

Bruner, Jerome. "Narrative Construction of Reality." *Critical Inquiry* 18 (1991): 1–21.

Burroughs, Bruce. "Indian Summer: Marian Anderson Profile." *Opera News* 69, no. 3 (2004): 61.

Burton, Louise. "Angelina Jordan, Age 7, Channels Billie Holiday's 'Gloomy Sunday' on 'Norway's Got Talent' Audition." *Music Times*, March 15, 2014. http://www .musictimes.com/articles/4805/20140315/angelina-jordan-age-7-channels-billie -holidays-gloomy-sunday-on-norways-got-talent-audition.htm.

Butler, Judith. *Bodies That Matter: On the Discursive Limits of "Sex."* New York: Routledge, 1993.

Butler, Judith. *Gender Trouble: Feminism and the Subversion of Identity*. New York: Routledge, 1999.

Butler, Shane. *The Ancient Phonograph*. New York: Zone Books, 2015.

Carpenter, Faedra Chatard. *Coloring Whiteness: Acts of Critique in Black Performance*. Ann Arbor: Michigan University Press, 2014.

Carvalho, John M. "Strange Fruit: Music between Violence and Death." *Journal of Aesthetics and Art Criticism* 71, no. 1 (2013): 111–19.

Cavarero, Adriana. *For More Than One Voice: Toward a Philosophy of Voice*. Stanford: Stanford University Press, 2005.

Cawotte. "Hibikase." YouTube, September 24, 2014. Accessed June 1, 2015. https:// www.youtube.com/watch?v=383HwPMvaQo (source discontinued).

"Celebrating Billie Holiday's Centennial with Cassandra Wilson." *Jazz Night in America*, NPR, April 17, 2015. https://www.npr.org/event/music/400178603 /celebrating-billie-holidays-centennial-with-cassandra-wilson.

Chessa, Luciano. *Luigi Russolo, Futurist: Noise, Visual Arts, and the Occult*. Berkeley: University of California Press, 2012.

Chybowski, Julia. "The 'Black Swan' in England." *American Music Research Center Journal* 14 (2006): 8–25.

Cook, Mercer. "The Negro Spiritual Goes to France." *Music Educators Journal* 40, no. 5 (1954): 42–48.

Cook, Perry R. "Singing Voice Synthesis: History, Current Work, and Future Directions." *Computer Music Journal* 20, no. 3 (1996): 38–46.

Cooke, Mervyn. *Jazz*. London: Thames and Hudson, 1998.

Cooper, B. Lee. "Wade in the Water: A Soul Chronology, 1927–1951. Get Your Soul Right: The Gospel Quartets and the Roots of Soul Music." *Popular Music and Society* 39, no. 2 (2016): 279–81.

Craft, William, and Ellen Craft. *Running a Thousand Miles for Freedom: The Escape of William and Ellen Craft from Slavery*. Athens: University of Georgia Press, 1999.

Crenshaw, Kimberlé. "Mapping the Margins: Intersectionality, Identity Politics, and Violence against Women of Color." *Stanford Law Review* 43, no. 6 (1991): 1241–99.

Cruz, Jon. *Culture on the Margins: The Black Spiritual and the Rise of American Cultural Interpretation*. Princeton: Princeton University Press, 1999.

Cusick, Suzanne G. "On Musical Performances of Gender and Sex." In *Audible Traces: Gender, Identity and Music*, edited by Elaine Barkin and Lydia Hamessley, 25–48. Los Angeles: Carciofoli Verlagshaus, 1999.

Cusick, Suzanne G. "'You Are in a Place That Is Out of the World . . .': Music in the Detention Camps of the 'Global War on Terror.'" *Journal of the Society for American Music* 2, no. 1 (2008): 1–26.

Damesukekun. "Kasane Teto 'Yamete yaruyo utaite nanka' (I'll Quit Singing) English Subtitles." YouTube, May 27, 2010. https://www.youtube.com/watch?v=oKulEbupof8.

Daubney, Kate. "Songbird or Subversive? Instrumental Vocalisation Technique in the Songs of Billie Holiday." *Journal of Gender Studies* 11, no. 1 (2002): 17–28.

Daughtry, J. Martin. "Afterword: From Voice to Violence and Back Again." In *Music, Politics, and Violence*, edited by Kip Pegley and Susan Fast, 243–63. Middletown, CT: Wesleyan University Press, 2012.

Daughtry, J. Martin. "Atmospheric Pressures: Reflections on Voice in the Anthropocene." UCLA Department of Musicology Distinguished Lecture Series, Los Angeles, May 25, 2017.

Davis, Angela Y. *Blues Legacies and Black Feminism: Gertrude "Ma" Rainey, Bessie Smith, and Billie Holiday*. New York: Pantheon Books, 1998.

Deguchi, Shinji. "Mechanism of and Threshold Biomechanical Conditions for Falsetto Voice Onset." *PLoS ONE* 6, no. 3 (2011): e17503.

Demers, Joanna. *The Anatomy of Thought-Fiction: CHS Report, April 2214*. Alresford, UK: Zero Books, 2017.

Denes, Peter B., and Elliot N. Pinson. *The Speech Chain: The Physics and Biology of Spoken Language*. New York: W. H. Freeman, 1993.

Devine, Richard. "iOS 7.1 Makes British Siri More Human, and Female!" *iMore*, March 11, 2014. http://www.imore.com/ios-71-makes-british-siri-more-human-and-female.

Dobson, Andrew. *Listening for Democracy: Recognition, Representation, Reconciliation*. Oxford: Oxford University Press, 2014.

Doyle, Jennifer. *Hold It Against Me: Difficulty and Emotion in Contemporary Art*. Durham, NC: Duke University Press, 2013.

Drott, Eric. "The End(s) of Genre." *Journal of Music Theory* 57, no. 1 (2013): 1–45.

Du Bois, W. E. B. *The Souls of Black Folk.* New York: Dover, 1994.

Edgerton, Michael Edward. *The 21st-Century Voice: Contemporary and Traditional Extra-Normal Voice.* 2nd ed. Lanham, MD: Rowman and Littlefield, 2015.

Eidsheim, Nina Sun. "Maria Callas's Waistline and the Organology of Voice." *Opera Quarterly*, July 22, 2017. https://doi.org/10.1093/oq/kbx008.

Eidsheim, Nina Sun. "Marian Anderson and 'Sonic Blackness' in American Opera." *American Quarterly* 63, no. 3 (2011): 641–71.

Eidsheim, Nina Sun. "Musical Aesthetics of Race and Ethnicity." Paper presented at the national meeting of the American Musicological Society, Philadelphia, November 13, 2009.

Eidsheim, Nina Sun. *Sensing Sound: Singing and Listening as Vibrational Practice.* Durham, NC: Duke University Press, 2015.

Eidsheim, Nina Sun. "Synthesizing Race: Towards an Analysis of the Performativity of Vocal Timbre." *Revista Transcultural de Musica* 13 (2009). http://www.sibetrans.com/trans/article/57/synthesizing-race-towards-an-analysis-of-the-performativity-of-vocal-timbre.

Eidsheim, Nina Sun. "Voice as Action: Towards a Model for Analyzing the Dynamic Construction of Racialized Voice." *Current Musicology* 93, no. 1 (2012): 7–31.

Eidsheim, Nina Sun. "Voice as a Technology of Selfhood: Towards an Analysis of Racialized Timbre and Vocal Performance." PhD diss., University of California, San Diego, 2008.

Eidsheim, Nina Sun, and Katherine Meizel, eds. *The Oxford Handbook of Voice Studies.* New York: Oxford University Press, forthcoming.

Eliot, T. S. *The Cocktail Party.* London: Faber and Faber, 1958.

Fales, Cornelia. "The Paradox of Timbre." *Ethnomusicology* 46, no. 1 (2002): 56–95.

Fay, Stephen. *The Ring: The Anatomy of an Opera.* Dover, NH: Longwood, 1984.

Feldman, Martha. *The Castrato: Reflections on Natures and Kinds.* Berkeley: University of California Press, 2014.

5ninthavenueproject. "Joey Arias in His Debut Performance as Billie Holiday in 1986." YouTube, July 5, 2014. https://www.youtube.com/watch?v=JyZQPKbdomA.

Foucault, Michel. *Discipline and Punish: The Birth of the Prison.* 2nd ed. New York: Vintage Books, 1995.

Francis, Fu Ka-Man. "Playing with the Voice: Hatsune Miku and Vocaloid Culture in Contemporary Japan." MA thesis, University of Hong Kong, 2014.

François, Anne-Lise. "Fakin' It/Makin' It: Falsetto's Bid for Transcendence in 1970s Disco Highs." *Perspectives of New Music* 33, nos. 1–2 (1995): 442–57.

Freitas, Roger. *Portrait of a Castrato: Politics, Patronage, and Music in the Life of Atto Melani.* Cambridge: Cambridge University Press, 2009.

Frisell, Anthony. *The Baritone Voice: A Personal Guide to Acquiring a Superior Singing Technique.* Boston: Branden, 2007.

Gelfer, Marylou Pausewang, and Kevin J. Schofield. "Comparison of Acoustic and Perceptual Measures of Voice in Male-to-Female Transsexuals Perceived as Female versus Those Perceived as Male." *Journal of Voice* 14, no. 1 (2000): 22–33.

Gillespie, Michael Boyce. *Film Blackness: American Cinema and the Idea of Black Film.* Durham, NC: Duke University Press, 2016.

Goffman, Erving. *Presentations of Self in Everyday Life.* Garden City, NY: Doubleday, 1959.

Goodman, Steve. *Sonic Warfare: Sound, Affect, and the Ecology of Fear.* Cambridge, MA: MIT Press, 2010.

GoogleChromeJapan. "Google Chrome: Hatsune Miku (初音ミク)." YouTube, December 14, 2011. https://www.youtube.com/watch?v=MGt25mv4-2Q.

Gordon, Bonnie. *Monteverdi's Unruly Women: The Power of Song in Early Modern Italy.* Cambridge: Cambridge University Press, 2004.

Graceinliife. "[VOCALOID 1] Obsoletion→Retirement [MIRIAM, LOLA, & LEON]." YouTube, December 31, 2013. https://www.youtube.com/watch?v=be-8LprsELc (not available in the United States).

Graziano, John. "The Early Life and Career of the 'Black Patti': The Odyssey of an African American Singer in the Late Nineteenth Century." *Journal of the American Musicological Society* 53, no. 3 (2000): 543–96.

Greatmuta0402. "SUPER GT 2014 GSR 初音ミクZ4 Drag the Ground Feat Hatsune Miku." YouTube, December 2, 2014. https://www.youtube.com/watch?v=wLuDRdvsjRE.

Greenberg, Jonathan. "Singing Up Close: Voice, Language, and Race in American Popular Music, 1925–1935." PhD diss., University of California, Los Angeles, 2008.

Grey, Herman. "Black Masculinity and Visual Culture." *Callaloo* 18, no. 2 (1995): 401–5.

Griffin, Farah Jasmine. *If You Can't Be Free, Be a Mystery: In Search of Billie Holiday.* New York: Free Press, 2001.

Griffin, Farah Jasmine. "When Malindy Sings: Meditation on Black Women's Vocality." In *Uptown Conversation: The New Jazz Studies,* edited by Robert G. O'Meally, Brent Hayes Edwards, and Farah Jasmine Griffin, 102–25. New York: Columbia University Press, 2004.

Guillory, Monique. "Black Bodies Swingin': Race, Gender, and Jazz." In *Soul: Black Power, Politics, and Pleasure,* edited by Monique Guillory and Richard C. Green, 191–215. New York: New York University Press, 1998.

Haeckel, E. *Die Natürliche Schöpfungs-geschichte: Gemeinverständliche wissenschaftliche Vorträge über die Entwickelungs-Lehre im Allgemeinen und diejenige von Darwin, Goethe und Lamarck im Besonderen.* Berlin: Druck und Verlag von Georg Reimer, 1889.

Haggin, Bernard H. *Music and Ballet, 1973–1983.* New York: Horizon House, 1984.

Halberstam, Judith. *In a Queer Time and Place: Transgender Bodies, Subcultural Lives.* New York: New York University Press, 2005.

Halberstam, Judith. "Queer Voices and Musical Genders." In *Oh Boy! Masculinities and Popular Music,* edited by Freya Jarman-Ivens, 183–96. New York: Routledge, 2007.

Hall, Stuart. "Cultural Identity and Diaspora." In *Identity: Community, Culture, Difference,* edited by Jonathan Rutherford, 222–37. London: Lawrence and Wishart, 1990.

Hall, Stuart. *Stuart Hall: Critical Dialogues in Cultural Studies.* Edited by David Morley and Kuan-Hsing Chen. New York: Routledge, 1996.

Haraway, Donna. "Situated Knowledge: The Science Question in Feminism and the Privilege of Partial Perspective." *Feminist Studies* 14, no. 3 (1988): 575–99.

Hari, Johann. "The Hunting of Billie Holiday: How Lady Day Found Herself in the Middle of the Federal Bureau of Narcotics' Early Fight for Survival." *Politico*, January 17, 2015. http://www.politico.com/magazine/story/2015/01/drug-war-the-hunting-of -billie-holiday-114298_Page4.html#.VdvUz9NVikq.

Harkness, Nicholas. "Anthropology at the Phonosonic Nexus." *Anthropology News* 52, no. 1 (2011): 5.

Hawkins, Stan, and Sarah Niblock. *Prince: The Making of a Pop Music Phenomenon.* Burlington, VT: Ashgate, 2011.

Helmholtz, Hermann von. *On the Sensations of Tone.* 1885; New York: Dover, 1954.

Henderson, Clayton W. "Minstrelsy, American." In *The New Grove Dictionary of Music and Musicians,* 2nd ed., vol. 16, edited by Stanley Sadie, 736–40. London: Macmillan, 2001.

Hillenbrand, James M., and Michael J. Clark. "The Role of F0 and Formant Frequencies in Distinguishing the Voices of Men and Women." *Attention, Perception, and Psychophysics* 71, no. 5 (2009): 1150–66.

Hobson, Janell. "Everybody's Protest Song: Music as Social Protest in the Performances of Marian Anderson and Billie Holiday." *Signs* 33, no. 2 (2008): 443–48.

Holiday, Billie, and William Dufty. *Lady Sings the Blues.* New York: Avon, 1976.

Hollien, Harry, Paul Moore, Ronald W. Wendahl, and John F. Michel. "On the Nature of Vocal Fry." *Journal of Speech, Language, and Hearing Research* 9 (June 1966): 245–47.

Huang, Hao, and Rachel Huang. "She Sang as She Spoke: Billie Holiday and Aspects of Speech Intonation and Diction." *Jazz Perspectives* 7, no. 3 (2013): 287–302.

Huron, David. *Sweet Anticipation: Music and the Psychology of Expectation.* Cambridge, MA: MIT Press, 2006.

Hutcheon, Linda, and Michael Hutcheon. *Bodily Charm: Living Opera.* Lincoln: University of Nebraska Press, 2000.

Itō, Mizuko, Daisuke Okabe, and Izumi Tsuji, eds. *Fandom Unbound: Otaku Culture in a Connected World.* New Haven: Yale University Press, 2012.

Iyer, Vijay. "5 Expansive Wadada Leo Smith Recordings, Picked by Vijay Iyer." *A Blog Supreme,* November 17, 2010. http://www.npr.org/sections/ablogsupreme/2010/11/16 /131366498/5-expansive-wadada-leo-smith-recordings-picked-by-vijay-iyer.

Jackson, Roland. *Performance Practice: A Dictionary-Guide for Musicians.* New York: Routledge, 2005.

Johnson, E. Patrick. "Black." In *Keywords for American Cultural Studies,* vol. 2, edited by Bruce Burgett and Glen Hendler, 30–34. New York: New York University Press, 2014.

Jones, Victoria Garrett. *Marian Anderson: A Voice Uplifted.* New York: Sterling, 2008.

Joyce, Jimmy, Francis Hobbs, and Betty Joyce. *Scoring for Voice: A Guide to Writing Vocal Arrangements.* Van Nuys, CA: Alfred, 1972.

June, Sara. "Nyan Cat [original]." YouTube, April 6, 2011. https://ru-clip.com/video
/QH2-TGUlwu4/video.html.

Kane, Brian. *"L'Objet Sonore Maintenant*: Pierre Schaeffer, Sound Objects and the Phe-
nomenological Reduction." *Organised Sound* 12, no. 1 (2007): 15–24.

Kane, Brian. *Sound Unseen: Acousmatic Sound in Theory and Practice*. Oxford: Oxford
University Press, 2014.

Keiler, Allan. *Marian Anderson: A Singer's Journey*. New York: Scribner, 2000.

Kenmochi, Hideki. "Singing Synthesis as a New Musical Instrument." In *Proceedings of
the International Conference on Acoustics, Speech and Signal Processing (ICASSP) 2012*,
5385–5388. Piscataway, NJ: IEEE, 2012. Accessed June 1, 2015. https://ieeexplore.ieee
.org/stamp/stamp.jsp?arnumber=6289138.

Kenmochi, Hideki. "VOCALOID and Hatsune Miku Phenomenon in Japan." In *Proceedings of the First Interdisciplinary Workshop on Singing Voice*, 1–4. N.p.: InterSing-
ing, 2010.

Kessler, Sarah Rebecca. "Anachronism Effects: Ventriloquism and Popular Media."
PhD diss., University of California, Irvine, 2016.

King, Jason. "The Sound of Velvet Melting: The Power of 'Vibe' in the Music of Roberta Flack." In *Listen Again: A Momentary History of Pop Music*, edited by Eric
Weisbard, 172–99. Durham, NC: Duke University Press, 2007.

Kinney, Katherine. "The Resonance of Brando's Voice." *Postmodern Culture* 24, no. 3
(2015). doi:10.1353/pmc.2014.0019.

Kinney, William Howland. *Recorded Music in American Life*. New York: Oxford University Press, 1999.

Kisekikui. "Hatsune Miku—Thoughtful Zombie (English Subbed)." YouTube, June 29
2010. https://www.youtube.com/watch?v=mujvVHUdrKE.

Koth, Michelle S. *Uniform Titles for Music*. Lanham, MD: Scarecrow Press, 2008.

Kreiman, Jody, Bruce R. Gerratt, Marc Garellek, Robin Samlam, and Zhaoyan Zhang.
"Toward a Unified Theory of Voice Production and Perception." *Loquens* 1, no. 1
(2014): 1–9.

Kreiman, Jody, Soo Jin Park, Patricia A. Keating, and Abeer Alwan. "The Relationship
between Acoustic and Perceived Interspeaker Variability in Voice Quality." Paper
presented at the annual *InterSpeech* conference, Dresden, Germany, September 6–10,
2015.

Kreiman, Jody, and Diana Sidtis. *Foundations of Voice Studies: An Interdisciplinary Approach to Voice Production and Perception*. Malden, MA: Wiley-Blackwell, 2011.

Kun, Josh. *Audiotopia: Music, Race, and America*. Berkeley: University of California
Press, 2005.

Lacey, Kate. *Listening Publics: The Politics and Experience of Listening in the Media Age*.
Cambridge: Polity Press, 2013.

Lawrence, Vera Brodsky, and George Templeton Strong. *Strong on Music: The New
York Music Scene in the Days of George Templeton Strong*. New York: Oxford University Press, 1987.

LeBrew, Arthur R. *The Black Swan: Elizabeth Taylor Greenfield Songstress*. Detroit: La
Brew, 1969.

"Let Me Down Easy: Interview with Anna Deavere Smith." *Great Performances*, PBS, January 12, 2012. http://video.pbs.org/viralplayer/2185803105.

Levin, Theodore Craig, and Valentina Süzükei. *Where Rivers and Mountains Sing: Sound, Music, and Nomadism in Tuva and Beyond*. Bloomington: Indiana University Press, 2006.

Lhamon, W. T. *Raising Cain: Blackface Performance from Jim Crow to Hip Hop*. Cambridge, MA: Harvard University Press, 1998.

Lindsay, R. Bruce. "Lindsay's Wheel of Acoustics." *Journal of the Acoustical Society of America* 36 (1964): 2241–43.

Lippi-Green, Rosina. *English with an Accent: Language, Ideology, and Discrimination in the United States*. London: Routledge, 1997.

Lipsitz, George. *The Possessive Investment in Whiteness: How White People Profit from Identity Politics*. Philadelphia: Temple University Press, 1998.

Lochbaum, C., and J. Kelly. "Speech Synthesis." In *Proceedings of the Fourth International Congress on Acoustics*, paper G42, 1–4. Copenhagen: Organization Committee of the Fourth International Congress on Acoustics, 1962. https://www.icacommission.org/Proceedings/ICA1962Copenhagen/ICA04%20Proceedings%20Vol1.pdf.

Lordi, Emily J. *Black Resonance: Iconic Women Singers and African American Literature*. New Brunswick, NJ: Rutgers University Press, 2013.

Lott, Eric. *Love and Theft: Blackface Minstrelsy and the American Working Class*. New York: Oxford University Press, 1993.

Mabry, Sharon. *Exploring Twentieth-Century Vocal Music: A Practical Guide to Innovations in Performance and Repertoire*. Oxford: Oxford University Press, 2002.

Makhoul, John. "Linear Prediction: A Tutorial Review." In *Proceedings of the IEEE* 63, 561–80. New York: Springer, 1975.

Margolick, David. *Strange Fruit: The Biography of a Song*. New York: Ecco Press, 2001.

Marshall, Caitlin. "Crippled Speech." *Postmodern Culture* 24, no. 3 (2015). 10.1353/pmc.2014.0020.

Massey, Douglas, and Garvey Lundy. "Use of Black English and Racial Discrimination in Urban Housing Markets: New Methods and Findings." *Urban Affairs Review* 36, no. 4 (2001): 452–69.

Mauss, Marcel. *Sociology and Psychology: Essays*. Translated by Ben Brewster. New York: Routledge, 1979.

McCracken, Allison. *Real Men Don't Sing: Crooning in American Culture*. Durham, NC: Duke University Press, 2015.

McDaniel, Melodie, director. *Little Jimmy Scott: Why Was I Born?* DVD. Bravo Profiles, Jazz Masters, 1998.

McDermott, J. Cynthia, and Lois Bridges Bird. *Beyond the Silence: Listening for Democracy*. Portsmouth, NH: Heinemann, 1999.

MegaConcertLove. "Nikki Yanofsky's Impression of Billie Holiday." YouTube, March 25, 2011. https://www.youtube.com/watch?v=2QVK4G9gkYY.

Meizel, Katherine. "A Powerful Voice: Investigating Vocality and Identity." *A World of Voice: Voice and Speech across Culture* 7 (2011): 267–75.

Merriam, Alan P., and Valerie Merriam. *The Anthropology of Music.* Evanston, IL: Northwestern University Press, 1980.

Merton, Robert K. "The Self-Fulfilling Prophecy." *Antioch Review* 8, no. 2 (1948): 193–210.

Meyer, Jan H. F., and Ray Land. "Threshold Concepts and Troublesome Knowledge: An Introduction." In *Overcoming Barriers to Student Understanding: Threshold Concepts and Troublesome Knowledge,* 3–18. London: Routledge, 2006.

Miller, Michael. *The Complete Idiot's Guide to Music Theory.* 2nd ed. New York: Penguin Group, 2005.

Miller, Richard. *National Schools of Singing.* Lanham, MD: Scarecrow Books, 1997.

Miller, Richard. *Solutions for Singers: Tools for Performers and Teachers.* Oxford: Oxford University Press, 2004.

Moon, Kristyn R. "Lee Tung Foo and the Making of a Chinese American Vaudevillian, 1900s–1920s." *Journal of Asian American Studies* 8, no. 1 (2005): 23–48.

Morton, Brian. *Prince: A Thief in the Temple.* Edinburgh: Canongate Books, 2007.

Moten, Fred. *In the Break: The Aesthetics of the Black Radical Tradition.* Minneapolis: University of Minnesota Press, 2003.

Mount, Kay H., and Shirley Salmon. "Changing the Vocal Characteristics of a Post-Operative Transsexual Patient: A Longitudinal Study." *Journal of Communication Disorder* 21 (1988): 229–38.

MovieClips. "Amazing Seven Year Old Sings Fly Me to the Moon (Angelina Jordan) on Senkveld 'The Late Show.'" YouTube, March 21, 2014. https://www.youtube.com/watch?v=rFWs2Z_RZ3Y.

MovieClips. "Amazing Seven Year Old Sings Gloomy Sunday/Billy Holiday (Angelina Jordan) Eng Sub." YouTube, March 7, 2014. https://www.youtube.com/watch?v=2da7N6ADm9s.

Muers, Rachel. *Keeping God's Silence: Towards a Theological Ethics of Communication.* Malden, MA: Blackwell, 2004.

Muniz, Gabriel. "Computer Programs and Humans in the Movie *Her.*" Research Center on Computing and Society, August 15, 2014. http://rccs.southernct.edu/computer-programs-and-humans-in-the-movie-her/.

Muñoz, José Esteban. *Disidentifications: Queers of Color and the Performance of Politics.* Minneapolis: University of Minnesota Press, 1999.

Muzehack. "Muzehack—Destruction ft. Vocaloid Leon." YouTube, October 21, 2011. https://www.youtube.com/watch?v=SQxwo22uEno.

Neal, Mark Anthony. *Songs in the Key of Black Life: A Rhythm and Blues Nation.* London: Routledge, 2003.

The New Harvard Dictionary of Music. Cambridge, MA: Belknap Press of Harvard University Press, 1986.

Nicholson, Stuart. *Billie Holiday.* Boston: Northeastern University Press, 1995.

Nicholson, Stuart. "Billie Holiday: Celebrate the Centenary of the Great Lady Day." *Jazzwise,* April 10, 2015. http://www.jazzwisemagazine.com/breaking-news/13529-billie-holiday-explore-the-albums-of-the-great-lady-day.

Noë, Alva. *Action in Perception.* Cambridge, MA: MIT Press, 2004.

Norton, Kay. *Singing and Wellbeing: Ancient Wisdom, Modern Proof.* New York: Routledge, 2016.

Nott, Josiah Clark, and George R. Gliddon. *Types of Mankind.* Philadelphia: Lippin-
cott, Gramb, 1854.

Obadike, Mendi. "Low Fidelity: Stereotyped Blackness in the Field of Sound." PhD
diss., Duke University, 2005.

Oby, Jason. *Equity in Operatic Casting as Perceived by African American Male Singers.*
Lewiston, NY: Edwin Mellen Press, 1998.

Ochoa Gautier, Ana María. *Aurality: Knowledge and Listening in Nineteenth-Century
Colombia.* Durham, NC: Duke University Press, 2014.

Omi, Michael, and Howard Winant. *Racial Formation in the United States: From the
1960s to the 1990s.* 2nd ed. New York: Routledge, 1994.

Pa1189j. "Angelina Jordan—Fly Me to the Moon—The View 2014." YouTube, September 19, 2014. https://www.youtube.com/watch?v=nBGMQ9Kx9iI.

Pavel Vu. "(Lola) Light Comes My Way (Original)." YouTube, April 3, 2014. https://
www.youtube.com/watch?v=yHisitISxqI.

Peirce, Charles S. *The Essential Peirce: Selected Philosophical Writings, Volume 2
(1893–1913).* Bloomington: Indiana University Press, 1998.

Piekut, Benjamin. "Actor-Networks in Music History: Clarifications and Critiques."
Twentieth-Century Music 11, no. 2 (2014): 191–215.

Potter, John. *Vocal Authority: Singing Style and Ideology.* New York: Cambridge University Press, 1998.

powell, john a. *Racing to Justice: Transforming Our Conceptions of Self and Other to
Build an Inclusive Society.* Bloomington: Indiana University Press, 2012.

Powers, Richard. *In the Time of Our Singing.* New York: Farrar, Straus and Giroux,
2003.

Purnell, Thomas, William Idsardi, and John Baugh. "Perceptual and Phonetic Experiments on American English Dialect Identification." *Journal of Language and Social
Psychology* 18, no. 1 (1999): 10–30.

Radano, Ronald. "Black Music Labor and the Animated Properties of Slave Sound."
boundary 2 43, no. 1 (2016): 173–208.

Radano, Ronald. *Lying Up a Nation: Race and Black Music.* Chicago: University of
Chicago Press, 2003.

Radano, Ronald. "The Secret Animation of Black Music." Paper presented at the Institute for Research in the Humanities, Madison, WI, January 25, 2016.

Radano, Ronald. "The Sound of Racial Feeling." *Dædalus* 142, no. 4 (2013): 126–34.

Rahaim, Matthew. *Musicking Bodies: Gesture and Voice in Hindustani Music.* Middletown, CT: Wesleyan University Press, 2012.

Ramshaw, Sara. "'He's My Man!': Lyrics of Innocence and Betrayal in *The People v. Billie Holiday.*" *Canadian Journal of Women and the Law* 16, no. 1 (2004): 86–105.

Redmond, Shana. *Anthem: Social Movements and the Sound of Solidarity in the African
Diaspora.* New York: New York University Press, 2013.

Redmond, Shana. "Black Music and the Aesthetics of Protest." Paper presented at the
UCLA Hammer Museum, Los Angeles, June 2, 2015.

Reneau, April Christine. "Determining Basic Voice Classification of High School Choir Students." PhD diss., University of Texas at El Paso, 2008.

Risset, Jean-Claude. *An Introductory Catalogue of Computer Synthesized Sounds (with Sound Examples)*. Murray Hill, NJ: Bell Laboratories, 1969.

Ritz, David. *Faith in Time: The Life of Jimmy Scott*. Cambridge, MA: Da Capo Press, 2002.

Rubin, D. L. "Nonlanguage Factors Affecting Undergraduates' Judgments of Nonnative English-Speaking Teaching Assistants." *Research in Higher Education* 33, no. 4 (1992): 511–31.

Rūmī Jalāl al-Dīn and Coleman Barks. *Rumi: The Big Red Book: The Great Masterpiece Celebrating Mystical Love and Friendship*. New York: HarperOne, 2010.

Sampson, Sarah Fuchs. "Operatic Artifacts." Paper presented at Inertia: A Conference on Sound, Media, and the Digital Humanities, Los Angeles, April 30–May 2, 2015.

Satie, Erik. *A Mammal's Notebook: Collected Writings of Erik Satie*. Edited by Ornella Volta. Translated by Anton Melville. London: Atlas Press, 1996.

Schaeffer, Pierre. *Traité des Objets Musicaux*. Paris: Éditions du Seuil, 1966.

Schechner, Richard. *Performance Studies: An Introduction*. London: Routledge, 2002.

Schlichter, Annette. "Do Voices Matter? Vocality, Materiality, Gender Performativity." *Body and Society* 17, no. 1 (2011): 31–52.

Schlichter, Annette. "Un/Voicing the Self: Vocal Pedagogy and the Discourse-Practices of Subjectivation." *Postmodern Culture* 24, no. 3 (2014). doi:10.1353/pmc.2014.0011.

Schmidt, Leigh Eric. *Hearing Things: Religion, Illusion, and the American Enlightenment*. Cambridge, MA: Harvard University Press, 2000.

Sedaris, David. "Music Lessons." *This American Life*, produced by Ira Glass, Julie Snyder, Alix Spiegel, and Nancy Updike. June 5, 1998. https://www.thisamericanlife.org/radio-archives/episode/104/transcript.

Sheean, Vincent. *Between the Thunder and the Sun*. New York: Kessinger, 2005.

Shirley, George. "The Black Performer." *Opera News* 35, no. 11 (1971): 6–13.

Silverman, Kaja. *The Acoustic Mirror: The Female Voice in Psychoanalysis and Cinema*. Bloomington: Indiana University Press, 1988.

Smalls, Dawn L. "Linguistic Profiling and the Law." *Stanford Law and Policy Review* 15, no. 2 (2004): 579–604.

Smith, Chris. "Susan Boyle First Audition—Britain's Got Talent—'I Dreamed a Dream.'" YouTube, July 25, 2010. https://www.youtube.com/watch?v=aRiJNS8Oz6E.

Smith, Jacob. *Vocal Tracks: Performance and Sound Media*. Berkeley: University of California Press, 2008.

Smith, Jeff. "Black Faces, White Voices: The Politics of Dubbing in Carmen Jones." *Velvet Light Trap* 51 (2003): 29–42.

Soph. "(Leon) I'll Quit Singing (Vocaloid)." YouTube, August 1, 2010. https://www.youtube.com/watch?v=axVcQrfJE_Q.

Spivak, Gayatri Chakravorty, and Ellen Rooney. "'In a Word': Interview." *differences* 1, vol. 2 (1989): 124–56.

Stein, Gertrude. *Everybody's Autobiography*. New York: Cooper Square, 1971.

Sterne, Jonathan. *The Audible Past.* Durham, NC: Duke University Press, 2006.

Stevens, Kenneth N., and Arthur S. House. "Development of a Quantitative Description of Vowel Articulation." *Journal of the Acoustical Society of America* 27, no. 3 (1955): 484–93.

Stoever, Jennifer Lynn. "The Contours of the Sonic Color-Line: Slavery, Segregation, and the Cultural Politics of Listening." PhD diss., University of Southern California, 2007.

Stoever, Jennifer Lynn. *The Sonic Color Line: Race and the Cultural Politics of Listening.* New York: New York University Press, 2016.

Stoever-Ackerman, Jennifer. "Reproducing U.S. Citizenship in *Blackboard Jungle*: Race, Cold War Liberalism, and the Tape Recorder." *American Quarterly* 63, no. 3 (2011): 781–806.

Stoever-Ackerman, Jennifer. "Splicing the Sonic-Color-Line: Tony Schwartz Remixes Postwar *Nueva York*." *Social Text* 28, no. 1 (2010): 59–85.

Story, Rosalyn. *And So I Sing: African-American Divas of Opera and Concert.* New York: Warner Books, 1990.

Stras, Laurie. "The Organ of the Soul: Voice, Damage and Affect." *Sounding Off: Theorizing on Disability in Music*, edited by Neil Lerner and Joseph Straus, 173–84. New York: Routledge, 2006.

Sundberg, Johan. *The Science of the Singing Voice.* DeKalb: Northern Illinois University Press, 1987.

Sutton, Matthew. "Bitter Crop: The Aftermath of Lady Sings the Blues." *a/b: Auto/Biography Studies* 27, no. 2 (2012): 294–315.

Szendy, Peter. *Listen: A History of Our Ears.* Translated by Charlotte Mandell. New York: Fordham University Press, 2008.

Szwed, John F. *Billie Holiday: The Musician and the Myth.* New York: Viking, 2015.

Taylor, Timothy Dean. "World Music in Television Ads." *American Music* 18, no. 2 (2000): 162–92.

Teolee. "Miku on Letterman." YouTube, October 8, 2014. https://www.youtube.com/watch?v=wzG5paboCnU.

Thomaidos, Konstantinos, and Ben Macpherson, eds. *Voice Studies: Critical Approaches to Process, Performance and Experience.* London: Routledge, 2015.

Thomson, Virgil. *Virgil Thomson.* New York: Knopf, 1966.

Thomson, Virgil, and Gertrude Stein. *Four Saints in Three Acts.* Edited by H. Wiley Hitchcock and Charles Fussell. Middleton, WI: American Musicological Society / A-R Editions, 2008.

Thurman, Kira. "The German Lied and Songs of Black Volk." *Journal of the American Musicological Society* 67, no. 2 (2014): 543–81.

To, Kit Yan. "The Voice of the Future: Seeking Freedom of Expression through Vocaloid Fandom." MA thesis, University of Texas, Austin, 2014.

Toll, Robert. *Blacking Up.* New York: Oxford University Press, 1974.

Trotter, James M. *Music and Some Highly Musical People.* Boston: Lee and Shepard, 1881.

Tukaram. "Landlocked in Fur." Accessed April 1, 2015. http://cliffarnold.com/landlockedinfur.html.

Turner, Patricia. "Marian Anderson." In *Notable Black American Women*, edited by Jessie Carney Smith and Shirelle Phelps, 18. Detroit: Gale Research, 1992.

Various Artists. *The Historical CD of Digital Sound Synthesis*. Computer Music Currents 13. Wergo 2033–2, 1995, compact disc.

Vazquez, Alexandra T. *Listening in Detail: Performances of Cuban Music*. Durham, NC: Duke University Press, 2013.

Vechten, Carl Van. "A Few Notes about *Four Saints in Three Acts*." In *Four Saints in Three Acts: An Opera to Be Sung*, by Gertrude Stein, 5–10. New York: Random House, 1934.

Vehanen, Kosti, and George J. Barnett. *Marian Anderson: A Portrait*. Westport, CT: Greenwood Press, 1970.

Vennard, William. *Singing: The Mechanism and the Technic*. New York: Carl Fischer, 1968.

Vocaloid Ruby. "(Ruby) Hands—heart*breaker (Demo)." YouTube, June 24, 2015. https://www.youtube.com/watch?v=yqxa1IdsPqE.

Voca Vamp. "(Hatsune Miku) Mikusabbath (UtsuP) (English and Romaji Subs)." YouTube, October 8, 2013. https://www.youtube.com/watch?v=qCxSpkL5jvI.

Vorperian, Houri K., Ray D. Kent, Mary J. Lindstrom, Cliff M. Kalina, Lindell R. Gentry, and Brian S. Yandell. "Development of Vocal Tract Length during Early Childhood: A Magnetic Resonance Imaging Study." *Journal of the Acoustical Society of America* 117, no. 1 (2005): 338–50.

Wald, Gayle. *It's Been Beautiful: "Soul!" and Black Power Television*. Durham, NC: Duke University Press, 2015.

Watson, Steven. *Prepare for Saints: Gertrude Stein, Virgil Thomson, and the Mainstreaming of American Modernism*. New York: Random House, 1998.

Weidman, Amanda. "Anthropology and Voice." *Annual Review of Anthropology* 43 (2014): 37–51.

Weidman, Amanda J. *Singing the Classical, Voicing the Modern: The Postcolonial Politics of Music in South India*. Durham, NC: Duke University Press, 2006.

Weidman, Amanda J. "Voice." In *Keywords in Sound*, edited by David Novak and Matt Sakakeeny, 232–40. Durham, NC: Duke University Press, 2015.

Wellesz, Egon, ed. *The New Oxford History of Music*. Vol. 1: *Ancient and Oriental Music*. Oxford: Oxford University Press, 1957.

West, Michael J. "What I Am Interested in Is Sound: A Conversation with Wadada Leo Smith." *Washington City Paper*, November 19, 2010. http://www.washington citypaper.com/arts/music/blog/13074613/what-im-interested-in-is-sound-a -conversation-with-wadada-leo-smith.

Whiteside, Sandra P. "A Comment on Women's Speech and Its Synthesis." *Perceptual and Motor Skills* 88 (1999): 110–12.

Williams-Jones, Pearl. "Afro-American Gospel Music: A Crystallization of the Black Aesthetic." *Ethnomusicology* 19, no. 3 (1975): 373–85.

Wilson, Olly. "Black Music as an Art Form." *Black Music Research Journal* 3 (1983): 1–22.

Wolk, Lesley, Nassima B. Abdelli-Beruh, and Dianne Slavin. "Habitual Use of Vocal Fry in Young Adult Female Speakers." *Journal of Voice* 26, no. 3 (2012): e111–16.

Woodson, Carter Godwin. *The Mis-Education of the Negro.* San Diego: Book Tree, 2006.

Woolfork, Lisa. *Embodying American Slavery in Contemporary Culture.* Urbana: University of Illinois Press, 2009.

Wright, Michelle M. *Physics of Blackness: Beyond the Middle Passage Epistemology.* Minneapolis: University of Minnesota Press, 2015.

Young, William S. *The Black Swan at Home and Abroad, or, A Biographical Sketch of Miss Elizabeth Taylor Greenfield, the American Vocalist.* Philadelphia: W. S. Young, 1855.

Index

Arias, Joey, 159–65
Aristotle, 18
Arroyo, Martina, 83, 87–88
ARTPOP/ARTRAVE tour (Lady Gaga), 137
Atlantic Records, 97
audile techniques, 26; African American music and, 40–43
audio-racial imagination, 26–27
authenticity: ethnosympathy and, 75–76; of slave music, 234n2; vocal imitation and, 166–69; vocal timbre and, 45–49
autobiographical voice, Billie Holiday and, 156–59

Baber, Katherine, 169
Baldwin, James, 10, 26–27, 177
Barber, Samuel, 84
Barg, Lisa, 78
Barlow, William, 220n91
Beahrs, Robbie, 17
bel canto school, 73–74, 213n27
beliefs, sound as projection of, 49
Bell Labs, 228n11
Bennett, Tony, 157–58
Bernheimer, Martin, 61
Beulah (radio program), 220n91
Big Al (Vocaloid character), 135, 137–39
Bing, Rudolf, 88
biological determinism, 156–58
blackness: acousmatics and, 7–9; African American singers identified with, 67–69, 190–93; American Operatic timbre and, 61–63; Anderson's singing linked to, 81–83, 88–90; animation of, 31–32; classical timbre and, 87–90; figure of sound and, 50–52; in film, 21–22; gender and, 35–36; imitations of Holiday and, 167–69; masculinity and, 101–5; micropolitics of listening and, 24–27, 58–60; phantom genealogy of slave music and, 75–77; popular music and, 215n17; racialized casting and, 83–86; vocal masculinity and, 92–93; vocal pedagogy and, 51–52; in vocal synthesis software, 120–26
Black Patti's Troubadours, 74
Blues Legacies and Black Feminism: Gertrude "Ma" Rainey, Bessie Smith, and Billie Holiday (Davis), 20–21

bodies: in dissent, 238n65; intermaterial dynamic of sound and, 195–200; technologies and, 42–43
Boghetti, Giuseppi (Joe Bogash), 81
Bogle, Donald, 82, 219n77
Briggs, Hope, 86
Brooks, Daphne, 26, 31, 169, 238n65
Bryant, Bil, 135, 142–43
Bumbry, Grace, 83
But Beautiful (Scott album), 95
Butler, Shane, 17

Cage, John, 113
Caldonia (Estella Young), 94
California v. O.J. Simpson, 1, 4, 9
Calloway, Cab, 95
Calvino, Italo, 3
Camellia (source vocalist), 139
Cameron, James, 135–36
Cantor synthesis software, 121–24
Carpenter, Faedra Chatard, 26
Cartoon Network, 141–42
Carvalho, John M., 155, 157
castrato singers, 99, 222n14
Cavarero, Adriana, 3, 33
channeling the ancestors, 156–58
channel vocoder (VOice CODER), 228n11
CHANT (formant wave function synthesis), 228n11
Charles, Ray, 94, 99
"Check It Out" (Vocaloid demo), 126–32
Chen, Lena, 142, 144–46
Cheng, Anne Anlin, 31
choice in listening, racialization of voice and, 181–84
Chybowski, Julia, 76, 217n32
Cincinnati Enquirer, 72
civil rights: Anderson as symbol for, 82–83, 88–89; black vocal timbre and, 61–63
Clarey, Cynthia, 86
classical voice pedagogy: American opera timbre and, 69; construction of timbre and, 52–57, 211nn6–8; early African American singers and, 69–75; race and, 43–49
Clifford, Charles, 39
Clifford v. Commonwealth of Kentucky, 58–60

fidelity, cult of; impersonation and, 164–65, 167–69, 172–75; listeners and, 181–84; voice identification and, 190–93

figure of sound (FoS), 50–52; listening against, 58–60; Vocaloid synthesis and, 116–17; vocal pedagogy and, 54–57; voice identification and, 190–93

film, blackness in, 21–22

Fisk Jubilee Singers, 76–77

Flack, Roberta, 207n31

Flying Dutchman (Wager), 85

formant wave function synthesis, 228n11

Foster, Mark, 100

Foucault, Michel, 13–14

Four Saints in Three Acts (Thomson), 67, 70, 78–84

4'33" (Cage), 113

Fox News, 190

François, Anne-Lise, 226n52

French, J. P. (Peter) (Dr.), 240n15

frequency, vocal masculinity and, 105

frequency modulation synthesis, 228n11

Fujita, Saki, 132, 227n2

Fulton, Sybrina, 240n16

Gawker (website), 161, 163

Gaye, Marvin, 105, 202, 224n38

gender: African American opera singers and, 67, 216n23; Billie Holiday impersonators and, 159–65; black masculinity and, 101–5; masculine vocality and, 91–93, 220nn1–2, 226n60; timbre and, 35–36; vocal pedagogy and, 51, 53, 58–60, 212n23; vocal signaling, 105–10; in vocal synthesis software, 124–26; voice and identification of, 6–7, 19–24, 39–43, 189–93, 206n26

Gershwin, George, 67, 79, 161, 218n67

Giddins, Gary, 96

GigaP, 137

Gillespie, Michael Boyce, 21

Gilliam, Rob, 144, 146

Giroux, Henry, 57–58

glassness, performance of, 196–200

Gleason, Ralph J., 157–58

"Gloomy Sunday" (song), 151, 172

Goff, Phillip, 238n71

Goodman, Steven, 55, 212n26

Goodsmile Racing, 139–40

Gordon, Bonnie, 99

Graziano, John, 74

Green, Ryan Speedo, 70, 89, 216n24

Greenberg, Jonathan, 215n18

Greenfield, Elizabeth Taylor, 70–76, 79, 81, 89, 216n25, 217n30, 217n32

Grey, Herman, 101

Griffin, Farah Jasmine, 10, 23, 68, 156–58, 168, 177, 207n31

Grove Music Online, 105

growth and development, vocal range and, 105–10, 220n2

Guardian, 93

Gunzberger, Deborah, 106

Hagana Miku (steel sound), 139

Haggins, Bernard H., 84–85

Halberstam, Judith, 102, 223n33

Hall, Peter (Sir), 85

Hampton, Lionel, 96

Hamrick, Hugh, 161

Hanks, Tom, 99

Hari, Johann, 235n16

Harkness, Nicholas, 206n17

Hatsune Miku voice bank, 116–17, 132–34, 227n2, 231n48

Hayes, Roland, 81, 218n71

Heaven (Scott album), 95

Henderson, W. J., 79

Hendricks, Barbara, 87

Her (film), 121, 229n17

Heyward, Dorothy, 78

Heyward, DuBose, 78–79

"Hibikase" (song), 137

Hitchcock, Henry-Russell, 78

Hobson, Janell, 156, 167

Hogan, Joe, 126

Holding Back the Years (Scott album), 95

Holiday, Billie, 20–21, 23; drug prosecution of, 235n16; impersonations of, 151–55, 159–65, 172–75; Jimmy Scott and, 94; life and career of, 155–59; listeners' perceptions of, 181–84, 191–93; mythification of, 180; style and technique of, 36–37, 169–72; vocal imitations of, 165–69

hologram production, 135–39

Horne, Marilyn, 87

Huang, Hao, 170

Huang, Rachel, 170
Hurston, Zora Neale, 169
Hutcheon, Linda, 42
Hutcheon, Michael, 42
hypermasculinity, 226n52; blackness linked
    with, 101–5

identity and identification: autobiography
    and, 153–55; labeling and, 185–88; mic-
    ropolitics of listening and, 56–57; through
    voice, 189–93, 240nn14–16; vocal imita-
    tion and, 167–69
imperialism, cultural theft and, 31
impersonation: of Billie Holiday, 151–55,
    159–65; listeners' role in, 165–69
Incidents in the Life of a Slave Girl (Jacobs), 20
intention, of vocal sound, 168–69
intermaterial vibration, 193–200
International Phonetic Alphabet (IPA),
    127–32, 216n19
international singing style, 213n27
interpretation: hermeneutics of, 213n41;
    vocal imitation and, 166–69
In the Time of Our Singing (Powers), 215n16
Inventing the Family of Man, 17
Invisible Children (film), 124
I Pagliacci (Leoncavallo), 84
Ito, Hiroyuki, 132, 134, 231n43

Jacobs, Harriet, 20
Japan: acousmatic question and, 146–50;
    Vocaloid fandom in, 134–39
Jaxon, Frankie "Half-Pint," 101
jazz music: black masculinity and, 101;
    Scott's contributions to, 95–101
Jenkins, Karl, 121, 124
Jewel, James, 220n91
Jolson, Al, 80
Jones, Alisha, 108
Jones, Matilda Sissieretta, 70–76, 81, 89,
    217n41
Jonze, Spike, 229n17
Jordan, Angelina, 151–55, 159, 161, 163–65,
    167–69, 172, 174–75, 191–93, 237n51

Kallmann syndrome, 35, 93–95, 99, 222n7
Kane, Brian, 205n4

Kei (Japanese graphic novelist), 137
Kelley, Robin, 226n52
Kessler, Sarah, 17
King, Jason, 207n31
King, Michael, 135
Kinney, Katherine, 17
Kisner, Jordan, 206n26
Klangfarbe (tone-color), 5
knowledge, vocal timbre as, 42–43
Kreiman, Jody, 6, 17, 106–7, 201–3, 206n13
Kun, Josh, 26, 197–200

Lady Day at Emerson's Bar and Grill (play),
    161–65
Lady Gaga, 137
Lady in Satin (song), 157–58
Lamperti, G. B., 213n28
Land, Ray, 8
"Last Night, Good Night (Re:Dialed)"
    (song), 137–39
Lee, Johnny, 220n91
Lee, Peggy, 159
Lee, Sylvia, 87
Lee Tung Foo, 212n18
legibility, vocal work and, 54–57
LEON Vocaloid voice banks, 116–17, 146–50;
    development of, 120–24, 141; soul singing
    and, 126–32; source sounds for, 125–26
Levin, Theodore, 17
Lhamon, W. T., 164
light, intermaterial dynamic of sound and,
    195–200
Lind, Jenny, 71, 73
linear predictive coding (LPC), 228n11
linguistic profiling, 39
listener disbelief, impersonation and,
    164–65
listener-speaker model, 12–13
listening: as agency, 177–80; classical voice
    pedagogy and, 47–49, 211n11; identifi-
    cation and, 56–57; impersonation and,
    165–69; to listening, 27–33, 57–60; mi-
    cropolitics of, 24–27, 190–93; Peirce's
    model of sign and, 209n53; through
    phantom genealogy, 86–90; practice of
    the pause and, 181–84; voice's source and,
    11–13, 18–24, 178–80
"LOLA Is Here" (Vocaloid demo), 126–32

LOLA Vocaloid voice banks, 116–17, 146–50;
development of, 120–24; soul singing and,
126–32; source sounds for, 125–26; users'
perceptions of, 124–26
London Philharmonic Orchestra, 124
Lone Ranger, The (radio program), 220n91
Lordi, Emily, 23, 26, 169
Lott, Eric, 31, 164
Lulu and Leander (radio series), 220n91
Luo Tianyi (Vocaloid character), 134
Lynch, David, 95, 100

Madame Butterfly (Puccini), 84
Madonna, 95
Magic and Loss (Reed tour), 95
Marcuse, Herbert, 20
Marshall, Caitlin, 17
Martin, Tracy, 240n16
Martin, Trayvon, 189–90, 240nn14–16
masculinity: African American opera sing-
ers and, 67; blackness and, 101–5; Scott's
career and definitions of, 95–101; timbre
and, 35–36; vocal hallmarks of, 91–93,
226n51
Mauss, Marcel, 13, 42
Maynor, Dorothy, 83
McCracken, Allison, 226n60
McDonald, Audra, 161–65
McDonough, Jimmy, 95
McFerrin, Bobby, 218n67
McFerrin, Robert, Sr., 83, 218n67
Mead, Margaret, 177
meaning: Derrida on deferrals and search for,
21; of vocal sound, 168–69
measurable aspects of voice, 14–24; pause
and, 181–84
Medicine for Melancholy (Gillespie), 22
Meiko synthesis software, 132, 228n15
Meizel, Katherine, 236n45
Merli (Vocaloid character), 134
Merriam, Alan P., 47–48
Merriam, Valerie, 47–48
Merton, Robert, 51
Metropolitan Opera, 80; desegregation of,
61–63, 87–89
Meyer, Jan, 8
"micropolitics of frequency," 212n26
micropolitics of listening, 24–27, 56–57,

212n26; Holiday impersonations and,
172–75; voice identification and, 190–93
Mikunopolis (Crypton Vocaloid concert),
137–39
Mikupa (Hatsune Miku Live Party), 137–39
"Mikusabbath" (song), 139
Miller, Richard, 53, 213n28
mimicry, of racial mimicry, 31–33
minstrelsy: American opera and, 69–71,
73–74, 79–80, 88–89; impersonation
and, 164–65, 234n2; recording media and,
216n26
Mirabelles drag group, 111
MIRIAM synthesis software, 120–24,
130–32
Misha (source vocalist), 139, 142–46
Mitchell, Leona, 85–86
Monty Python's Flying Circus, 1, 9
Morgenstern, Dan, 96
Moten, Fred, 26, 64, 209n67
Muñoz, José Esteban, 32, 110–13
"Music: Saints in Cellophane," 61
musique acousmatique, 1–2

Nader, Ralph, 1
naming-through-listening, 181–84
National Association of Music Merchants
(NAMM), 117, 227n5
national schools of singing: Anderson's reper-
toire and, 82–83; teacher genealogies and,
64–66; vocal pedagogy and, 53–57, 212n13,
213n28
native language, American opera singers and
role of, 68–69, 214n3, 216n19
Neal, Lem, 94
Neal, Mark Anthony, 226n52
New Bird (album), 96
Newsome, Chubby, 96
New York City Opera, 84
New York Herald, 71
New York Times, 62, 93, 117, 124, 159, 161
Nicholson, Stuart, 157–58
Niconico Douga (website), 232n61
niji sousaku (secondary creativity), 134
Noë, Alva, 208n36
nonsonorous criteria: impersonation and,
166–69; vocal timbre and, 67–69, 217n34
Norman, Jessye, 219n88

1-24